by Thomas R. Beyer, Jr., Ph.D.
C.V. Starr Professor of Russian
Dean, The Russian School
Middlebury College
Middlebury, Vermont

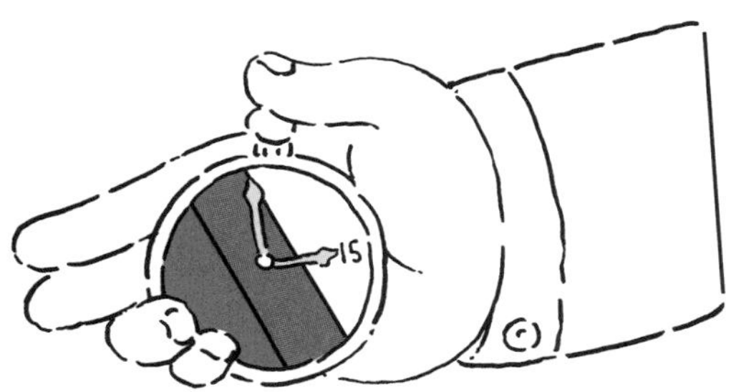

To help you pace your learning, we've included stopwatches *like the one above* throughout the book to mark each 15-minute interval. You can read one of these units each day or pace yourself according to your needs.

CONTENTS

All inquiries should be addressed to:
Barron's Educational Series, Inc.
250 Wireless Boulevard
Hauppauge, New York 11788

International Standard Book No. 0-8120-4846-6

Library of Congress Catalog Card No. 92-28052
Cover and Book Design Milton Glaser, Inc.
Illustrations Juan Suarez

PRINTED IN THE UNITED STATES OF AMERICA
456 880 9876543

Library of Congress Cataloging-in-Publication Data

Beyer, Thomas R.
Learn Russian the fast and fun way: the activity kit that makes learning a language quick and easy! / by Thomas R. Beyer, Jr.
p. cm.

ISBN 0-8120-4846-6
1. Russian language—Self-instruction. 2. Russian language—Textbooks for foreign speakers—English.
I. Title.
PG2112.5.B46 1993 92-28052
491.782'421—dc20 CIP

For Dorothea, Carina, Stefanie and Alexandra.

With gratitude to all my Russian friends, to countless key ladies, shop clerks, hairdressers, diplomats, scholars, colleagues, and all those lovely people who have made Russian fun for me.

Russia (**Россия**), even after the breakup of the Soviet Union in 1991, has emerged as still the largest country in the world, occupying almost one-sixth of our planet's land mass. The vast expanses of Russia cover eleven separate time zones on two continents: Europe and Asia. Russia and ten other former republics of the U.S.S.R. are now sovereign states or countries that have united in a loosely knit Commonwealth of Independent States (**Содружество Независимых Государств**). Russia has approximately 150 million people, almost half of the inhabitants of the former Soviet Union. All are citizens of Russia (**россияне**), and many are ethnic Russians (**русские**). Russia, however, is a multinational state and home to over one hundred nationalities and languages.

The Russian language was a mandatory subject in Soviet schools and almost all of the 280 million people inhabiting the former republics know and speak Russian, either as their native or second language. In fact, a Georgian who wishes to speak with an Uzbek is likely to use Russian for communication. While English and other languages are now gaining popularity, Russian will remain, for at least a generation, the one mutually understandable language for those who live in Armenia, Azerbaijan, Belarus, Kazakhstan, Kyrgyzstan, Moldova, Russia, Tajikistan, Turkmenistan, Ukraine, Uzbekistan and the countries not part of the Commonwealth, Estonia, Georgia, Latvia, and Lithuania.

Knowing Russian can open up a window onto a fascinating and enchanting nation, from the fairytale cupolas of Saint Basil's Cathedral to the majesty and power of Red Square and the Kremlin. Moscow, Russia's capital, is home to more than eight and one-half million people and the world-renowned Bolshoi Ballet. Far to the north, Saint Petersburg, capital to the tsars from Peter the Great until Nicholas II, offers a marvelous blend of picturesque architecture highlighted by the White Nights of summer. Here too are the glorious palaces—the magnificent Winter Palace and Hermitage Art Museum.

Russians take great pride in their culture and country and they appreciate the efforts of those who try to speak their language. For many, the Russian alphabet is a major stumbling block to getting to know the country and its people better. With our *Fast and Fun Way* you'll be reading the signs and ready to talk with real Russians in just a matter of days. When you do get an opportunity to use your new language skills, you'll notice that your efforts will be truly rewarded. So let's begin!

PRONUNCIATION

You know you're in Russia when the simple sign for a restaurant looks like **РЕСТОРАН**. Actually, the Russian alphabet has only a few more letters than English. But to get started, look at the list below. Read aloud the pronunciation in the first column and then look at the Russian letters in the middle column. At the far right you will see the translation, and you'll be pleasantly surprised to learn how many of them you already know. After the first three words we'll add only one new letter per word.

Pronunciation	Russian	English
DA	**ДА**	yes
NYET	**НЕТ**	no
BANK	**БАНК**	bank
BAR	**БАР**	bar
PARK	**ПАРК**	park
KAsa	**КАССА**	cashier
taKSI	**ТАКСИ**	taxi
kiOSK	**КИОСК**	kiosk, newsstand
kaFE	**КАФЕ**	café
buFYET	**БУФЕТ**	buffet, snack bar
miTRO	**МЕТРО**	metro, subway
maskVA	**МОСКВА**	Moscow
aeraPORT	**АЭРОПОРТ**	airport
aeraFLOT	**АЭРОФЛОТ**	Aeroflot
ZAL	**ЗАЛ**	hall
FKHOT	**ВХОД**	entrance
VYkhat	**ВЫХОД**	exit
TSENTR	**ЦЕНТР**	center
byuRO	**БЮРО**	bureau
gardiROP	**ГАРДЕРОБ**	garderobe, coat check
POCHta	**ПОЧТА**	post office
RYAT	**РЯД**	row
STOYtye	**СТОЙТЕ**	Stand!
nye kuRIT'	**НЕ КУРИТЬ**	No Smoking
bal'SHOY	**БОЛЬШОЙ**	the Bolshoi, big
ZHENski	**ЖЕНСКИЙ**	ladies' (room)
muSHKOY	**МУЖСКОЙ**	men's (room)
yiSCHO	**ЕЩЁ**	more, else

Now that you have seen most of the Russian letters, let's look at the whole system. What we commonly call the Russian alphabet is officially known as the Cyrillic alphabet. The Russians adopted the Cyrillic alphabet created in the ninth century when the monks Cyril and Methodius developed a written language for the Slavs. The Cyrillic alphabet has thirty-three letters and has much in common with the Greek alphabet. As you have seen, many letters are familiar to you from English and several others resemble Greek letters. As in English, each letter is only an approximation of how a sound is pronounced. The guide below should get you started in speaking Russian.

VOWELS

Russian has five vowel sounds, but ten vowel letters. Five of the letters are "hard" and five are "soft." The one vowel sound in each word that is stressed receives special emphasis. As you speak Russian, try in the beginning to exaggerate your pronunciation.

Russian Letter	Russian Sound	English Symbol	Example
	Hard Vowels		
а	**a** as in f**a**ther	A	**да** *DA*
э	**e** as in **e**cho	E	**эхо** *Ekho*
ы	**y** as in hair**y**	Y	**мы** *MY*
о	**o** as in hell**o**	O	**но** *NO*
у	**u** as in r**u**le	U	**ну** *NU*
	Soft Vowels		
я	**ya** as in **ya**hoo	YA	**я** *YA*
е	**ye** as in **ye**s	YE	**нет** *NYET*
и	**ee** as in b**ee**	I	**ива** *Iva*
ё	**yo** as in **yo**-yo	YO	**полёт** *paLYOT*
ю	**u** as in **u**nion	YU	**юмор** *YUmar*

CONSONANT LETTERS

Russian Letter	Russian Sound	English Symbol	Example
б	**b** as in **b**at	B	**банк** *BANK*
в	**v** as in **v**ote	V	**вот** *VOT*
г	**g** as in **g**o	G	**гол** *GOL*
д	**d** as in **d**og	D	**да** *DA*
ж	**zh** as in a**z**ure	ZH	**жена** *zhiNA*
з	**z** as in **z**oo	Z	**за** *ZA*
й	**y** as in bo**y**	Y	**мой** *MOY*
к	**k** as in **k**ayak	K	**касса** *KAsa*
л	**l** as in **l**ot	L	**лампа** *LAMpa*
м	**m** as in **m**all	M	**муж** *MUSH*
н	**n** as in **n**ote	N	**нос** *NOS*
п	**p** as in **p**apa	P	**парк** *PARK*
р	**r** as in **r**abbit	R	**рот** *ROT*
с	**s** as in **s**un	S	**суп** *SUP*
т	**t** as in **t**oe	T	**такси** *taKSI*
ф	**f** as in **f**und	F	**фунт** *FUNT*
х	**ch** as in Ba**ch**, lo**ch**	KH	**ах** *AKH*
ц	**ts** as in **ts**ar	TS	**царь** *TSAR'*
ч	**ch** as in **ch**eap	CH	**читает** *chiTAyit*
ш	**sh** as in **sh**ow	SH	**шапка** *SHAPka*
щ	**sh** as in **sh**eep	SCH	**щи** *SCHI*
ъ	hard sign		not pronounced
ь	soft sign		not pronounced

STRESS

Each Russian word has only one syllable that is stressed or under accent. Russians simply know where the stress is and do not write the accent marks. We will indicate the stressed syllable in our transcription with capital letters as an aid for your pronunciation.

THREE RULES OF PRONUNCIATION

1. Russians pronounce the **o** sound only when it is stressed. When some other vowel is stressed in a word, the letter **o** is pronounced as an **a** **кот** (*KOT*) but **кота́** (*kaTA*). When the letters **е, я** and sometimes **а** are not stressed, they are pronounced as **i** in the English word "it."

2. Consonants can be hard **ну** (*NU*) or soft **нет** (*NYET*). The soft **n** is like the sound in the word "onion." A consonant is hard unless it is followed by a soft vowel letter **я, е, и, ё, ю** or by the soft sign **ь**.

3. At the end of a word, or before voiced consonants, **б, в, г, д, ж**, and **з**, become their voiceless counterparts, **б→п, в→ф, г→к, д→т, ж→ш, з→с**. Examples: **год**→*GOT,* **баб**→*BAP,* **ног**→*NOK,* **автомат**→*aftaMAT,* **водка**→*VOTka.*

Now look at the following Russian signs and see if you can write their meanings in the blanks.

1. **СУВЕНИРЫ** ______________________________
2. **ТЕЛЕФОН** ______________________________
3. **РЕСТОРАН** ______________________________
4. **ТУАЛЕТ** ______________________________
5. **ТЕАТР** ______________________________

ANSWERS

1. SOUVENIRS 2. TELEPHONE 3. RESTAURANT 4. RESTROOM (TOILET/WC) 5. THEATER

THE RUSSIAN ALPHABET

Now that we know how to pronounce Russian letters and words, it's time to learn how to recognize the letters of the alphabet and to write them. As in English, Russian has printed or **block** letters and script or *italic* letters. One major difference, however, is that Russians do not print. So while you want to be able to recognize both sets of letters, you'll want to use the script letters when you write. Below is the Russian alphabet in its alphabetical order. Next to it we have given the English. Finally, there are spaces for you to try your hand at writing Russian.

Russian		English		Your turn
А а	*А а*	**A a**	*A a*	________
Б б	*Б б*	**B b**	*B b*	________
В в	*В в*	**V v**	*V v*	________
Г г	*Г г*	**G g**	*G g*	________
Д д	*Д д*	**D d**	*D d*	________
Е е	*Е е*	**Ye ye**	*Ye ye*	________
Ё ё	*Ё ё*	**Yo yo**	*Yo yo*	________
Ж ж	*Ж ж*	**Zh zh**	*Zh zh*	________
З з	*З з*	**Z z**	*Z z*	________
И и	*И и*	**I i**	*I i*	________
Й й	*Й й*	**Y y**	*Y y*	________
К к	*К к*	**K k**	*K k*	________
Л л	*Л л*	**L l**	*L l*	________

М м	*М м*	**M m**	*M m*	
Н н	*Н н*	**N n**	*N n*	
О о	*О о*	**O o**	*O o*	
П п	*П п*	**P p**	*P p*	
Р р	*Р р*	**R r**	*R r*	
С с	*С с*	**S s**	*S s*	
Т т	*Т т*	**T t**	*T t*	
У у	*У у*	**U u**	*U u*	
Ф ф	*Ф ф*	**F f**	*F f*	
Х х	*Х х*	**Kh kh**	*Kh kh*	
Ц ц	*Ц ц*	**Ts ts**	*Ts ts*	
Ч ч	*Ч ч*	**Ch ch**	*Ch ch*	
Ш ш	*Ш ш*	**Sh sh**	*Sh sh*	
Щ щ	*Щ щ*	**Sch sch**	*Sch sch*	
ъ	*ъ ъ*			
ы	*ы*	**y**	*y*	
ь	*ь ь*			
Э э	*Э э*	**E e**	*E e*	
Ю ю	*Ю ю*	**Yu yu**	*Yu yu*	
Я я	*Я я*	**Ya ya**	*Ya ya*	

GETTING TO KNOW PEOPLE

(znaKOMSTva)
Знакомство

1

(daVAYtye) *(paznaKOmimsya)*
Давайте познакомимся.
Let's Get Acquainted.

Knowing how to greet people and start a conversation is very important. Read the following dialogue several times, pronouncing each line carefully aloud. The dialogue contains basic words and expressions that will be useful to you.

Mark Smith, his wife, Caroline, their daughter, Stephanie, and their son, Alex, have just arrived at **Шереметьево** (Sheremetevo) airport in **Москва** (Moscow) and are looking for their luggage. Mark approaches an airline employee.

MARK	*(ZDRASTvuytye)* **Здравствуйте.**	Hello.
CLERK	**Здравствуйте.**	Hello.
	(paMOCH) **Как вам помочь?**	How may I help you?
MARK	*(GDYE) (NAshi) (chimaDAny)* **Где наши чемоданы?**	Where are our suitcases?
CLERK	*(zaVUT)* **Как вас зовут?**	What is your name?
MARK	*(miNYA)* **Меня зовут "Mark Smith."**	My name is Mark Smith.

CLERK	*(atKUda)* **Откуда вы?**	Where are you from?
MARK	*(YA) (IS) (SA SHA A)* **Я из США.**	I'm from the USA.
CLERK	*(NOmir) (VAshiva) (RYEYsa)* **Номер вашего рейса?**	Your flight number?
MARK	**Аэрофлот 62.**	Aeroflot 62.

As the clerk looks through some papers on her desk, **Иван** (Ivan), Mark's host in Moscow, approaches.

ИВАН	*(priVYET) (diLA)* **Привет, Марк. Как дела?**	Hi, Mark. How are things?
MARK	*(kharaSHO) (spaSIba)* **Хорошо, спасибо.**	Fine, thanks.
ИВАН	*(BYL) (paLYOT)* **Как был ваш полёт?**	How was your flight?
MARK	*(maYA) (siMYA)* **Вот моя семья,**	Here is my family,
	(zhiNA) **моя жена.**	my wife
ИВАН	*(Ochin') (priYATna)* **Очень приятно.**	A pleasure to meet you.
MARK	*(DOCHka)* **И это дочка**	And here are my daughter
	(SYN) **и сын.**	and son.
CLERK	*(izviNItye) (paZHAlusta)* **Извините, пожалуйста.**	Excuse me, please.
	Ваши чемоданы	Your suitcases
	(aSTAlis') **остались в Вашингтоне.**	stayed behind in Washington.
MARK	*(tiPYER') (DYElat')* **А теперь что нам делать?**	And now what are we to do?
CLERK	*(valNUYtyes')* **Не волнуйтесь.**	Don't worry.
	(aNI) (BUdyt) **Они будут в Москве**	They'll be in Moscow
	(ZAFtra) **завтра.**	tomorrow.
MARK	*(LUche) (POZna) (CHEM) (nikagDA)* **Лучше поздно, чем никогда.**	Better late than never.
CLERK	*(PRAvy)* **Вы правы.**	
ИВАН	*(paSHLI)* **Ну пошли.**	Well, let's get going.

	(da) (sviDAniya)	
MARK	**До свидания.**	Goodbye.
CLERK	**До свидания.**	Goodbye.

Now here is your first exercise based on the dialogue you have practiced. Try to match the Russian expressions from the dialogue with their English equivalents. No peeking until you've tried.

1. **Хорошо, спасибо.**
2. **Здравствуйте.**
3. **Как вам помочь?**
4. **До свидания.**
5. **Не волнуйтесь.**
6. **Как вас зовут?**
7. **Ну, пошли.**
8. **Лучше поздно, чем никогда.**
9. **Извините, пожалуйста.**
10. **Очень приятно.**

a. Don't worry.
b. What's your name?
c. Better late than never.
d. Fine, thanks.
e. Excuse me, please.
f. How may I help you?
g. Goodbye.
h. Hello.
i. A pleasure (to meet you).
j. Well, let's get going.

ANSWERS

Matching **1.** d **2.** h **3.** f **4.** g **5.** a **6.** b **7.** j **8.** c **9.** e **10.** i

(LYUdi) (i) (VYEschi)

ЛЮДИ И ВЕЩИ

People and Things

One of the first things you'll have to know in Russian is how to name people and things. These are the *nouns*, the naming words. Russian nouns belong to one of three grammatical genders. They can be masculine, feminine, or neuter, and you can usually tell the gender of a noun by the ending. Masculine nouns end in a consonant. Feminine nouns end in **а** or **я**. Neuter nouns end in **о** or **е**. Some nouns end in the soft sign **ь**; most of these are feminine except for ones ending in **-ель**, which are masculine. The gender is only a grammatical category. The Russian word for chair, *(STUL)* **стул**, is masculine. River, *(riKA)* **река**, is feminine. A letter, *(pis'MO)* **письмо**, is neuter.

English forms the plural by adding the letter **s (es)** to the end of a word. Russian plurals can be formed by ending **ы (и)** or **а (я)**.

If the noun ends in a consonant, add **ы** to the ending, *(stuDYENT)* **студент**→*(stuDYENty)* **студенты**.

If the noun ends in **а**, replace the **а** with **ы**, *(KOMnata)* **комната**→*(KOMnaty)* **комнаты**.

If the noun ends in the soft sign **ь** or the letter **я**, add **и**, *(TYOtya)* **тётя**→*(TYOti)* **тёти**.

For neuter nouns that end in **о**, change the **о** to **а**, *(pis'MO)* **письмо**→*(PIS'ma)* **письма**.

If the ending was **е** change that **е** to **я**, *(ZDAniye)* **здание**→*(ZDAniya)* **здания**.

> Russian has only a few spelling rules. One of them is as follows: after the letters **г, к, х, ч, ш, щ, ж**, you may not write the letter **ы**. Instead, you must write an **и**.
>
> EXAMPLE: *(MAL'chik)* **мальчик**→*(MAL'chiki)*, **мальчики**, *(stuDYENTka)* **студентка**→*(stuDYENTki)* **студентки**

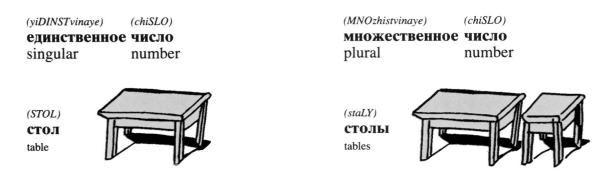

Singular and Plural

(yiDINSTvinaye) **единственное** singular *(chiSLO)* **число** number

(STOL) **стол**
table

____

(MNOzhistvinaye) **множественное** plural *(chiSLO)* **число** number

(staLY) **столы**
tables

____

единственное число		**множественное число**	
(afTObus) **автобус** bus		*(afTObusy)* **автобусы** buses	
(LAMpa) **лампа** lamp		*(LAMpy)* **лампы** lamps	
(gaZYEta) **газета** newspaper		*(gaZYEty)* **газеты** newspapers	
(MAL'chik) **мальчик** boy		*(MAL'chiki)* **мальчики** boys	
(DYEvushka) **девушка** girl		*(DYEvushki)* **девушки** girls	
(naGA) **нога** leg	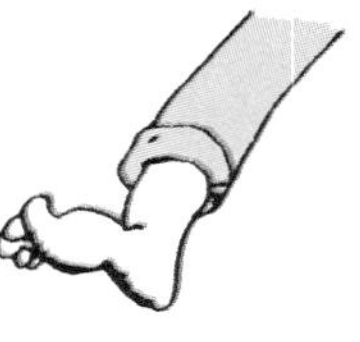	*(NOgi)* **ноги** legs	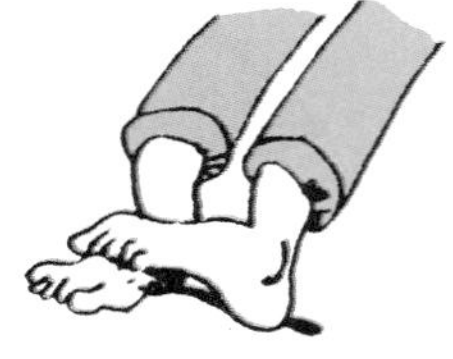

единственное число | **множественное число**

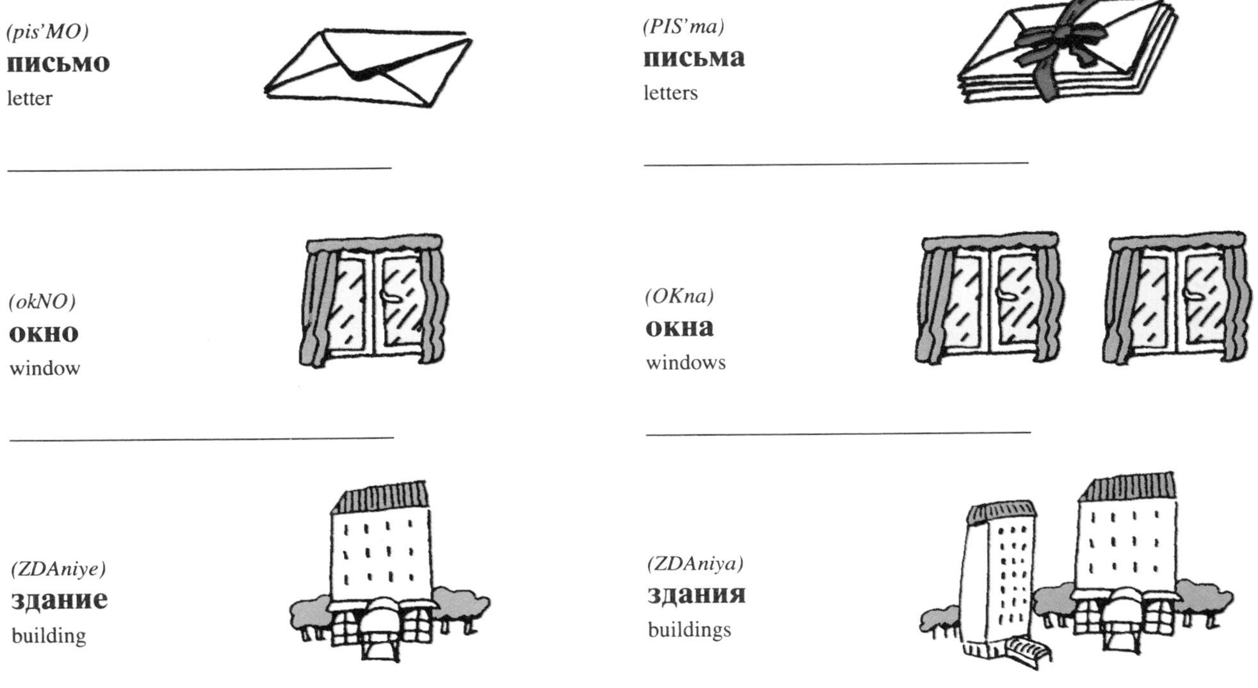

(pis'MO)
письмо
letter

(PIS'ma)
письма
letters

(okNO)
окно
window

(OKna)
окна
windows

(ZDAniye)
здание
building

(ZDAniya)
здания
buildings

Before going on, review the above words and write them out in the blanks provided.

Just as English has its "child" but "children," "woman" but "women," Russian has some plurals that simply should be learned. Here are a few of the most important ones. Repeat them to yourself and then write them out.

(MAT')
мать
mother

(MAtiri)
матери
mothers

(aTYETS)
отец
father

(aTSY)
отцы
fathers

единственное число

(DOCH)
дочь
daughter

(SYN)
сын
son

(riBYOnak)
ребёнок
child

множественное число

(DOchiri)
дочери
daughters

(synaV'YA)
сыновья
sons

(DYEti)
дети
children

Now, give the name of the famous Russian novel *Fathers and Sons.*

(Hint: It was actually *Fathers and Children.*) ______________________

(ON) (aNA) (aNO)
он, она, оно
he/it she/it it

We now know that Russian nouns are identified by their grammatical gender. Examine the following questions and answers.

(GDYE) (afTObus) **Где автобус?** Where's the bus?	*(ON) (TAM)* **Он там.** It's over there.
(GDYE) (STANtsiya) (miTRO) **Где станция метро?** Where's the Metro station?	*(aNA) (TAM)* **Она там.** It's over there.
(GDYE) (pis'MO) **Где письмо?** Where's the letter?	*(aNO) (TAM)* **Оно там.** It's over there.

ANSWER

Novel Отцы и дети

In the plural, all of the genders are replaced by only one form of the pronoun: *(aNI)* **они**.

(GDYE) (gaZYEty) **Где газеты?** Where are the newspapers?	*(aNI) (TAM)* **Они там.** They're over there.

Now try to fill in the blanks with the correct form of **он, она, оно, они**.

1. *(GDYE) (stuDYENT)* **Где студент?** Where's the student? ____________ *(TAM)* **там.** there.

2. *(GDYE) (DYEriva)* **Где дерево?** Where's the tree? ____________ *(TAM)* **там.** there.

3. *(GDYE) (KNIga)* **Где книга?** Where's the book? ____________ *(TAM)* **там.** there.

4. *(GDYE) (YAblaka)* **Где яблоко?** Where's the apple? ____________ *(TAM)* **там.** there.

5. *(GDYE) (DYEti)* **Где дети?** Where are the children? ____________ *(TAM)* **там.** there.

6. *(GDYE) (MAma)* **Где мама?** Where's Mama? ____________ *(TAM)* **там.** there.

ANSWERS

Fill in **1.** Он **2.** Оно **3.** Она **4.** Оно **5.** Они **6.** Она

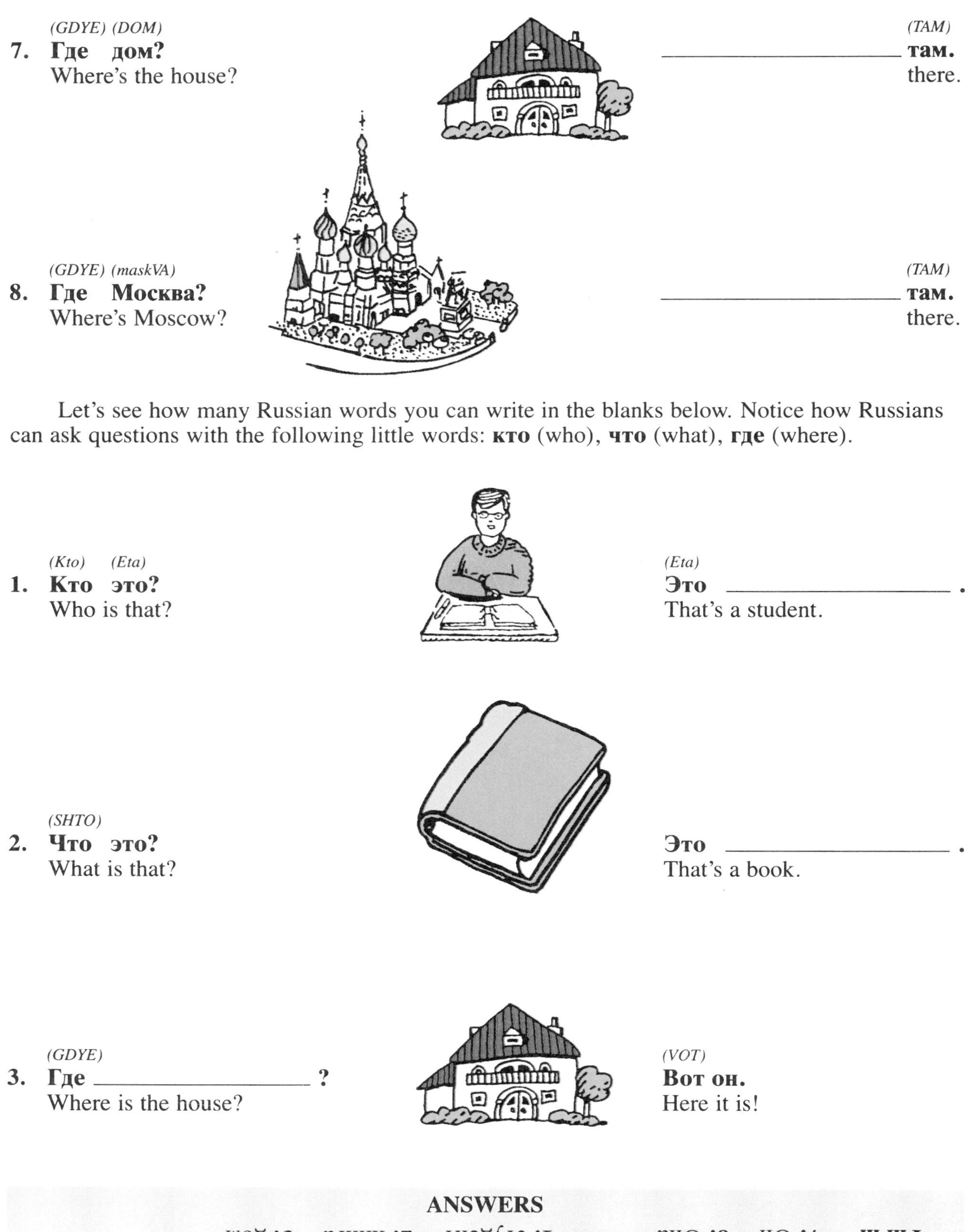

(GDYE) (DOM)
7. Где дом?
Where's the house?

(TAM)
________________ **там.**
there.

(GDYE) (maskVA)
8. Где Москва?
Where's Moscow?

(TAM)
________________ **там.**
there.

Let's see how many Russian words you can write in the blanks below. Notice how Russians can ask questions with the following little words: **кто** (who), **что** (what), **где** (where).

(Kto) (Eta)
1. Кто это?
Who is that?

(Eta)
Это ________________ **.**
That's a student.

(SHTO)
2. Что это?
What is that?

Это ________________ **.**
That's a book.

(GDYE)
3. Где ________________ **?**
Where is the house?

(VOT)
Вот он.
Here it is!

ANSWERS

Fill in **7.** Он **8.** Она **1.** студент **2.** книга **3.** дом

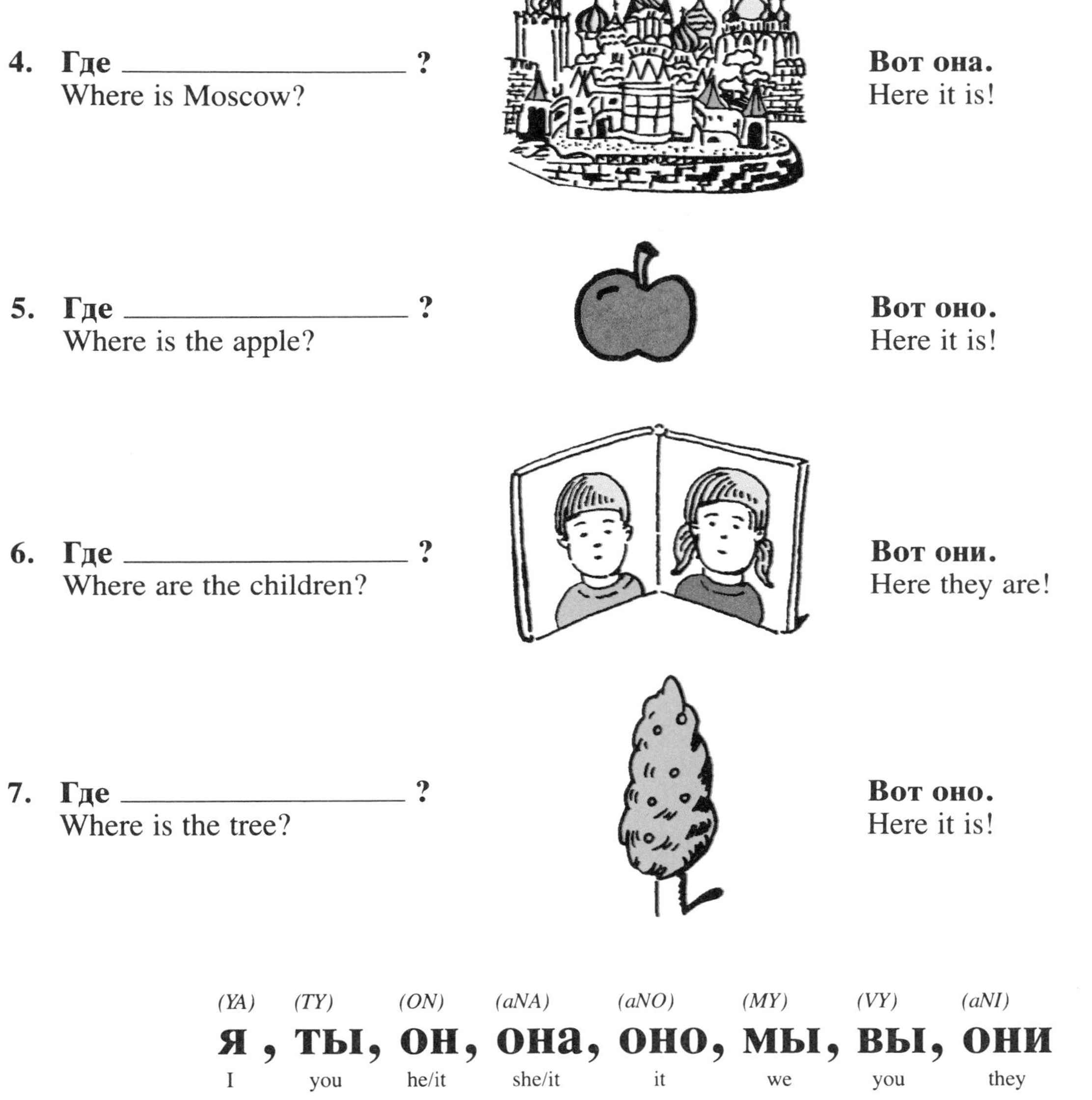

4. Где ________________ **?**
Where is Moscow?

Вот она.
Here it is!

5. Где ________________ **?**
Where is the apple?

Вот оно.
Here it is!

6. Где ________________ **?**
Where are the children?

Вот они.
Here they are!

7. Где ________________ **?**
Where is the tree?

Вот оно.
Here it is!

(YA)	*(TY)*	*(ON)*	*(aNA)*	*(aNO)*	*(MY)*	*(VY)*	*(aNI)*
я ,	**ты,**	**он,**	**она,**	**оно,**	**мы,**	**вы,**	**они**
I	you	he/it	she/it	it	we	you	they

We use personal pronouns to relate to one another. Thus, they are essential if you are to understand and speak Russian. Keep your ears attuned for the word **вы**, the polite form of addressing "you." You'll answer with the form **я**, "I," which is in fact the last letter of the Russian alphabet; it is only capitalized if it begins a sentence. The **ты**, "you," form is used between family members and friends, to animals, and between young people of similar ages. When in doubt, you'll be better off using **вы** so as not to offend anyone.

ANSWERS

Fill in **4.** Москва **5.** яблоко **6.** дети **7.** дерево

(NAshi) (ROTSTviniki)

НАШИ РОДСТВЕННИКИ

Our Relatives

This is **Иван**'s family tree. Note the word for each of his relatives.

(maRIya) (anDRYEyevna)
Мария Андреевна
(BAbushka)
бабушка
grandmother

(sirGYEY) (alikSANdravich)
Сергей Александрович
(DYEdushka)
дедушка
grandfather

(mikhaIL) (sirGYEyevich)
Михаил Сергеевич
(aTYETS)
отец
father

(Ana) (piTROVna)
Анна Петровна
(MAT')
мать
mother

(baRIS) (piTROvich)
Борис Петрович
(DYAdya)
дядя
uncle

(VYEra) (sirGYEyevna)
Вера Сергеевна
(TYOtya)
тётя
aunt

(NIna) (miKHAYlavna)
Нина Михайловна
(DOCH)
дочь
daughter
(siSTRA)
сестра
sister

(vaSIli) (miKHAYlavich)
Василий Михайлович
(SYN)
сын
son
(BRAT)
брат
brother

(iRIna) (baRIsavna)
Ирина Борисовна
(dvaYUradnaya)
двоюродная сестра
female cousin

(PYOTR) (baRIsavich)
Пётр Борисович
(dvaYUradny)
двоюродный брат
male cousin

(iVAN) (miKHAYlavich)
Иван Михайлович

Find the following family members in the family tree and write in the relationship in the blank space.

1. **Нина —** ______________________ **Василия.**
   sister of
2. **Борис Петрович —** ______________________ **Нины.**
   uncle of
3. **Мария Андреевна —** ______________________ **Михаила Сергеевича.**
   mother of
4. **Василий Михайлович —** ______________________ **Анны Петровны.**
   son of
5. **Сергей Александрович —** ______________________ **Нины.**
   grandfather of

In the word search puzzle we have placed the words for "father," "aunt," "uncle," "grandfather," and "sister." See how many you can find.

я	о	е	ь	т	н	т	а	й	к	л	ж
д	т	ё	т	я	т	ё	д	я	д	я	с
х	е	ф	с	д	е	д	у	ш	к	а	л
м	ц	ч	ф	з	т	с	е	с	т	р	а
н	ж	я	ь	щ	я	ш	р	г	ф	с	х

Each family is unique. Use the spaces below to write out some of the Russian words you will need to describe your own family situation.

______________________ ______________________

______________________ ______________________

______________________ ______________________

______________________ ______________________

Отчим (stepfather), **мачеха** (stepmother), **пасынок** (stepson), **падчерица** (stepdaughter), **сводная сестра** (stepsister), **сводный брат** (stepbrother)

ANSWERS

Family 1. сестра **2.** дядя **3.** мать **4.** сын **5.** дедушка

Word search отец, тётя, дядя, дедушка, сестра

Look at the Russian words below for an apartment. Repeat each of the words several times and then practice writing them in the spaces below.

(kvarTIRA)
КВАРТИРА
An Apartment

(KUKHnya)
кухня
kitchen

(DVYER')
дверь
door

(VAnaya)
ванная
bathroom

(khalaDIL'nik)
холодильник
refrigerator

(VAna)
ванна
bathtub

(duKHOFka)
духовка
oven

(RAkavina)
раковина
sink

(gaSTInaya)
гостиная
living room

(SPAL'nya)
спальня
bedroom

(diVAN)
диван
sofa

(SHKAF)
шкаф
closet

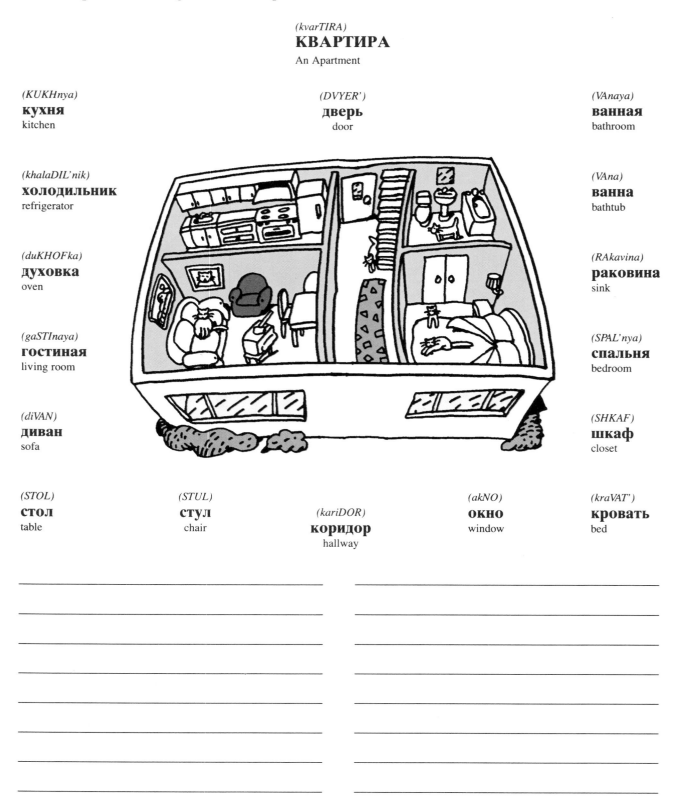

(STOL)
стол
table

(STUL)
стул
chair

(kariDOR)
коридор
hallway

(akNO)
окно
window

(kraVAT')
кровать
bed

ARRIVAL

(priYEST

Приезд

2 Где ночевать?

(GDYE) (nachiVAT')

Where to Spend the Night

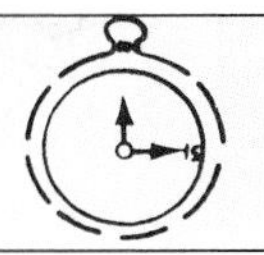

You'll probably already have booked a room either in a hotel or with a private family from home — at least for your first few days in Russia. In fact, unless you have been invited by someone who will arrange for your accommodations, you should not leave home without a reservation. Even so, you'll want to know some basic words and phrases that describe the services and facilities you can expect to find. Learn these words first, and notice how they are used in the dialogues you will read later.

(gaSTInitsa)
гостиница
hotel

(NOmir)
номер
hotel room

(STOimast')
стоимость
cost

(VAnaya)
ванная
bathroom

(DUSH)
душ
shower

(zabraNIravat')
забронировать
to reserve

(diZHURnaya)
дежурная
key lady (floor clerk)

(adminiSTRAtar)
администратор
administrator

(GORnichnaya)
горничная
maid

(PASpart)
паспорт
passport

(KLYUCH)
ключ
key

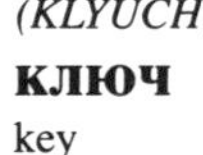

(LIFT)
лифт
elevator

(SKOL'ka)

Сколько?

How much/many?

The numbers are absolutely essential if you wish to get by in Russian. Take a look and try to pronounce the following numbers from one to ten. Then practice your writing in the spaces supplied.

Number	Russian	Pronunciation
0	**нуль** ____________	*NUL'*
1	**один** ____________	*aDIN*
2	**два** ____________	*DVA*
3	**три** ____________	*TRI*
4	**четыре** ____________	*chiTYrye*
5	**пять** ____________	*PYAT'*
6	**шесть** ____________	*SHEST'*
7	**семь** ____________	*SYEM'*
8	**восемь** ____________	*VOsim'*
9	**девять** ____________	*DYEvit'*
10	**десять** ____________	*DYEsit'*

Let's see if you can fill in the blanks after the numerals with their correct names. Solve the problems along the way. Note: Plus is **плюс**, Minus is **минус**, Equals is **будет**.

а. 2 ________ + (**плюс** *PLYUS*) 3 ________ = **будет** *BUdit* ________

б. 5 ________ + (**плюс**) 2 ________ = **будет** ________

в. 6 ________ + (**плюс**) 4 ________ = **будет** ________

г. 8 ________ – (**минус** *MInus*) 7 ________ = **будет** ________

д. 9 ________ – (**минус**) 6 ________ = **будет** ________

(NOmir) (v) (gaSTInitse)

НОМЕР В ГОСТИНИЦЕ

A Room in the Hotel

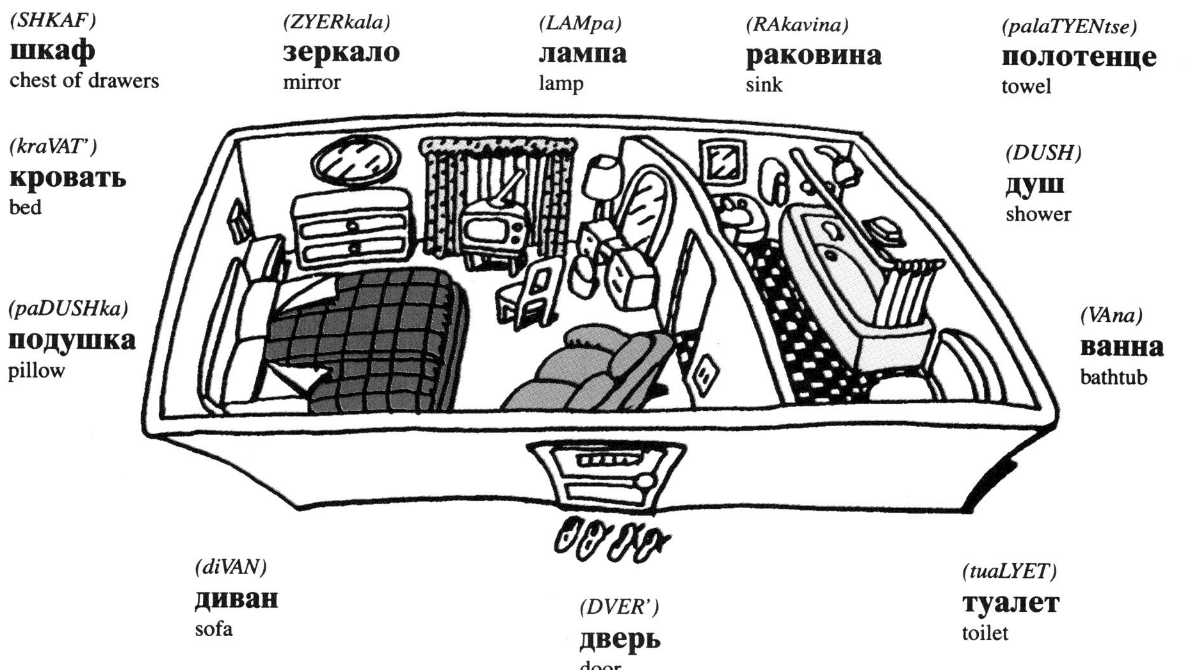

ANSWERS

Numbers а. два + три = пять **б.** пять + два = семь **в.** шесть + четыре = десять
г. восемь – семь = один **д.** девять – шесть = три

(KAK) (zadaVAT) (vaPROS)

Как задавать вопрос

How to ask a question

Just like English, Russian has a few essential question words. If most of ours begin with **wh**o, **wh**en, **wh**ere, **wh**at, the Russian question words have **к**то, **к**огда, **к**уда and words derived from those forms, like **г**де and **ч**то.

Look at the words below and repeat them aloud several times. When you feel comfortable that you know them, try writing them out.

Russian word	Pronunciation	English
Кто	*KTO*	Who
Когда	*kagDA*	When
Куда	*kuDA*	Where to
Где	*GDYE*	Where
Что	*SHTO*	What
Как	*KAK*	How
Сколько	*SKOL'ka*	How much, how many

____________ ____________ ____________ ____________

________________ ________________ ________________

We hope that everything will be perfect, but if something is out of order you may need the following phrases.

(SHTO) (Eta)		*(NYE)(raBOtait)*
Что это?	____________	**не работает.**
What is this?	____________	doesn't work.

Can you get the following items repaired?

1. **Что это? Это лампа.**  ____________ **не работает.**

ANSWER

Repairs 1. Лампа не работает.

2. **Что это?** **Это телевизор.**  ________________ **не работает.**

3. **Что это?** **Это душ.**  ________________ **не работает.**

Let's watch the Smith family check into their hotel. Look at the words carefully and then try to read them aloud to practice your pronunciation.

MARK	**Здравствуйте.**	Hello.
	(zabraNIravali)	
	Мы забронировали два	We reserved two
	(NOmira) (siVOdnya)	
	номера на сегодня.	rooms for today.
	(DObraye) (Utra)	
CLERK	**Доброе утро.**	Good morning.
	(faMIliya)	
	Как ваша фамилия?	What's your last name?
MARK	**Меня зовут Марк Смит.**	My name is Mark Smith.
	(gaspaDIN)	
CLERK	**Да, господин Смит.**	Yes, Mister Smith.
	(DUshem)	
	Два номера с душем.	Two rooms with a shower.
	(sazhaLYEniyu) (adNOM)	
	К сожалению, в одном	Unfortunately, in one
	номере душ не работает.	room the shower isn't working.
	(nichiVO)	
MARK	**Ничего. Мы все будем**	It doesn't matter. We'll all
	(priniMAT') (druGOM)	
	принимать душ в другом номере.	take a shower in the other room.
CLERK	**Хорошо. Но есть ещё**	Fine. But there is still
	(MAlinikaya) (praBLYEma)	
	одна маленькая проблема.	one small problem.
	(Imina)	
MARK	**Что именно?**	What exactly?

ANSWERS

Repairs 2. Телевизор не работает. **3.** Душ не работает.

CLERK	**В другом номере** (akNO) (atkryVAitsa) **окно не открывается.**	In the other room the window doesn't open.
MARK (to Caroline)	(DYElat') **Что будем делать?**	What shall we do?
	(DYEti) (uSTAli) **Поздно. Дети устали.**	It's late. The children are tired.
	(SvaBODnykh) **Нет свободных номеров во всей Москве.**	There are no available rooms in all of Moscow.
CAROLINE	(daVAYtye) (aSTAnimsya) (ZDYES') **Давайте останемся здесь.**	Let's stay here.
CLERK	(pasparTA) **Хорошо. Ваши паспорта,** (paZHAluysta) **пожалуйста.**	Fine. Your passports, please.
MARK	(naSCHOT) **Вот они. А как насчёт** (ZAFtraka) **завтрака?**	Here they are. And how about breakfast?
CLERK	(buFYEtye) **Завтрак в буфете** (chiSOF) **в восемь часов.**	Breakfast is served in the snack bar at 8:00 AM.
	(prapuSKA) **Вот ваши пропуска.**	Here are your passes.*
MARK	(KLYUCH) **А где ключ?**	And where is the key?
CLERK	(shiSTOM) (etaZHE) **На шестом этаже.**	On the sixth floor.
	Номер 615.	Room 615.
CAROLINA	(SKAzhitye) **Вы не скажете,** (LIFT) **где лифт?**	Could you tell me where the elevator is?
CLERK	(iDItye) (PRYAma) **Идите прямо,** (paTOM) (naPRAva) **а потом направо.**	Go straight ahead, and then to the right.
MARK	(spaSIba) (bal'SHOye) **Спасибо большое.**	Thank you very much.
CLERK	**Пожалуйста.**	You're welcome.

* In most Russian hotels you will receive a **пропуск** (hotel pass) which you must show to the doorman and to your key lady. The key lady on your floor will give you your key and collect it when you leave the room.

After you have reviewed the dialogue a few times, see if you can fill in the blanks with the correct Russian words.

1. **Ваши ________________________ , пожалуйста.**

2. **Но есть ещё одна маленькая ________________________ .**

3. **________________________ не открывается.**

4. **А как ________________________ завтрака?**

5. **Давайте ________________________ здесь.**

(DVA) *(SLOva)*

Два слова

Two words

If you want to make friends and get along with people on your trip, you will want to learn and use these two little words.

(spaSIba)	*(paZHAluysta)*
спасибо	**пожалуйста***
thank you	please, you're welcome

* This word can mean either "please" or "you're welcome," according to the situation.

ANSWERS

Fill in **1.** паспорта **2.** проблема **3.** Окно **4.** насчёт **5.** останемся

Circle these important words along with five other words related to your hotel stay in the word maze below. (HINT: Look for the Russian words for *please, thank you, elevator, passport, key, key lady, toilet.)*

а б в д к т к л и м

п о ж а л у й с т а

а р с у ю а ш щ о ю

с о н т ч л я б т я

п г ж е э е а с т и

о о ж а л т л и ф т

р й с п а с и б о а

т ё р ъ е д м о м ю

д е ж у р н а я т ь

ANSWERS

Word maze пожалуйста, спасибо, лифт, паспорт, ключ, дежурная, туалет

PLACES OF INTEREST

(dastaprimiCHAtil'nasti)
Достопримечательности

3 *(KAK) (tuDA) (prayTI)* Как туда пройти?

How to Get There (on Foot)

"How do I get to . . . ?" "Where is the nearest subway?" "Is the museum straight ahead?" You'll be asking directions and getting answers wherever you travel. Get to know the words and phrases that will make getting around easier. Write in the new words and say them aloud several times.

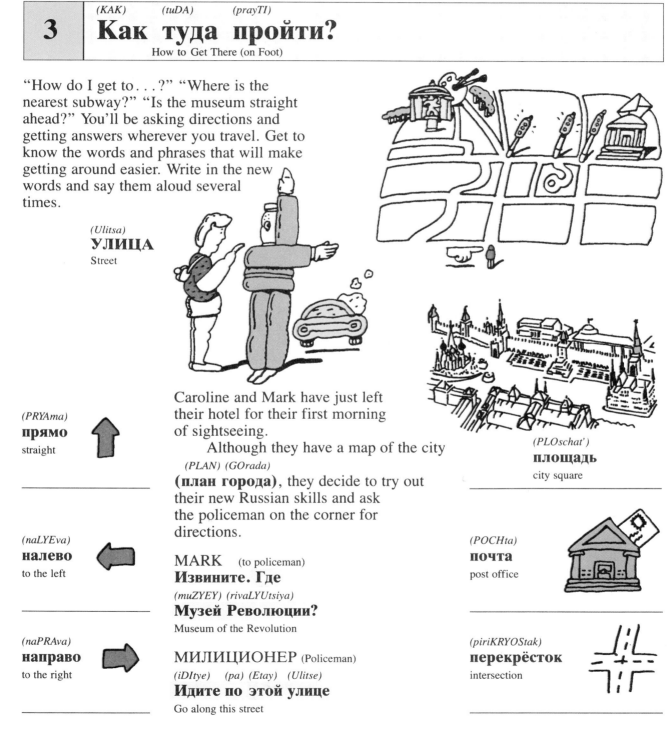

(Ulitsa)
УЛИЦА
Street

(PLOschat')
площадь
city square

(PRYAma)
прямо
straight

(naLYEva)
налево
to the left

(naPRAva)
направо
to the right

Caroline and Mark have just left their hotel for their first morning of sightseeing.

Although they have a map of the city *(PLAN) (GOrada)* **(план города)**, they decide to try out their new Russian skills and ask the policeman on the corner for directions.

MARK (to policeman)
(muZYEY) (rivaLYUtsiya)
Извините. Где Музей Революции?
Museum of the Revolution

МИЛИЦИОНЕР (Policeman)
(iDItye) (pa) (Etay) (Ulitse)
Идите по этой улице
Go along this street

(POCHta)
почта
post office

(piriKRYOStak)
перекрёсток
intersection

(da) (svitaFOra) (paTOM) (naLYEva)
до светофора, потом налево
until the traffic signal, then to the left

(svitaFOR)
светофор
traffic light

(da) (uGLA) (TAM) (pavirNItye) (naPRAva)
до угла. Там поверните направо.
to the corner. There you turn to the right.

(iDItye) (DAL'she) (i) (PYErit) (VAmi)
Идите дальше и перед вами
Go a bit farther and in front of you

(BUdit) (muZYEY)
будет музей.
will be the museum.

CAROLINE **Спасибо.**

МИЛИЦИОНЕР **Пожалуйста.**

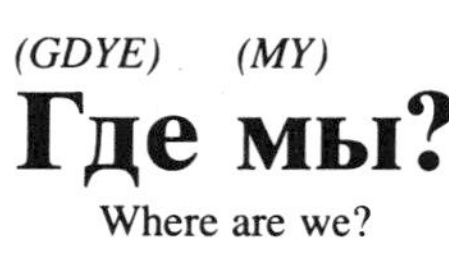

(GDYE) (MY)
Где мы?
Where are we?

(STOL)
стол ____________________
table

(KOSHka)
кошка ____________________
cat

Look at the words and phrases used in Russian to describe location. Write out each of these important little words. Notice that the noun for "table" has different endings according to the prepositions that precede it. You will not need to learn all of these endings. Pay closer attention to the highlighted forms.

(ZA) (staLOM)
за столом
behind

____

(PYErit) (staLOM)
перед столом
in front of

____

(NA) (staLYE)
на столе
on

____

(U) (staLA)
у стола
next to

(Okala) (staLA)
около стола
near

(daliKO) (OT) (staLA)
далеко от стола
far away

Now take a look at the **мальчик** (boy) and the **дом** (house). Can you write in the proper words to locate him?

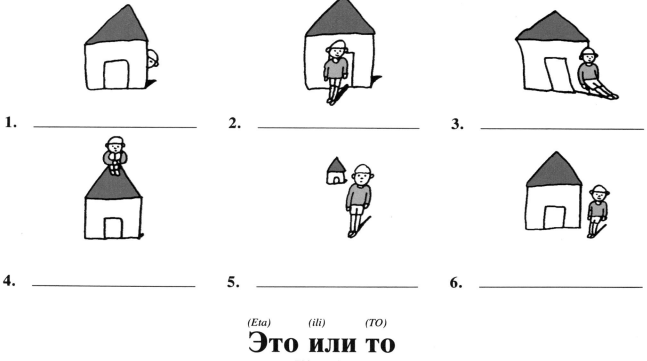

1. ______________________

2. ______________________

3. ______________________

4. ______________________

5. ______________________

6. ______________________

(Eta) (ili) (TO)

Это или то

This or that

You can do lots of things in Russian by using your finger to point and these two little words. Let's try it for fun. Fill in the blanks with the correct response.

(khaTItye)

1. **Вы хотите это или то?** ______________________ **, пожалуйста.**
   Would you like this one or that one? This one, please.

(pritpachiTAitye)

2. **Вы предпочитаете это или то?** ______________________ **, пожалуйста.**
   Do you prefer this one or that one? That one, please.

ANSWERS

This or That **1.** Это **2.** То

Fill in **1.** за **2.** перед **3.** у **4.** на **5.** далеко от **6.** около

(NUZHniye) *(slaVA)*

Нужные слова

Necessary words

Write the Russian words in the space provided and say them aloud.

(TSERkaf')
церковь
church

____

(kiNO)
кино
movie

____

(magaZIN)
магазин
store

____

(BANK)
банк
bank

____

(Ulitsa)
улица
street

____

(maSHYna)
машина
car

____

(apTYEka)
аптека
pharmacy

____

(kiOSK)
киоск
kiosk

____

(iTI) *(pishKOM)*

Идти пешком

Coming and going (on foot)

Russian verbs have endings to indicate who is performing the action. Remember back to the personal pronouns and look at the following table. Then write out the expressions in the blanks. NOTE: Russians use the same word for "Coming" and "Going!"

я иду́	______________	I am going
ты идёшь	______________	you are going
он/она идёт	______________	he/she is going
мы идём	______________	we are going
вы идёте	______________	you are going
они иду́т	______________	they are going

(GDYE) (ili) (kuDA)

Где или куда

Where or where to

We have already seen examples of the ending of a noun changing because of a preposition. We say the noun is in a specific *case*. The **nominative** (naming) case is the form of a noun found in dictionaries and word lists. Russian has six cases. To express location, Russians use the **prepositional or the accusative case**.

In answer to the question **«Где?»** ("Where?") Russians use the preposition **в** (in) or **на** (at) plus the prepositional case, which for most nouns has the ending **е**.

Где мама? ________	**Она в магазине.** ________
Где папа? ________	**Он в банке.** ________
Где Иван? ________	**Он в аптеке.** ________
Где Ирина? ________	**Она на почте.** ________

In answer to the question **«Куда?»** ("Where to?"), Russians reply with the preposition **в** (in) or **на** (at) plus the accusative case. The accusative endings for masculine and neuter nouns are the same as the nominative. For feminine nouns, those that end in **а** will have the accusative case ending **у**, those ending in **я** will end in **ю.**

Куда идёт мама? ________	**Она идёт в магазин.** ________
Куда идёт папа? ________	**Он идёт в банк.** ________
Куда ты идёшь? ________	**Я иду в аптеку.** ________
Куда вы идёте? ________	**Мы идём на почту.** ________

That's an awful lot to learn. Go back over the section above and practice writing out in the spaces provided the new words and phrases. Then let's see if you can fill in the blanks below.

1. Папа и мама ________ (are going) **в город** *(GOrat)*. **2. Мама должна пойти** *(dalZHNA)* (has to go) ________ (to the bank).

ANSWERS

Fill in **1.** идут **2.** в банк

3. Папа идёт ______________ **на почту.**
is going

4. Там ______________ **работает Ирина.**
at the post office — works *(raBOtait)*

5. Ирина и папа идут ______________ **.**
to a store

6. Мама уже ______________ **.**
at the store.

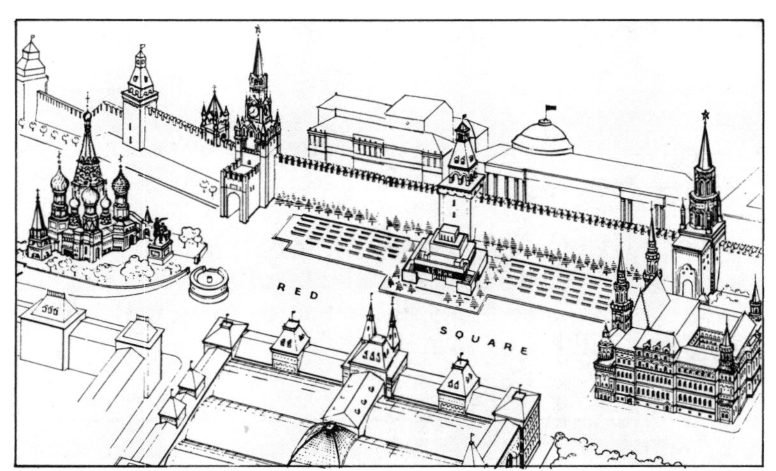

ANSWERS

Fill in **3.** идёт **4.** на почте **5.** в магазин **6.** в магазине.

4 Виды транспорта / Как туда проехать

(VIdy) (TRANsparta) (KAK) (tuDA) (praYEkhat')

Means of Transportation / How to Get There (by Vehicle)

You will certainly want to use the public transportation systems in **Москва** or **Санкт-Петербург** (Saint Petersburg). The following dialogue contains some words and expressions you will find useful. Read the dialogue aloud several times to familiarize yourself with the meaning and pronunciation of the words. *And don't forget to take a ride on the* **Метро**.

CAROLINE	*(paYEdim) (takSI)* **Поедем на такси** *(tiATR)* **в театр.**	Let's ride in a taxi to the theater.
MARK	*(SLISHkam) (DOraga)* **Нет. Слишком дорого.**	No. That's too expensive.
CAROLINE	**Как насчёт метро?** *(uDOBna) (BYStra)* **Это удобно и быстро.**	How about the metro? That's comfortable and quick.

MARK	(nichiVO) (VIDna) **Да. Но ничего не видно.**	Yes. But you can't see anything.
CAROLINE	(Edim) (afTObusye) **Едем на автобусе?**	Should we take the bus?
MARK	(priKRASna) **Прекрасно! У тебя** (biLYEty) **есть билеты?**	Splendid! Do you have any tickets?
CAROLINE	(kaNESHna) **Конечно, у меня есть.**	Of course. I have some.

На автобусе (On the bus).

PASSENGER	(vyKHOditye) **Вы выходите?**	Are you getting off?
CAROLINE	(SKAzhitye) **Нет. Вы не скажете,** (SKOL'ka) (astaNOvak) **сколько остановок** **до Большого театра?**	No. Could you tell us, how many stops until the Bolshoi Theater?
PASSENGER	(bal'SHOY) (CHEris) **Большой театр через** **две остановки.**	The Bolshoi Theater comes after two stops.

After listening to the conversation above, you should be able to choose the correct answer and write it in the blank spaces.

1. **Поедем ____________________ в театр.**
   а. на автобусе   б. на метро   в. на такси
2. **Нет. Слишком ____________________ .**
   а. хорошо   б. дорого   в. дешёво
3. **Едем __________ автобусе?**
   а. на   б. через   в. в
4. **Вы ____________________?**
   а. скажете   б. едете   в. выходите
5. **____________________ театр через две остановки.**
   а. Большой   б. наш   в. прекрасный

ANSWERS

Fill in 1. а 2. б 3. а 4. в 5. а

(KAK) (MY) (YEdim)

Как мы едем?

How will we go?

Look at the pictures below, repeat the phrases, and then write them in the blanks.

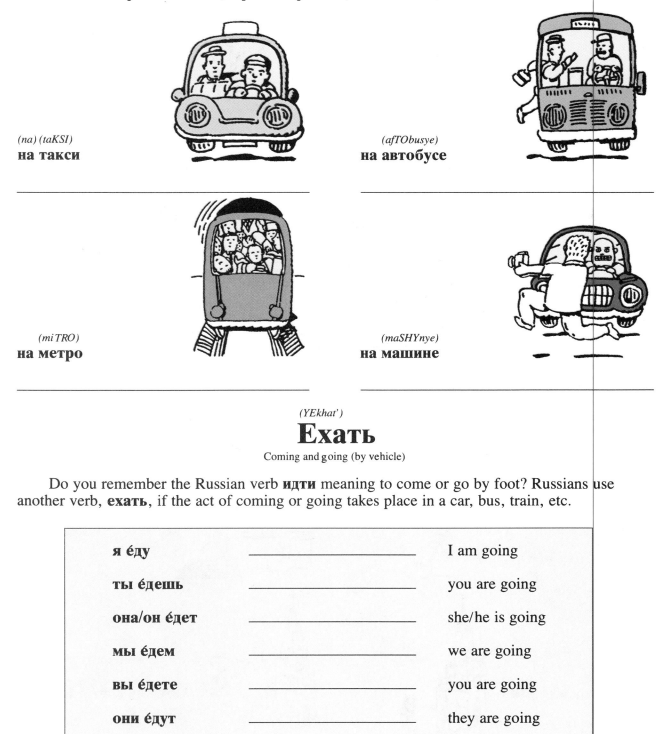

(na) (taKSI)
на такси

____

(afTObusye)
на автобусе

____

(miTRO)
на метро

____

(maSHYnye)
на машине

____

(YEkhat')

Ехать

Coming and going (by vehicle)

Do you remember the Russian verb **идти** meaning to come or go by foot? Russians use another verb, **ехать**, if the act of coming or going takes place in a car, bus, train, etc.

я éду	______________	I am going
ты éдешь	______________	you are going
она/он éдет	______________	she/he is going
мы éдем	______________	we are going
вы éдете	______________	you are going
они éдут	______________	they are going

(GDYE) (aNI) (kuDA) (aNI) (YEdut)
ГДЕ ОНИ? КУДА ОНИ ЕДУТ?
Where Are They? Where Are They Going?

Мужчина в Москве.

Мужчина едет в Москву.

Женщина в Вашингтоне.

Женщина едет в Вашингтон.

Мальчик в театре.

Мальчик едет в театр.

Девочка на балете.

Девочка едет на балет.

Молодой человек в кино.

Молодой человек едет в кино.

Девушка в Кремле.

Девушка едет в Кремль.

(CHEY) Чей, *(CH'YA)* Чья, *(CH'YO)* Чьё, *(CH'I)* Чьи

Whose?

You already know that Russian nouns can be masculine, feminine and neuter, and singular or plural. Some modifiers must agree with the noun. In the chart below you will see that the words for "mine, your, our" change according to the noun. Russians say:

(MOY) (DOM) (maYA) (kvarTIra) (maYO) (pis'MO) (maYI) (DYEti)
мой дом, моя квартира, моё письмо, мои дети
my house my apartment my letter my children

ENGLISH	MASCULINE	FEMININE	NEUTER	ALL PLURALS
My	**мой**	**моя**	**моё**	**мои**
Your	**твой**	**твоя**	**твоё**	**твои**
Her/His	**её/его**	**её/его**	**её/его**	**её/его**
Our	**наш**	**наша**	**наше**	**наши**
Your	**ваш**	**ваша**	**ваше**	**ваши**
Their	**их**	**их**	**их**	**их**

See how well you can do in filling in the missing modifiers:

1. **Это** ____________ (my) **кошка.** (cat)
2. **Это** ____________ (their) **улица.** (street)
3. **Это** ____________ (our) **собака.** (dog)
4. **Это** ____________ (her) **стол.** (table)
5. **Это** ____________ (your) **бабушка.** (grandmother)
6. **Это** ____________ (your (pl.)) **банк.** (bank)

ANSWERS

Modifiers 1. моя 2. их 3. наша 4. её 5. твоя 6. ваш

7. Это ________ **сын.** (his / son) **8. Это** ________ **машина.** (my / car) **9. Это** ________ **стул.** (our / chair)

10. Это ________ **яблоко.** (your / apple) **11. Это** ________ **дети.** (her / children) **12. Это** ________ **дом.** (their / house)

Let's take a break. You've had a lot of information to absorb. See how much Russian you already know by trying your hand at the **кроссворд** (crossword)

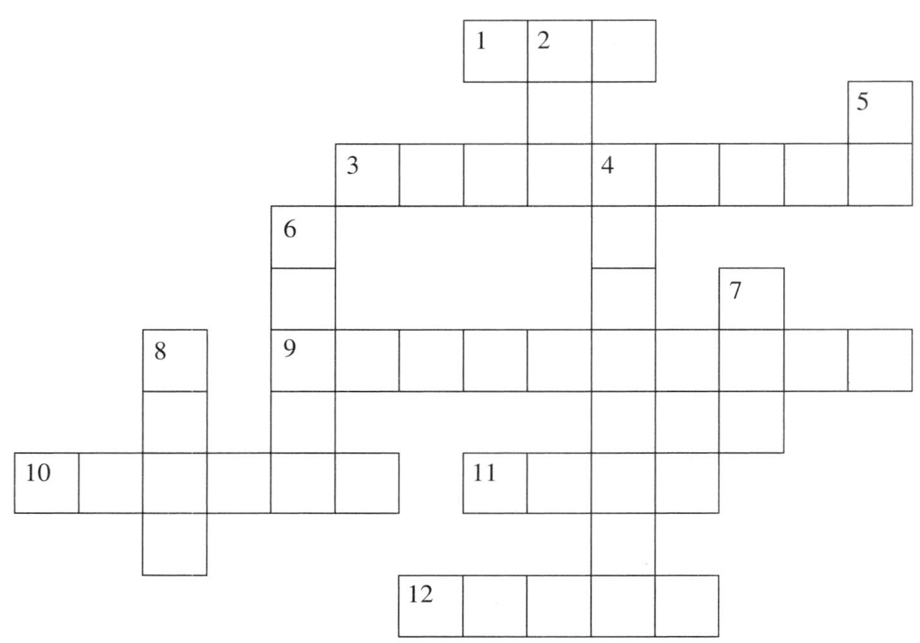

По горизонтали	**По вертикали**
Across	*Down*
1. They	**2.** No
3. Hotel	**4.** Excuse me
9. Policeman	**5.** Yes
10. Four	**6.** Room/number
11. One	**7.** She
12. Museum	**8.** Five

ANSWERS

Modifiers **7.** его **8.** моя **9.** наш **10.** твоё **11.** её **12.** их

Puzzle Across: **1.** они **3.** гостиница **9.** милиционер **10.** четыре **11.** один **12.** музей

Down: **2.** нет **4.** извините **5.** да **6.** номер **7.** она **8.** пять

(VRYEmya) (i) (CHIsla)

Время и числа

Time and Numbers

(SKOL'ka)

Сколько?

How much/many?

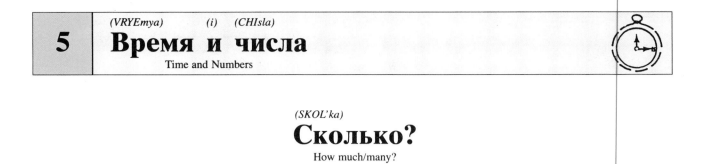

The numbers are essential if you wish to get by in Russian. Do you remember the numbers from one to ten in Chapter 2? Let's cover them again and write them out for practice along with two new important words for telling time.

Number	Russian		Pronunciation
0	**нуль**	______________	*NUL'*
1	**один**	______________	*aDIN*
2	**два**	______________	*DVA*
3	**три**	______________	*TRI*
4	**четыре**	______________	*chiTYrye*
5	**пять**	______________	*PYAT'*
6	**шесть**	______________	*SHEST'*
7	**семь**	______________	*SYEM'*
8	**восемь**	______________	*VOsim'*
9	**девять**	______________	*DYEvit'*
10	**десять**	______________	*DYEsit'*
11	**одиннадцать**	______________	*aDInatsat'*
12	**двенадцать**	______________	*dviNAtsat'*

(kaTOry) *(siyCHAS)* *(CHAS)*

КОТОРЫЙ СЕЙЧАС ЧАС?

What Time Is It Now?

Now you're ready to start telling time. Look at the clocks below.

В Токио девять часов.	**На Аляске три часа.**	**В Нью-Йорке восемь часов.**	**В Москве три часа.**	**В Париже час.**

In order to express the time, Russians use the number plus a form of the word "hour"—**час**. For one o'clock, simply say **час** (*CHAS*). After the numbers two, three, and four, say **часа** (*chiSA*): **два часа, три часа, четыре часа**. After the number five and through twenty use **часов** (*chiSOF*): **пять часов, шесть часов, и т.д.**

Can you count around the clock? Try it just once. To add precision to your times you might want to add the words for "in the morning"—**утра** (*uTRA*), "in the afternoon"—**дня** (*DNYA*), "in the evening"—**вечера** (*VYEchira*).

ANSWERS

Clock час, два часа, три часа, четыре часа, пять часов, шесть часов, семь часов, восемь часов, девять часов, десять часов, одиннадцать часов, двенадцать часов

(kagDA)

Когда?

When?

Now that you can tell time, it's easy to tell someone *when* or *at what time* something will or did happen. You simply add the preposition **в** before the time. Tell when you are coming and then we'll fill in the blank!

Я приду в час.

____

Я приду в три часа.

____

Я приду в семь часов.

____

Я приду в четыре часа.

____

Я приду в десять часов.

____

Now that we can get there on time, you'll want to learn the other important numbers. Notice that Russians make the word for eleven and twelve by adding one + ten—**один на десять = одиннадцать**, two + ten—**два на десять = двенадцать**. The same is true for the numbers from thirteen to nineteen. Once again, try to repeat them aloud and then write them in the blanks provided.

Number	Russian		Pronunciation
13	**тринадцать**	______________	*triNAtsat'*
14	**четырнадцать**	______________	*chiTYRnatsat'*
15	**пятнадцать**	______________	*pitNAtsat'*
16	**шестнадцать**	______________	*shistNAtsat'*
17	**семнадцать**	______________	*simNAtsat'*
18	**восемнадцать**	______________	*vasimNAtsat'*
19	**девятнадцать**	______________	*divitNAtsat'*

The numbers for twenty, thirty, fifty, sixty, seventy and eighty are really two tens—**два десять = двадцать**, three tens—**три десять = тридцать**, etc.

Number	Russian		Pronunciation
20	**двадцать**	____________	*DVAtsat'*
30	**тридцать**	____________	*TRItsat'*
40	**сорок**	____________	*SOrak*
50	**пятьдесят**	____________	*pidiSYAT*
60	**шестьдесят**	____________	*shizdiSYAT*
70	**семьдесят**	____________	*SYEM'disit*
80	**восемьдесят**	____________	*VOsim'disit*

To make the numbers twenty-one, twenty-two, etc., just add the single digits from above.

21	22	23
двадцать один	**двадцать два**	**двадцать три**
24	25	26
двадцать четыре	**двадцать пять**	**двадцать шесть**
27	28	29
двадцать семь	**двадцать восемь**	**двадцать девять**

Here are all of the other numbers you'll need to know to get around completely. Be sure to practice them often, until you get the hang of it.

Number	Russian		Pronunciation
90	**девяносто**	______________	*diviNOSta*
100	**сто**	______________	*STO*
101	**сто один**	______________	*STO aDIN*
110	**сто десять**	______________	*STO DYEsit'*
200	**двести**	______________	*DVYESti*
300	**триста**	______________	*TRISta*
400	**четыреста**	______________	*chiTYrista*
500	**пятьсот**	______________	*pit'SOT*
600	**шестьсот**	______________	*shist'SOT*
700	**семьсот**	______________	*sim'SOT*
800	**восемьсот**	______________	*vasim'SOT*
900	**девятьсот**	______________	*divit'SOT*
1000	**тысяча**	______________	*TYsicha*
2000	**две тысячи**	______________	*DVYE TYsichi*
5000	**пять тысяч**	______________	*PYAT' TYsich*
1,000,000	**миллион**	______________	*miliON*
2,000,000	**два миллиона**	______________	*DVA miliOna*
5,000,000	**пять миллионов**	______________	*PYAT' miliOnaf*
1,000,000,000	**миллиард**	______________	*miliART*

Ordinal Numbers

Write in the floors in the elevator by hand in the spaces provided and say them aloud.

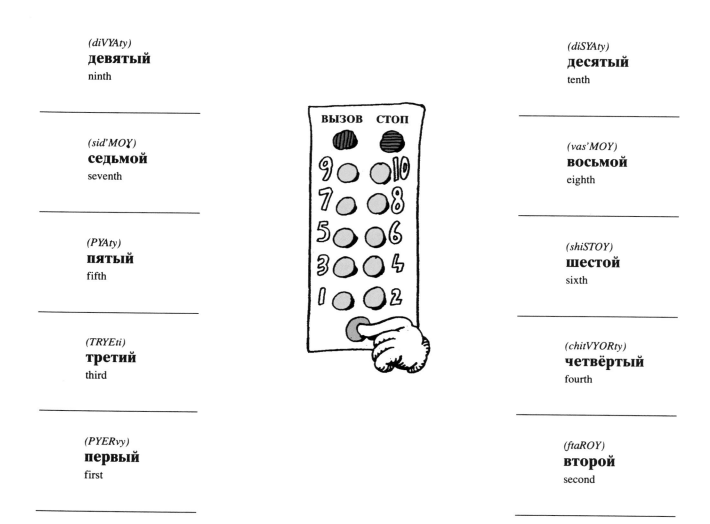

(diVYAty)
девятый
ninth

____

(diSYAty)
десятый
tenth

____

(sid'MOY)
седьмой
seventh

____

(vas'MOY)
восьмой
eighth

____

(PYAty)
пятый
fifth

____

(shiSTOY)
шестой
sixth

____

(TRYEti)
третий
third

____

(chitVYORty)
четвёртый
fourth

____

(PYERvy)
первый
first

____

(ftaROY)
второй
second

____

Sometimes, especially in plane and train schedules, Russians use the 24-hour clock, so that the numbers from 13 to 24 designate the P.M. hours.

One o'clock P.M. = **Тринадцать часов.** *(triNAtsat' chiSOF)*

In addition to saying twelve o'clock, **двенадцать часов**, Russians can say

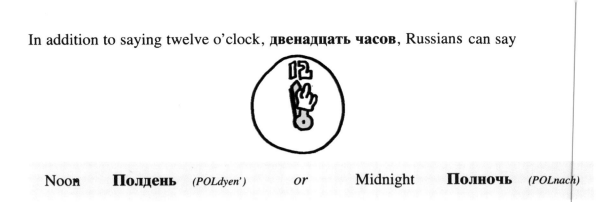

Noon **Полдень** *(POLdyen')* *or* Midnight **Полночь** *(POLnach)*

Once an hour has begun, Russians look forward to the next hour. Thus 1:05 is five minutes of the second hour. They also make use of these two useful quantities for a quarter: *(CHETvirt')* **четверть**, and a half: *(palaVIna)* **половина**.

(PYAT) (miNUT) (ftaROva)
пять минут второго

(DYEsit') (miNUT) (TRYEt'yiva)
десять минут третьего

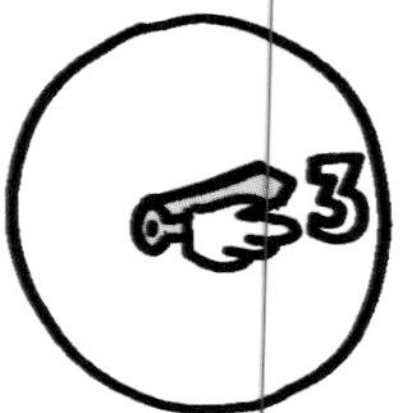

(CHETvirt') (chitVYORtava)
четверть четвёртого

(DVAtsat') (miNUT) (PYAtava)
двадцать минут пятого

(DVAtsat') (PYAT') (miNUT) (shiSTOva)
двадцать пять минут шестого

(palaVIna) (sid'MOva)
половина седьмого

After the half hour Russians count backwards; thus 7:35 is the eighth hour minus twenty-five minutes.

(byez) (dvatsaTI) (piTI) (VOsim')
без двадцати пяти восемь

(byez) (dvatsaTI) (DYEvit')
без двадцати девять

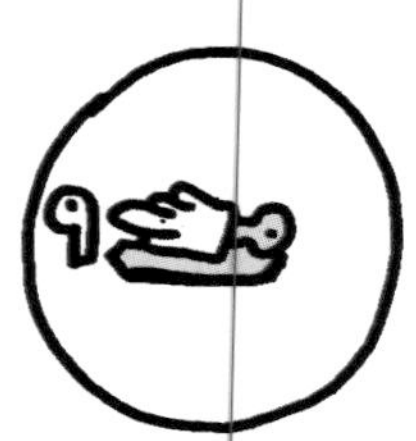

(byez) (CHETvirti) (DYEsit')
без четверти десять

(byez) (disiTI) (aDInatsat')
без десяти одиннадцать

(byez) (piTI) (dviNAtsat')
без пяти двенадцать

Can you give a set of numbers around the clock. Try to say the following times. Then answer the question, **который сейчас час?** Fill in the blanks.

а. 1:00 ________________

б. 2:05 ________________

в. 3:10 ________________

г. 4:15 ________________

д. 5:20 ________________

е. 6:25 ________________

ё. 7:30 ________________

ж. 8:35 ________________

з. 9:40 ________________

и. 10:45 ________________

й. 11:50 ________________

к. 12:55 ________________

ANSWERS

Time а. час **б.** пять минут третьего **в.** десять минут четвёртого **г.** четверть пятого **д.** двадцать минут шестого **е.** двадцать пять минут седьмого **ё.** половина восьмого **ж.** без двадцати пяти девять **з.** без двадцати десять **и.** без четверти одиннадцать **й.** без десяти двенадцать **к.** без пяти час

Let's watch Mark in the following encounter. Look over the text and then repeat the dialogue several times until you are comfortable with all the highlighted words and phrases.

MARK	**Извините, пожалуйста.**	Excuse me.
	(kaTOry) (siCHAS) **Который сейчас час?**	What time is it?
ГОСПОДИН	**Уже полночь.**	It's already midnight.
MARK	*(MOzhit) (BYT')* **Не может быть!**	That can't be!
	(SONtse) (SVYEtit) **Солнце светит.**	The sun is shining.
ГОСПОДИН	*(PRAvy)* **Вы правы.**	You're right.
	Тогда, уже полдень.	Then, it's noon.
MARK	*(SHUtitye)* **Вы шутите?**	Are you joking?
ГОСПОДИН	**Нет. Но мои часы**	No. But my watch
	(raBOtayut) **не работают.**	isn't working.
	(tuRIST) **Вы турист?**	Are you a tourist?
MARK	**Да, конечно.**	Yes, of course.
ГОСПОДИН	*(kuPIT')* **Вы хотите купить**	Do you want to buy a
	часы?	watch?
MARK	*(STOyat)* **Сколько они стоят?**	How much do they cost?
	(TOL'ka) **У меня только**	I only have
	тридцать рублей.	thirty rubles.
ГОСПОДИН	**Эти часы стоят**	This watch costs
	двадцать пять рублей.	twenty-five rubles.
MARK	*(vaz'MU)* **Хорошо. Я возьму.**	Fine. I'll take it.

Note: Did you notice how the word for "watch" (**часы**) is related to the word for hour **час**. Actually, the word for "watch" is made from a plural of "hours."

Can you write these phrases from the dialogue in Russian?

1. What time is it? ______________________________
2. It's already midnight. ______________________________
3. But my watch isn't working. ______________________________
4. Do you want to buy a watch? ______________________________

(kaKOY) КАКОЙ *(siVOdnya)* СЕГОДНЯ *(DYEN')* ДЕНЬ?

What Day Is Today?

(paniDYEL'nik)	*(FTORnik)*	*(sriDA)*	*(chitVYERK)*	*(PYATnitsa)*	*(suBOta)*	*(vaskriSYEn'ye)*
понедельник	**вторник**	**среда**	**четверг**	**пятница**	**суббота**	**воскресенье**

(siVOdnya) **сегодня** today

(fchiRA) **вчера** yesterday

(ZAFtra) **завтра** tomorrow

(uZHE) **уже** already

(yiSCHO) **ещё** still

(aPYAT') **опять** again

If you want to say when (on what day) you are coming, use the preposition **в** and the accusative case. Read the answers to the question:

When do you work?	**Когда вы работаете?**	*(kagDA) (VY) (raBOtaitye)*

ANSWERS

Dialogue **1.** Который сейчас час? **2.** Уже полночь. **3.** Но мои часы не работают. **4.** Вы хотите купить часы?

I work	**Я работаю**	
on Monday	**в понедельник.**	(f) (paniDYEL'nik)
on Tuesday	**во вторник.**	(va) (FTORnik)
on Wednesday	**в среду.**	(f) (SRYEdu)
on Thursday	**в четверг.**	(f) (chitVYERK)
on Friday	**в пятницу.**	(f) (PYATnitsu)
I don't work	**Я не работаю**	
on Saturday	**в субботу.**	(f) (suBOtu)
on Sunday	**в воскресенье.**	(v) (vaskriSYEn'ye)

Can you match up the following days of the week and adverbs of time with their English equivalents?

1. сегодня	**а.** tomorrow
2. вторник	**б.** already
3. завтра	**в.** Wednesday
4. среда	**г.** yesterday
5. уже	**д.** again
6. вчера	**е.** Tuesday
7. опять	**ё.** today

(RUskiye) *(glaGOly)*

РУССКИЕ ГЛАГОЛЫ

Russian Verbs

You have already seen the personal pronouns for I, you, he, etc. and the conjugation of the Russian verbs for motion on foot (**идти**) and by vehicle (**ехать**). Russian verbs belong to one of two classes or conjugations in the present tense. Look at the endings for the first conjugation.

ANSWERS

Matching 1. ё **2.** е **3.** а **4.** в **5.** б **6.** г **7.** д

Note how the forms change according to the subject of the sentence.

PRONOUN	VERB		VERB	
	рабóтать	(to work)	**жить**	(to live)
я	**рабóтаю**	(I work)	**живý**	(I live)
ты	**рабóтаешь**	(you work)	**живёшь**	(you live)
она/он	**рабóтает**	(she/he works)	**живёт**	(she/he lives)
мы	**рабóтаем**	(we work)	**живём**	(we live)
вы	**рабóтаете**	(you work)	**живёте**	(you live)
они	**рабóтают**	(they work)	**живýт**	(they live)

The endings vary slightly according to whether they come after a consonant or a vowel, and whether or not they are stressed.

You can form lots of verbs based on the chart above. Here are just a few examples:

ENGLISH	RUSSIAN INFINITIVE	CONJUGATED FORM
to rest	*(adyKHAT')* **отдыхать**	*(YA) (adyKHAyu)* **я отдыхаю**
to have breakfast	*(ZAFtrakat')* **завтракать**	*(TY) (ZAFtrakaish)* **ты завтракаешь**
to have lunch/dinner	*(aBYEdat')* **обедать**	*(aNA) (aBYEdait)* **она обедает**
to know	*(ZNAT')* **знать**	*(ON) (ZNAit)* **он знает**
to have supper	*(Uzhinat')* **ужинать**	*(MY) (Uzhinaim)* **мы ужинаем**
to be late	*(aPAZdyvat')* **опаздывать**	*(VY) (aPAZdyvaitye)* **вы опаздываете**
to understand	*(paniMAT')* **понимать**	*(aNI) (paniMAyut)* **они понимают**

Now try your own hand in writing in the correct endings of these verbs.

1. I understand. — **Я понима _____ .**
2. We are resting. — **Мы отдыха _____ .**
3. They are breakfasting. — **Они завтрака _____ .**
4. She is dining. — **Она обеда _____ .**
5. Don't you know? — **Вы не зна _____ ?**

It's time to stop and catch our breath. We already know a tremendous amount as the little narrative below will indicate. Just fill in the blanks with the proper verbal endings, and then try writing out a quick translation to indicate how much you've already mastered.

Вера и Андрей жив _____ (live) в Москве. Они завтрака _____ (breakfast) в семь часов утра. Андрей работа _____ (works) в Кремле и он ед _____ (goes) туда (there) на метро. Вера работа _____ (works) на почте (post office) и утром она ид _____ (goes) пешком (on foot) на почту. Сегодня (Today) она опаздыва _____ (is late) и она ед _____ (goes) на такси. Вечером (In the evening) Вера спрашива _____ (asks), «Где мы ужина _____ (supper) ?» Андрей не хочет (want) ужинать (to have supper) в ресторане (restaurant), и он отвеча _____ (replies) «Я не зна _____ (know), где ты ужина _____ (supper), но я сегодня вечером отдыха _____ (rest).».

ANSWERS

Verbs **1.** Я понимаю. **2.** Мы отдыхаем. **3.** Они завтракают. **4.** Она обедает. **5.** Вы не знаете?

Fill in живут, завтракают, работает, едет, идёт, опаздывает, едет, спрашивает, ужинаем, отвечает, знаю, ужинаешь, отдыхаю.

Translation Vera and Andrei live in Moscow. They eat breakfast at seven o'clock in the morning. Andrei works in the Kremlin and he rides there on the metro. Vera works at a post office and she walks to the post office. Today she is late and she rides in a taxi. In the evening Vera asks, "Where will we have supper?" Andrei doesn't want to have supper in a restaurant and he replies, "I don't know where you are having supper, but this evening I am resting."

6 (na POizde) На поезде
On the Train

Train Service

Traveling by train can be a pleasant way to travel between cities in Russia and to catch a glimpse of the countryside and the people. The overnight trains between **Москва** and **Санкт-Петербург** provide a reliable and comfortable opportunity to make acquaintances, avoid weather delays at airports, and get a good night's sleep. In Moscow there are several train stations depending upon your destination. Be sure to ask from which station your train departs.

The following dialogue contains important words and phrases connected with train travel. Read it aloud several times.

MARK	*(vagZAlye)* **Вот мы на вокзале.**	Here we are at the station.
STEFANIE	**Папа, мы едем на** *(KRASnoy) (striLYE)* **«Красной стреле»** **в Санкт-Петербург?**	Dad, are we riding on the "Red Arrow" to Saint Petersburg?
MARK	**Да.** (to the clerk)	Yes.
	(aBRATny) **Сколько стоит обратный** *(biLYET)* **билет в Петербург?**	How much does a round-trip ticket to Petersburg cost?
ДЕВУШКА (clerk)	**Билет в мягком вагоне?**	A first class ticket? (in the soft car)
MARK	*(CHETvira)* **Да. Нас четверо.**	Yes. There are four of us.

ДЕВУШКА	**Вам нужно** *(NUZHna)* **одно или два купе.** *(kuPYE)* **Это будет 500 или 700 рублей.** *(ruBLYEY)*	You'll need one or two compartments. That will be 500 or 700 rubles.
MARK	**А в купированном** *(kuPIravanam)* **вагоне?** *(vaGOnye)*	And in a sleeping car?
ДЕВУШКА	**350 рублей.**	350 rubles.
MARK	**Когда отправляется** *(atpraVLYAitsa)* **поезд?**	When does the train depart?
ДЕВУШКА	**В 23:45**	At 11:45 P.M. (23:45).
MARK	**С какой платформы?** *(platFORmy)*	From which platform?
ДЕВУШКА	**Платформа № 4. Вот ваши билеты.**	Track #4. Here are your tickets.
STEFANIE	**Папа, где наши места?** *(misTA)*	Dad, where are our places?
MARK	**Вагон 10, места 5-8.**	Car 10, seats 5-8.

You might find yourself on all sorts of trains. The famous Trans-Siberian Railway can be the adventure of a lifetime. Traveling out to or back from a country **dacha** (villa) you might take an Express train (**Скорый поезд**). For overnight trains, as Mark and his daughter, Stefanie, have just learned, there are several categories of service for comfort. In first class (**мягкий вагон**) you can have a compartment (**купе**) with two very comfortable beds or with four beds. There is also the regular sleeping car (**купированный вагон**).

Try reading aloud the names of some of Moscow's favorite train stations. Then see if you can pair them with their English equivalents.

1. **Казанский вокзал**	а. Riga Station
2. **Киевский вокзал**	б. Yaroslav Station
3. **Белорусский вокзал**	в. Kazan Station
4. **Рижский вокзал**	г. Kiev Station
5. **Ярославский вокзал**	д. Byelorussian Station

ANSWERS

Train stations 1. в 2. г 3. д 4. а 5. б

Look at the following train schedule from the **Ярославский вокзал** in **Москва**. From here trains depart across Siberia for the Far East. You can go to **Пекин** (Beijing) or **Владивосток** (Vladivostok). Notice how the information is presented. First comes the destination (**пункт назначения**), then the number and category of train (**наименования, категория поезда**), the distance in kilometers from Moscow (**расстояние в км. от Москвы**), departure time from Moscow (**Время отправления из Москвы**), time enroute to there in hours and minutes (**Время в пути (туда), часы, мин.**).

ОТ МОСКВЫ

Пункты назначения поездов	Наименование, № и категория поездов	Расстояние в км от Москвы	Время отправления из Москвы	Дни отправления из Москвы	Время в пути (туда), часы, мин.	Дни прибытия на конечный пункт	Время прибытия на конечный пункт	Наличие вагонов: СВ, ресторанов (ВР), с купе-буфетом (КБ), багажных (Б)
ЯРОСЛАВСКИЙ ВОКЗАЛ								
Пекин (вагоны: Улан-Батор)	**4** скорый	До Наушек 5902	**0.30**	ср.	88.02	пн.	Пр. в Наушки 16.32	П, СВ, ВР, Б
Пекин (вагоны: Байн-Тумэн, Пхеньян)	**20** скорый	До Забайкальска 6666	**1.20**	сб., вскр	104.55	пт., сб.	Пр. в Забайкальск 10.15	СВ, ВР, Б
Улан-Батор (вагоны: Эрдэнэт)	**6** скорый	До Наушек 5902	**21.30**	кр. ср.	88.50	кр. пн.	Пр. в Наушки 14.20	СВ, ВР, Б
Улан-Батор (вагоны: Баганур, Сайн-Шанда, Чойр)	**110** скорый	До Наушек 5902	**0.30**	вс., чт	88.02	чт., пн.	Пр. в Наушки 16.32	СВ, ВР
Архангельск (ч. Ярославль-Гл. — Вологду)	**16** скорый	1130	**12.10**	еж., с 5/IX неч.	19.20	еж., с 6/IX чет.	7.30	П, СВ, ВР
Архангельск (ч. Ярославль-Гл. — Вологду)	**218** пасс.	1130	**19.45**	ежедневно	21.05	ежедневно	16.50	П, СВ, ВР, Б
Архангельск (ч. Ярославль-Гл. — Вологду — Коношу — Обозерскую)	**404** пасс.	1130	**17.35**	с 6/VI вт., пт	21.50	с 7/VI ср., сб.	15.25	—
Архангельск (ч. Ярославль-Гл. — Вологду)	**420** пасс.	1130	**2.40**	*	26.00	*	4.40	—
Благовещенск (ч. Киров — Свердловск — Тюмень)	**350** пасс.	7982	**13.00**	по 2/IX ежедн.	147.02	по 8/IX еж.	16.02	ВР
Владивосток (ч. Ярославль-Гл. — Киров — Тюмень—Новосибирск)	**2** «Россия» скорый	9296	**15.05**	ежедневно	142.10	ежедневно	13.55	СВ, ВР, ВБ
Владивосток (вагоны: Пхеньян)	**42** скорый	9297	**17.35**	чт., сб с 5/VI нечетные	148.30	ср., пт с 12/VI четные	22.05	СВ, ВР
Владивосток (ч. Киров — Тюмень — Новосибирск)	**140** скорый	9296	**9.40**	с 25/VI ежедневно	163.48	с 2/VII ежедневно	5.28	ВР
Вологда (ч. Ярославль-Гл.)	**660** «Вологодские зори» пасс	496	**0.20**	ежедневно	8.35	ежедневно	8.55	П, СВ
Воркута (ч. Ярославль-Гл. — Вологду — Коношу)	**22** скорый	2268	**20.50**	ежедневно	39.11	ежедневно	12.01	П, СВ, ВР
Воркута (ч. Ярославль-Гл. — Вологду — Коношу)	**180** пасс	2282	**13.10**	ежедневно	45.51	ежедневно	11.01	П, ВР, Б
Воркута (ч. Ярославль-Гл. — Вологду — Коношу)	**424** пасс.	2268	**3.00**	*	44.30	*	23.30	—
Горький (ч. Монино — Петушки — Владимир)	**38** «Нижегородец» скорый	460	**23.25**	ежедневно	8.05	ежедневно	7.30	СВ
Горький (ч. Монино — Петушки — Владимир)	**608** пасс.	460	**22.55**	ежедневно	9.20	ежедневно	8.15	П, Б
Горький (ч. Монино — Петушки — Владимир)	**610** «Буревестник» пасс	460	**16.35**	ежедневно	6.55	ежедневно	23.30	КБ
Горький (ч. Монино — Петушки — Владимир)	**612** пасс.	460	**1.35**	ежедневно	8.10	ежедневно	9.45	—
Горький (ч. Монино — Петушки — Владимир)	**484** пасс.	460	**2.50**	*	8.10	*	11.00	—
Горький (ч. Монино — Петушки — Владимир)	**486** пасс.	460	**13.45**	четные	8.10	четные	21.55	—
Забайкальск (вагоны: Байн-Тумэн)	**146** «Забайкалье» скорый	6666	**1.20**	ср., чт., пт. по 1/IX	104.55	вск., пн., вт. по 5/IX	10.15	ВР
Иваново (ч. Бельково)	**658** «Красная Галка» пасс	317	**16.50**	ежедневно	6.37	ежедневно	23.27	КБ
Иваново (ч. Бельково)	**662** пасс	317	**1.10**	ежедневно	7.25	ежедневно	8.35	СВ, Б
Иваново (ч. Бельково)	**428** пасс.	317	**3.55**	*	8.15	*	12.10	—
Инта (ч. Ярославль-Гл. — Вологду — Коношу)	**450** пасс.	2000	**3.40**	со 2/VI по 4/VIII чет. по 31/VIII ежед	39.20	с 1/VI по 5/VIII неч. по 1/IX ежедн	19.00	—

Can you answer a few of these questions?

1. When do the express trains leave for Beijing?
2. How many kilometers is it to Arkhangelsk?
3. Which city is closer, Gorky or Ivanovo?
4. How many hours is the quickest trip to Vladivostok?

ANSWERS

Questions **1.** 0:30 (12:30 AM) and 1:20 AM **2.** 1130 (700 miles) **3.** Ivanovo
4. 142 hours (almost six full days).

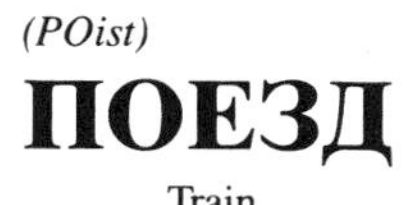

(POist)

ПОЕЗД

Train

(putiSHESTvavat')
путешествовать
to travel

(pasaZHYR)
пассажир
passenger

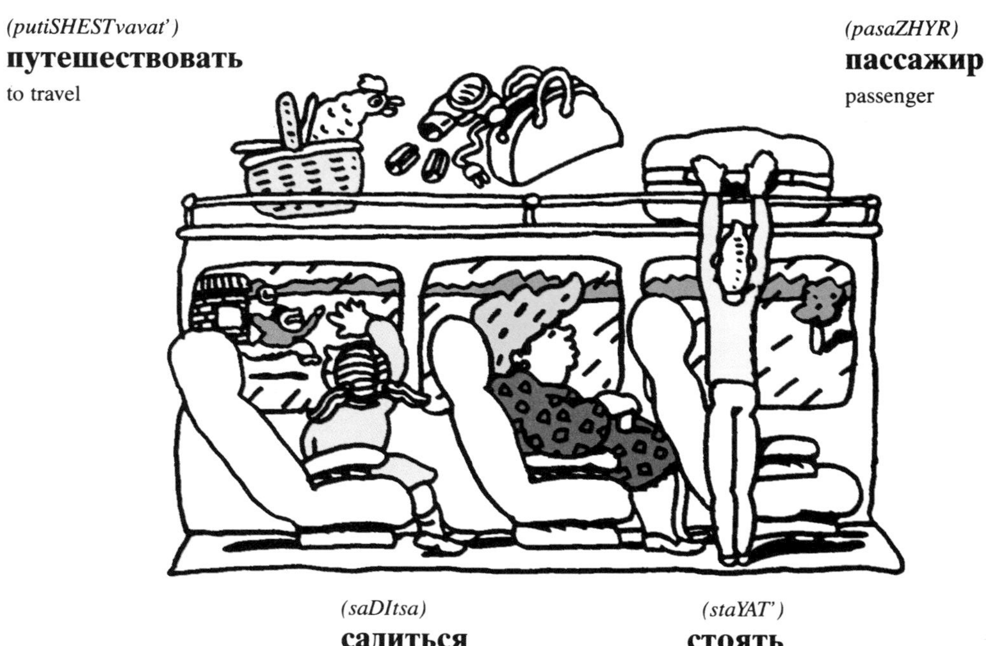

(saDItsa)
садиться
to sit down

(staYAT')
стоять
to stand

(ZAL azhiyDAniya)
зал ожидания
waiting lounge

(platFORma)
платформа
platform

(pravadNIK)
проводник
conductor

(raspiSAniye)
расписание
schedule

(tiLYESHka)
тележка
luggage cart

(naSIL'schik)
носильщик
porter

The Possessive Modifiers

(MOY)	(TVOY)	(yiVO)	(yiYO)	(NASH')	(VASH)	(IKH)
мой,	**твой,**	**его,**	**её,**	**наш,**	**ваш,**	**их**
my	your	his	her	our	your	their

On your journey you will certainly need to know how to distinguish your own belongings from those of others. Just as we use "my, your, his, her, our, their" in English, remember that Russians too have a way of expressing possession. The easiest category is the third person, "he, she and their," for which Russians use **его, её, их**.

This is his train and seat.	**Это его поезд и место.**
This is her train and seat.	**Это её поезд и место.**
This is their train and seat.	**Это их поезд и место.**

The forms for **его, её, их** remain unchanged regardless of the noun.

When we want to say "my, your, or our," the Russian word changes according to the gender of the noun. Look at the chart below.

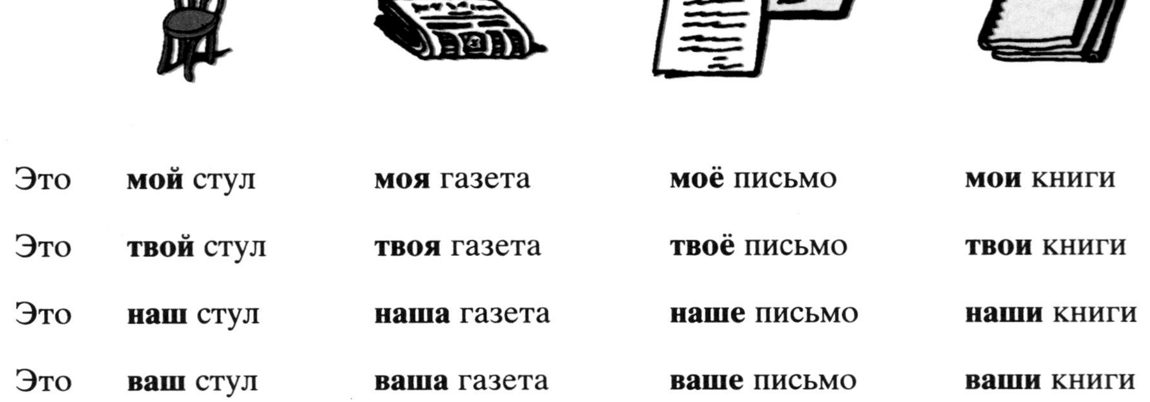

Это	**мой** стул	**моя** газета	**моё** письмо	**мои** книги
Это	**твой** стул	**твоя** газета	**твоё** письмо	**твои** книги
Это	**наш** стул	**наша** газета	**наше** письмо	**наши** книги
Это	**ваш** стул	**ваша** газета	**ваше** письмо	**ваши** книги

Caroline is having some trouble with her seats on the train. Can you help her fill in the blanks?

Извините, пожалуйста. Это ____________ (your) **место** (seat)**?** ____________ (Our) **места** (seats)**, номера 12, 13, 14, 15.**

Да, это ____________ (my) **место, номер 12. Нет, нет,** ____________ (my) **место, номер 19. Это** ____________ (your) **места.**

Марк, это ____________ (your) **место. Где Стефани и Александр? Это** ____________ (her) **место, и это** ____________ (his) **место.**

ANSWERS

Fill in ваше, Наши, моё, моё, ваши, твоё, её, его

7

(STRAny) (i) (yizyKI)

Страны и языки

Countries and Languages

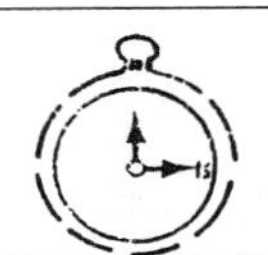

Now let's examine how Russians look at the rest of the world and learn how to say the names of the different countries in Russian. First look at the map and then match the Russian names with their English counterparts.

(kantiNYENty) (i) (STRAny)

Континенты и страны

Continents and countries

Africa	*(AFrika)* **Африка**	Asia	*(Aziya)* **Азия**
America	*(aMYErika)* **Америка**	Australia	*(afSTRAliya)* **Австралия**
North America	*(SYEvirnaya) (aMYErika)* **Северная Америка**	Europe	*(yiVROpa)* **Европа**
South America	*(YUZHnaya) (aMYErika)* **Южная Америка**	Afghanistan	*(afganiSTAN)* **Афганистан**

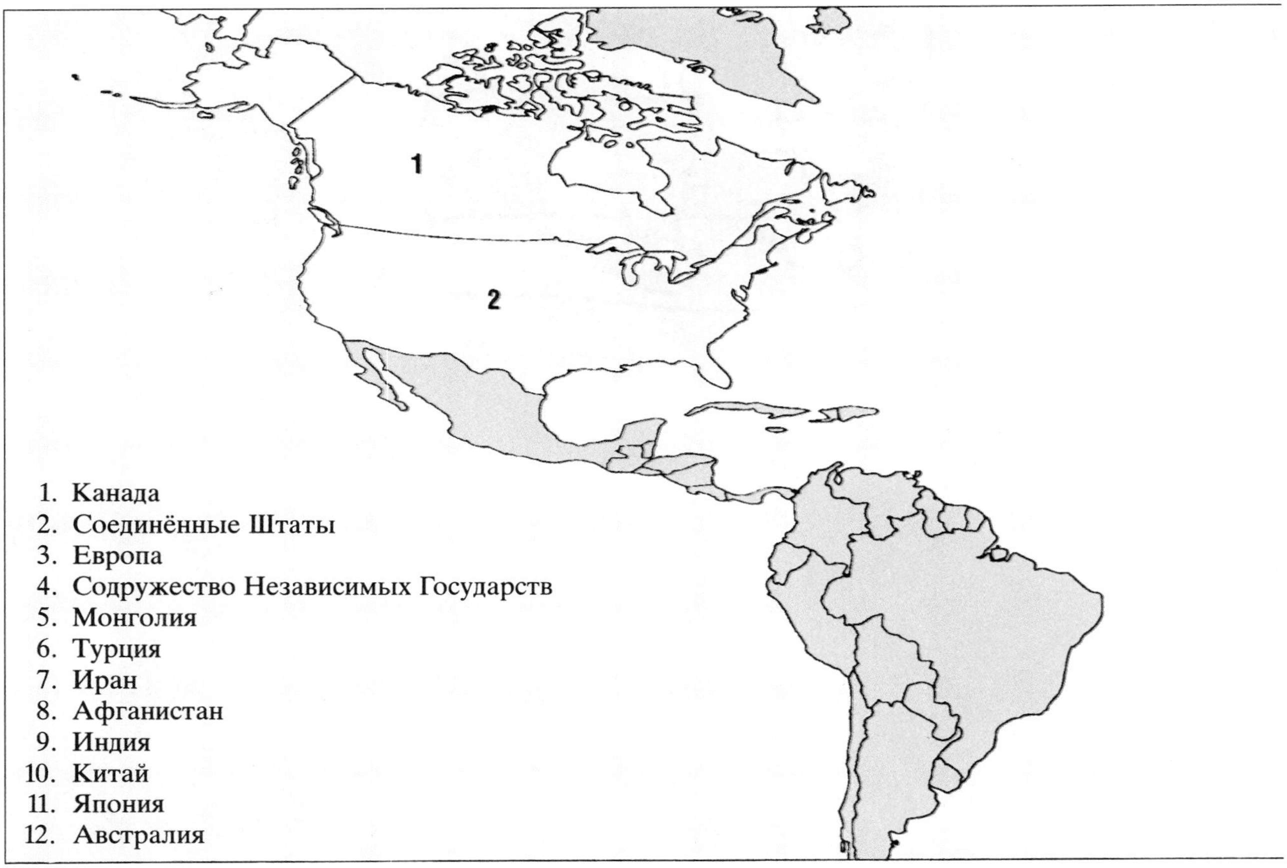

1. Канада
2. Соединённые Штаты
3. Европа
4. Содружество Независимых Государств
5. Монголия
6. Турция
7. Иран
8. Афганистан
9. Индия
10. Китай
11. Япония
12. Австралия

Austria	*(AFstriya)* **Австрия**	Germany	*(girMAniya)* **Германия**
Belgium	*(BYEL'giya)* **Бельгия**	Hungary	*(VYENgriya)* **Венгрия**
Canada	*(kaNAda)* **Канада**	India	*(INdiya)* **Индия**
China	*(kiTAY)* **Китай**	Iran	*(iRAN)* **Иран**
C.I.S.	*(ESENGA)* **СНГ**	Ireland	*(irLANdiya)* **Ирландия**
England	*(ANgliya)* **Англия**	Israel	*(izraIL')* **Израиль**
Estonia	*(eSTOniya)* **Эстония**	Italy	*(iTAliya)* **Италия**
Finland	*(finLYANdiya)* **Финляндия**	Japan	*(yaPOniya)* **Япония**
France	*(FRANtsiya)* **Франция**	Latvia	*(LATviya)* **Латвия**
Georgia	*(GRUziya)* **Грузия**	Lithuania	*(liTVA)* **Литва**

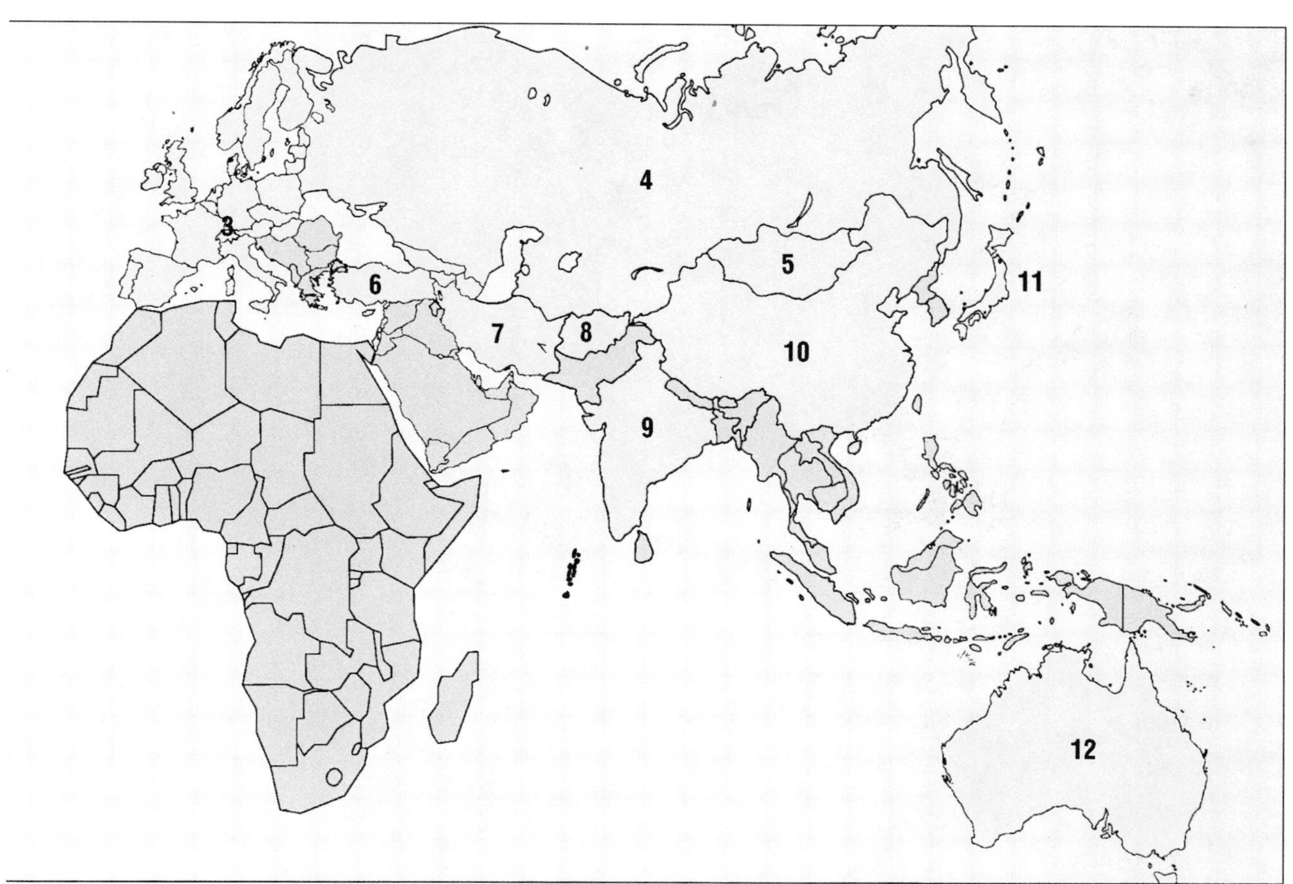

Mongolia	*(manGOliya)* **Монголия**	Spain	*(iSPAniya)* **Испания**
Norway	*(narVYEgiya)* **Норвегия**	Sweden	*(SHVYEtsiya)* **Швеция**
Poland	*(POL'sha)* **Польша**	Switzerland	*(shviyTSAriya)* **Швейцария**
Portugal	*(partuGAliya)* **Португалия**	Turkey	*(TURtsiya)* **Турция**
Scotland	*(shatLANdiya)* **Шотландия**	United States	*(sayidiNYOniye)* *(SHTAty)* **Соединённые Штаты**

СОДРУЖЕСТВО НЕЗАВИСИМЫХ ГОСУДАРСТВ

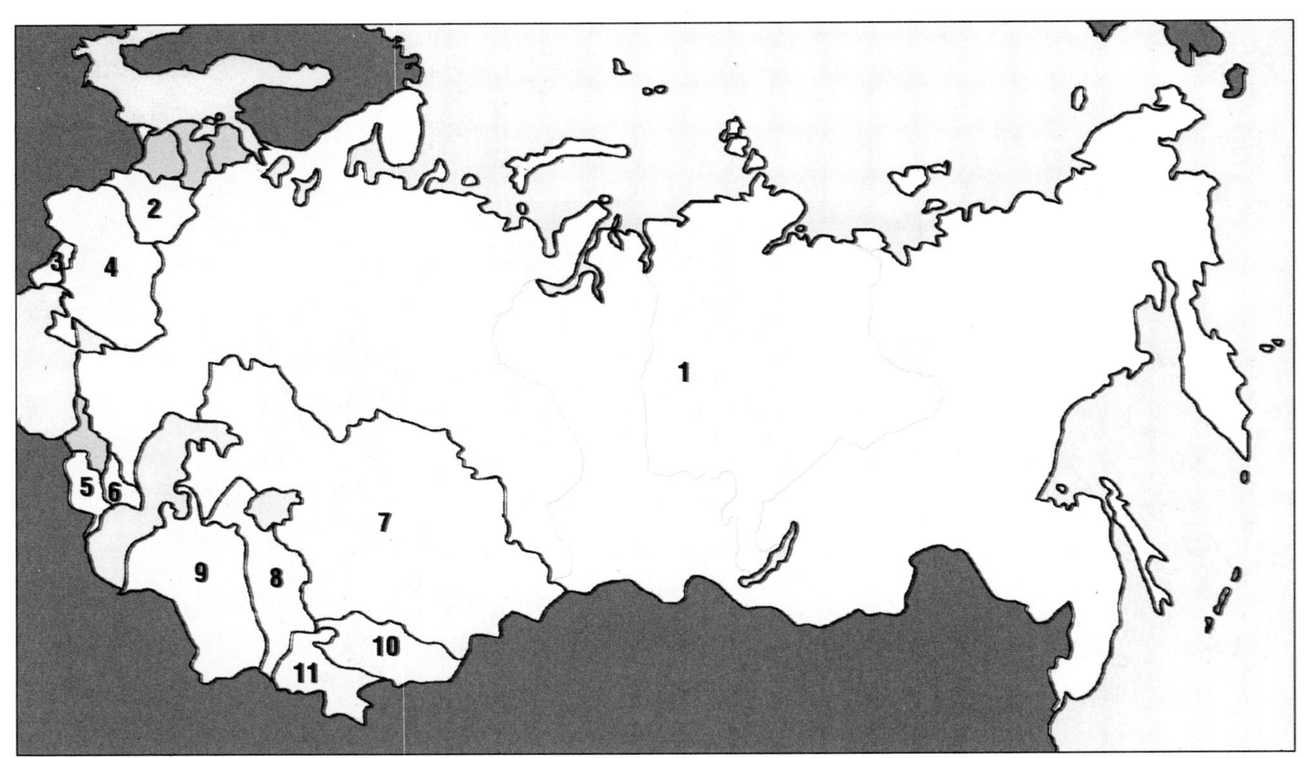

1. Россия
2. Беларусь
3. Молдова
4. Украина
5. Армения
6. Азербайджан
7. Казахстан
8. Узбекистан
9. Туркменистан
10. Кыргызстан
11. Таджикистан

(saDRUzhistva) (nizaVIsimykh) (gasuDARSTV)

Содружество Независимых Государств

Commonwealth of Independent States

In 1991 the fifteen republics *(riSPUbliki)* **(республики)** of the former Union of Soviet Socialist Republics (USSR) — *(saYUS) (saVYETskikh) (satsialiSTIchiskikh) (riSPUblik)* **Союз Советских Социалистических Республик** *(ES)(ES)(ES)(ER)* **(СССР)**, separated. In its place arose fifteen independent countries or states. Eleven states *(gasuDARSTva)* **(государства)** joined in the creation of a loose confederation called the Commonwealth of Independent States. The former Baltic republics are now the independent states of Estonia *(eSTOniya)* **(Эстония)**, Latvia *(LATviya)* **(Латвия)** and Lithuania *(litVA)* **(Литва)**. The former republic of Georgia, *(GRUziya)* **Грузия**, is also independent. The countries of the Commonwealth and their capitals are listed below.

English	Country (Russian)	Capital
Armenia (capital Yerevan)	*(arMYEniya)* **Армения**	**(Ереван)**
Azerbaijan (Baky)	*(azirbayDZHAN)* **Азербайджан**	**(Баку)**
Belarus (Mensk)	*(bilaRUS')* **Беларусь**	**(Минск)**
Kazakhstan (Almaty)	*(kazakhSTAN)* **Казахстан**	**(Алма-Ата)**
Kyrgyzstan (Bishkek)	*(kyrgySTAN)* **Кыргызстан**	**(Бишкек)**
Moldova (Chisinau)	*(malDOVa)* **Молдова**	**(Кишинёв)**
Russia (Moscow) Russian Federation	*(raSIya)* **Россия** **Российская Федерация**	**(Москва)**
Tajikistan (Dushanbe)	*(tadzhikiSTAN)* **Таджикистан**	**(Душанбе)**
Turkmenistan (Ashgabat)	*(turkminiSTAN)* **Туркменистан**	**(Ашхабад)**
Ukraine (Kiev)	*(ukraIna)* **Украина**	**(Киев)**
Uzbekistan (Toshkent)	*(uzbikiSTAN)* **Узбекистан**	**(Ташкент)**

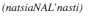

(natsiaNAL'nasti)

Национальности

Nationalities

It is very easy to tell someone your nationality in Russian. Simply use the pronoun **Я** and the proper masculine or feminine form:

(RUski) **Я русский.**	I'm a Russian.	*(RUskaya)* **Я русская.**

MASCULINE	ENGLISH	FEMININE
(azirbayDZHAnits) **Я азербайджанец.**	I'm Azerbaijanian.	*(azirbayDZHANka)* **Я азербайджанка.**
(amiriKAnits) **Я американец.**	I'm American.	*(amiriKANka)* **Я американка.**
(armiNIN) **Я армянин.**	I'm Armenian.	*(arMYANka)* **Я армянка.**
(afstraLIyits) **Я австралиец.**	I'm Australian.	*(afstraLIYka)* **Я австралийка.**
(angliCHAnin) **Я англичанин.**	I'm British.	*(angliCHANka)* **Я англичанка.**
(bilaRUS) **Я беларус.**	I'm Belarussian.	*(bilaRUSka)* **Я беларуска.**
(kaNAdits) **Я канадец.**	I'm Canadian.	*(kaNATka)* **Я канадка.**
(eSTOnits) **Я эстонец.**	I'm Estonian.	*(eSTONka)* **Я эстонка.**
(gruZIN) **Я грузин.**	I'm Georgian.	*(gruZINka)* **Я грузинка.**
(kaZAKH) **Я казах.**	I'm Kazakh.	*(kaZASHka)* **Я казашка.**
(kyrGYS) **Я кыргыз.**	I'm Kyrgyzian.	*(kyrGYSka)* **Я кыргызка.**

Male	English	Female
(laTYSH) **Я латыш.**	I'm Latvian.	*(laTYSHka)* **Я латышка.**
(liTOvits) **Я литовец.**	I'm Lithuanian.	*(liTOFka)* **Я литовка.**
(maldaVAnin) **Я молдованин.**	I'm Moldovian.	*(maldaVANka)* **Я молдованка.**
(taDZHIK) **Я таджик.**	I'm Tajik.	*(taDZHICHka)* **Я таджичка.**
(turkMYEN) **Я туркмен.**	I'm Turkmenian.	*(turkMYENka)* **Я туркменка.**
(ukraInits) **Я украинец.**	I'm Ukrainian.	*(ukraINka)* **Я украинка.**
(uzBYEK) **Я узбек.**	I'm Uzbek.	*(uzBYECHka)* **Я узбечка.**

(YA) (gavaRYU) (pa-RUski)

Я говорю по-русски.

I speak Russian.

You already know the first conjugation of Russian verbs. The verb *(gavaRIT')* **говорить** (to speak) belongs to the second conjugation. Look at the Russian forms for this verb and another second conjugation verb meaning "to hurry" — *(spiSHYT')* **спешить**.

Pronoun	Russian Verb	English	Russian Verb	English
	говорить		**спешить**	
я	**говорю́**	I speak	**спешу́**	I am hurrying
ты	**говори́шь**	you speak	**спеши́шь**	you are hurrying
она/он	**говори́т**	she/he speaks	**спеши́т**	she/he is hurrying
мы	**говори́м**	we speak	**спеши́м**	we are hurrying
вы	**говори́те**	you speak	**спеши́те**	you are hurrying
они	**говоря́т**	they speak	**спеша́т**	they are hurrying

Note how the endings very slightly according to a spelling rule in Russian which states that after **ш, щ, ч, ж** and **ч**, you may not write **я** or **ю** but must substitute for them the letters **а** and **у**.

To say "I speak Russian" use the form **Я говорю по-русски.**

How would you ask "Do you speak Russian?" ____________________________

This form — **по-русски** or **по-английски** (English) — is useful in a variety of expressions concerning language ability. You can combine the language you want to describe with the Russian verbs: **Я понимаю** (I understand), **Я читаю** (I read), and **Я пишу** (I write).

Now it's your turn to say the Russian sentences aloud and then practice writing them in the spaces below. Can you figure out the meanings for all of the sentences?

1. **Они говорят по-русски.** ____________________________
2. **Она говорит по-русски.** ____________________________
3. **Мы говорим по-английски.** ____________________________
4. **Ты понимаешь по-русски?** ____________________________
5. **Он читает по-английски.** ____________________________
6. **Вы читаете по-русски?** ____________________________
7. **Она говорит по-английски.** ____________________________
8. **Я говорю по-французски.** ____________________________
9. **Они понимают по-испански.** ____________________________
10. **Они говорят по-украински.** ____________________________

ANSWERS

Do you speak Russian? Вы говорите по-русски?

Speaking 1. They speak Russian. **2.** She speaks Russian. **3.** We speak English. **4.** Do you understand Russian? **5.** She reads English **6.** Do you read Russian? **7.** She speaks English. **8.** I speak French. **9.** They understand Spanish. **10.** They speak Ukrainian.

(RUskiye) (imiNA)

Русские имена

Russian names

Russians have three names: a first name, **имя**; a patronymic derived from one's father's name, **отчество**; and a family name, **фамилия**. The polite way to refer to recent acquaintances is with the name and patronymic; for example, **Борис Николаевич** (Boris Nikolaevich) (*baRIS nikaLAyivich*) or **Анна Петровна** (Anna Petrovna) (*Ana piTROVna*). When Russians use their first names, they are likely to have a nickname; for example, Ivan — **Иван** becomes Vanya — **Ваня**, Aleksandr — **Александр** becomes Sasha — **Саша**.

(YA) (patiRYAla) (maYU) (SUMku)

Я потеряла мою сумку.

I've lost my purse.

Caroline has lost her purse while out sightseeing. She approaches a policeman for help.

CAROLINE	(izviNItye) **Извините, пожалуйста.**	Excuse me please.
	Вы говорите по-английски?	Do you speak English?

МИЛИЦИОНЕР (Policeman)	(niMNOga) **Только немного.**	Just a little.
CAROLINE	(MOzhitye) (paMOCH) **Вы можете мне помочь?**	Can you help me?
МИЛИЦИОНЕР	(kaNYESHna) (sluCHIlas') **Конечно. Что случилось?**	Of course. What happened?
CAROLINE	**Я потеряла мою сумку.**	I've lost my purse.
МИЛИЦИОНЕР	**Ваша сумка? Как? Где?**	Your purse? How? Where?
CAROLINE	(ZNAyu) (byLA) **Я не знаю. Я была в** (DYElat') **метро. Что мне делать?**	I don't know. I was on the metro. What should I do?
МИЛИЦИОНЕР	(BYla) **Что было в сумке?**	What was in the purse?
CAROLINE	(PASpart) (VIza) **Мой паспорт, виза** (buMAZHnik) **и бумажник.**	My passport, visa, and wallet.
МИЛИЦИОНЕР	**Что ещё?**	What else?
CAROLINE	**Кредитные карточки и** (daROZHniye) (CHEki) **дорожные чеки.**	Credit cards and travelers' checks.
МИЛИЦИОНЕР	(pazvaNItye) (byuRO) **Позвоните в бюро** (naKHOdak) **находок.**	Call the Lost and Found Office.
CAROLINE	(saVYET) **Спасибо за совет.**	Thanks for the advice.
МИЛИЦИОНЕР	(zhiLAyu) **Не за что. Желаю вам** (uSPEkha) **успеха.**	Don't mention it. I wish you success.
CAROLINE	**До свидания.**	Goodbye.

8	*(na) (daROgye)* **На дороге** On the Road

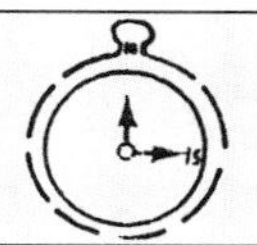

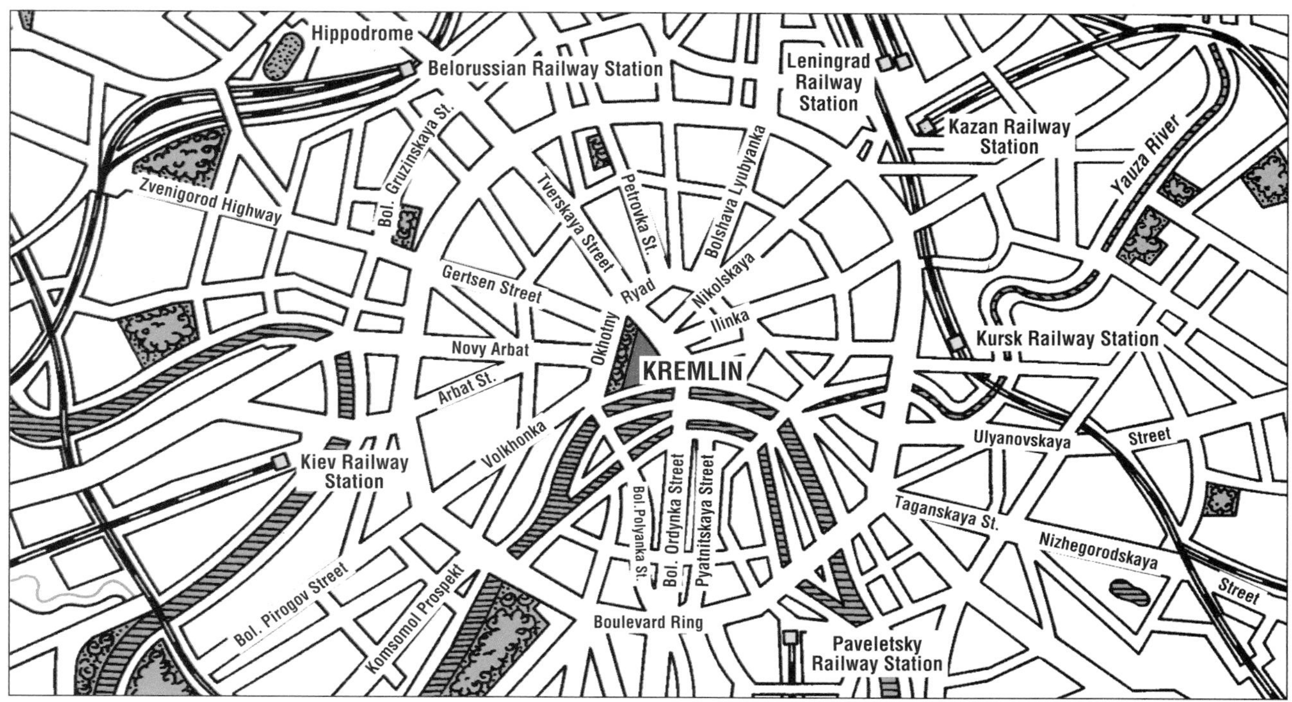

(VZYAT') (napraKAT) (maSHYnu)

ВЗЯТЬ НАПРОКАТ МАШИНУ

Renting a Car

To reserve a car for rental you might want to contact your travel bureau in advance. You can also rent a car at the major tourist hotels in Russia. Rates vary according to the car you choose and there will be a charge for rental including insurance, plus a mileage charge. You need a valid driver's license. You should ask if you can purchase special coupons for gasoline.

Mark has decided that he can get around and see more of the city with his family if he rents a car. Let's see how he goes about renting a car for the day.

MARK	*(khaTYEL)* **Доброе утро. Я хотел бы взять напрокат машину.**	Good morning. I would like to rent a car.
ДЕВУШКА (Young Woman)	*(DYEN')* **Пожалуйста. На один день?**	Certainly. For one day?
MARK	**Нет, на одну неделю.**	No, for one week.

ДЕВУШКА	*(pritpachiTAitye)* **Вы предпочитаете** *(MAlin'kuyu) (bal'SHUyu)* **маленькую или большую** **машину?**	Do you prefer a small or a large car?
MARK	*(mikraafTObus)* **Нам нужен микроавтобус.**	We need a minivan.
ДЕВУШКА	*(praBLYEma)* **Это не проблема.**	That's no problem.
MARK	*(binZIN) (FKHOdit) (STOimast')* **Бензин входит в стоимость?**	Is gas included in the price?
ДЕВУШКА	*(kuPIt')* **Нет, но можно купить** *(taLOny)* **у нас талоны.**	No, but you can buy gas coupons from us.
MARK	*(vaDItil'skiye) (praVA)* **Вот мои водительские права.**	Here is my driver's license.
ДЕВУШКА	*(kriDITnaya)* **У вас есть кредитная** *(KARtachka)* **карточка?**	Do you have a credit card?
MARK	**Конечно. Вот она.**	Of course. Here it is.
ДЕВУШКА	*(shasLIvava) (puTI)* **Счастливого пути!**	Have a good trip!

Pretend that you want to rent a car. Can you do it? Try to fill in the blanks below with the correct words or expressions.

1. **Я хотел бы ________________________ машину.**

2. **Нам нужен ________________________ .**

3. **Вот мои ________________________ права.**

4. **________________________ входит в стоимость?**

ANSWERS

Fill in 1. взять напрокат **2.** микроавтобус **3.** водительские **4.** Бензин

(daROZHnye) *(ZNAki)*

ДОРОЖНЫЕ ЗНАКИ

Road Signs

If you're planning to drive while you're abroad, it's important to spend some time memorizing the meanings of these signs.

Главная дорога
Right of Way

Опасность
Danger

Стоп
Stop

Максимальная скорость
Maximum Speed

Минимальная скорость
Minimum Speed

Конец ограничения
End of Speed Limit

Въезд запрещён
No Entrance

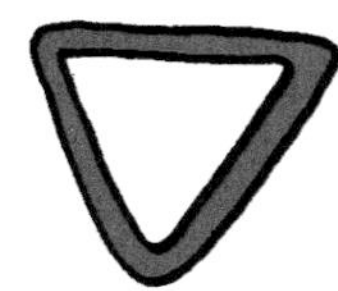

Уступите дорогу
Yield Right of Way

Двустороннее движение
Two-Way Traffic

Опасный поворот
Dangerous Curve

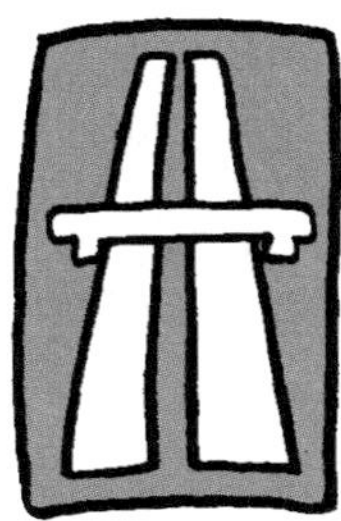

Автомагистраль
Expressway

Конец автомагистрали
End of Expressway

Таможня
Customs

Обгон запрещён
No Passing

Конец зоны запрещения обгона
End No Passing Zone

Одностороннее движение
One-way Traffic

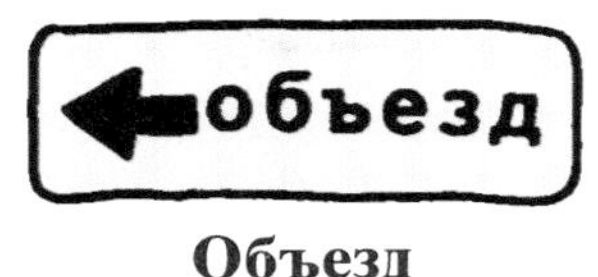

Объезд
Detour

Движение запрещено
Road Closed
(Traffic Prohibited)

Стоянка
Parking

Остановка запрещена
No Standing

Круговое движение
Roundabout

Место для разворота
Place for U-turn

Стоянка запрещена
No Parking

Велосипеды запрещены
Bicycles Prohibited

Пешеходный переход
Pedestrian Crossing

Железнодорожный переезд без шлагбаума
Railroad Crossing
(No Gate)

Железнодорожный переезд со шлагбаумом
Railroad Crossing
(With Gate)

(binzakaLONka)

БЕНЗОКОЛОНКА

The Service Station

Gasoline is sold by the liter in Russia. You may need coupons **(талоны)**, which can be purchased when you rent the vehicle. Credit for unused coupons is given. Most Europeans have a good idea of how many liters of gasoline they use per 100 kilometers. If you want to be safe, try to calculate your own mileage in the city and on the open road.

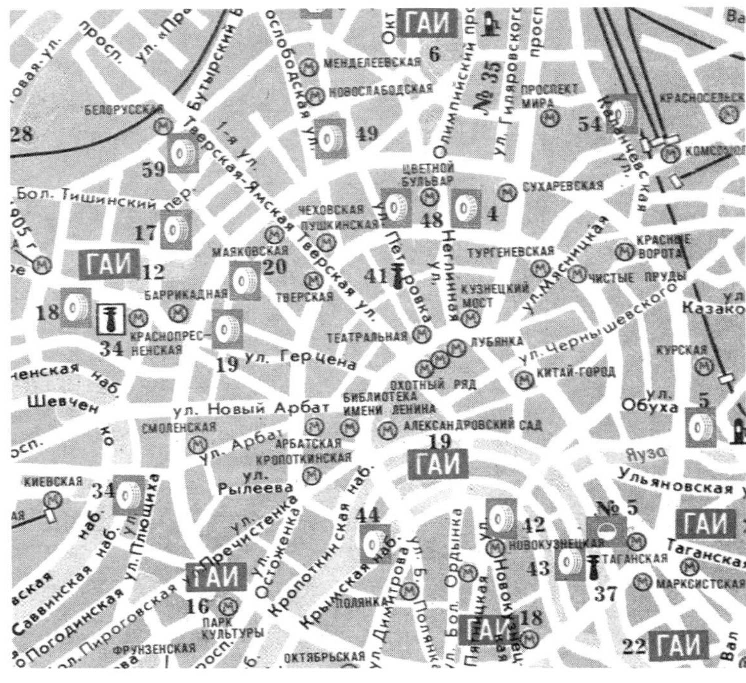

MARK	*(LItrav)* **Сорок литров, пожалуйста.**	Forty liters, please.
CASHIER	*(diviNOSta) (TRYEt'iva)* **Девяносто третьего** *(PYAtava)* **или девяносто пятого?**	Regular (93 octane) or super (95 octane)?
MARK	**Девяносто пятого.** *(praVYER'tye)* **Проверьте, пожалуйста,** *(masla) (VOdu) (SHYny)* **масло, воду и шины.**	Super (95 octane). Please check the oil, water, and tires.
CASHIER	**Всё в порядке.**	Everything's in order.
MARK	*(aftadaROZHnaya)* **У вас есть автодорожная** *(KARta)* **карта? Как проехать** *(aftaSYERvis)* **в автосервис?**	Do you have a road map? How do we get to the repair shop?
CASHIER	**Прямо десять километров,** **а потом направо.**	Straight ahead 10 kilometers, and then to the right.
MARK	**Спасибо. До свидания.**	Thank you. Good-bye.

(fpiRYOT)
вперёд
forward
(naLYEva)
налево
left
(naPRAva)
направо
right
(naZAT)
назад
backward
(SYEvir)
север
north
(ZApat)
запад
west
С
З
В
Ю
(vaSTOK)
восток
east
(YUK)
юг
south

(avtamaBIL') *(maSHYna)*

АВТОМОБИЛЬ - МАШИНА

Automobile Car

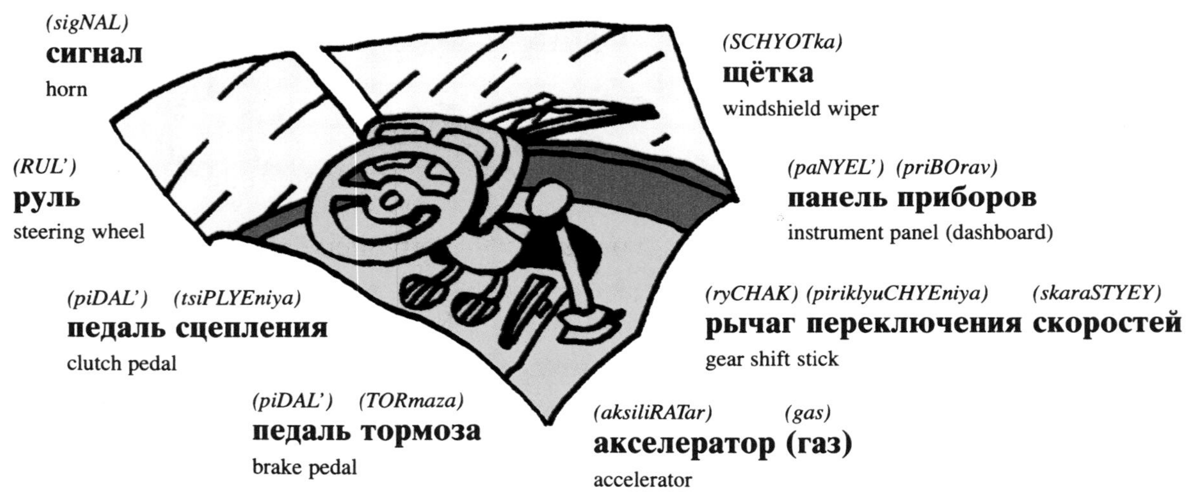
(signNAL)
сигнал
horn
(SCHYOTka)
щётка
windshield wiper
(RUL')
руль
steering wheel
(paNYEL') (priBOrav)
панель приборов
instrument panel (dashboard)
(piDAL') (tsiPLYEniya)
педаль сцепления
clutch pedal
(ryCHAK) (piriklyuCHYEniya) (skaraSTYEY)
рычаг переключения скоростей
gear shift stick
(piDAL') (TORmaza)
педаль тормоза
brake pedal
(aksiliRATar) (gas)
акселератор (газ)
accelerator

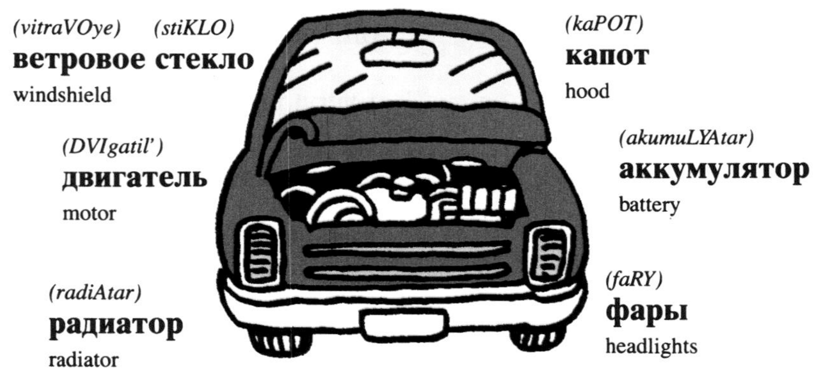
(vitraVOye) (stiKLO)
ветровое стекло
windshield
(kaPOT)
капот
hood
(DVIgatil')
двигатель
motor
(akumuLYAtar)
аккумулятор
battery
(radiAtar)
радиатор
radiator
(faRY)
фары
headlights

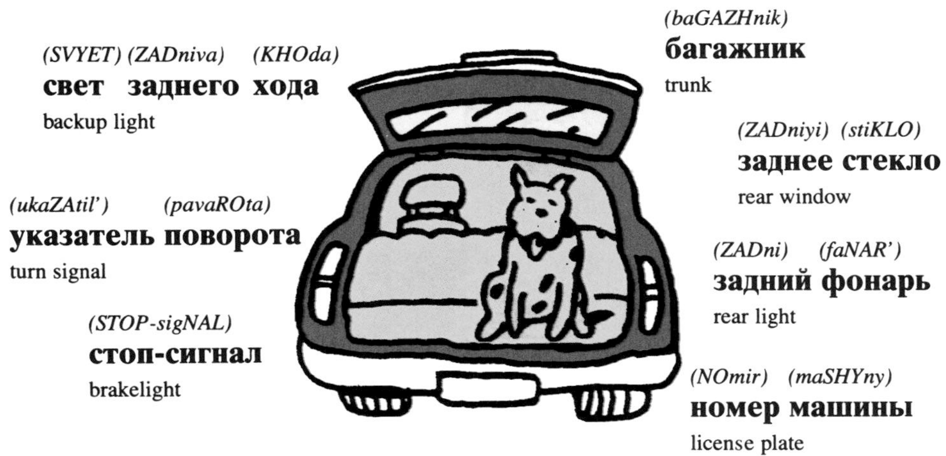
(SVYET) (ZADniva) (KHOda)
свет заднего хода
backup light
(baGAZHnik)
багажник
trunk
(ZADniyi) (stiKLO)
заднее стекло
rear window
(ukaZAtil') (pavaROta)
указатель поворота
turn signal
(ZADni) (faNAR')
задний фонарь
rear light
(STOP-sigNAL)
стоп-сигнал
brakelight
(NOmir) (maSHYny)
номер машины
license plate

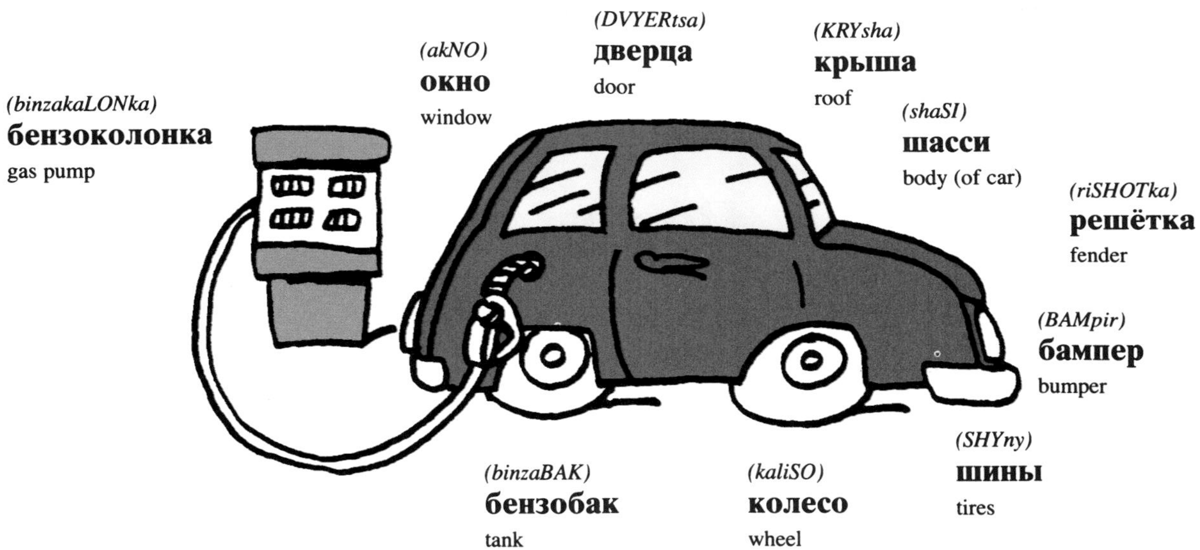
(DVYERtsa)
дверца
door
(KRYsha)
крыша
roof
(akNO)
окно
window
(binzakaLONka)
бензоколонка
gas pump
(shaSI)
шасси
body (of car)
(riSHOTka)
решётка
fender
(BAMpir)
бампер
bumper
(SHYny)
шины
tires
(binzaBAK)
бензобак
tank
(kaliSO)
колесо
wheel

Now fill in the names of the following auto parts.

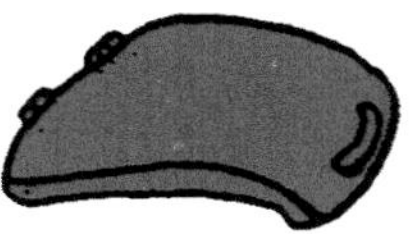

________________ ________________ ________________

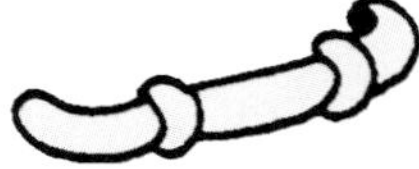

________________ ________________ ________________

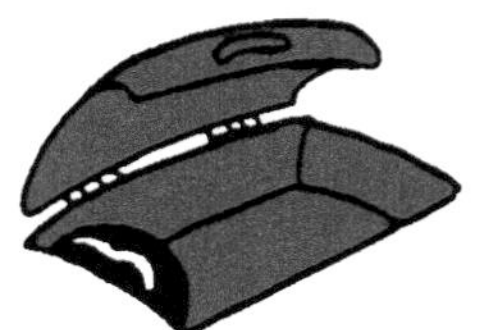

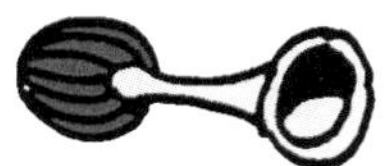

(pamaGItye)

Помогите!

Help!

Here are some useful phrases in case of problems:

(spuSTIlas') (SHYna) **У меня спустилась шина.**	I have a flat tire.
(zaVOditsa) **Машина не заводится.**	The car doesn't start.
Она не идёт.	It doesn't go.
(pirigriVAitsa) **Она перегревается.**	It overheats.
(KONchilsya) **Бензин кончился.**	There's no more gas.
(radiAtar) (pratiKAit) **Радиатор протекает.**	The radiator is leaking.
(akumuLYAtar) (SYEL) **Аккумулятор сел.**	The battery is dead.
Проверьте, пожалуйста,	Please check the
аккумулятор.	battery.
(tarmaZA) **тормоза.**	brakes.
(gluSHYtil') **глушитель.**	muffler.
масло.	oil.
шины.	tires.

(paviLItil'naye) *(naklaNYEniye)*

Повелительное наклонение

Imperative mood

If you want other people to do something, you will have to use the verb in the "command" or "imperative" way. You have already seen and used several of these imperative forms, and they are easily recognized. In the chart below, note that there is a form for the familiar and singular, and a second form for the formal, polite, or plural.

To form the imperative from Russian verbs you must know the form for the third person plural (the "they" form). First remove the ending **ут/ют** or **ат/ят**.

If you are left with a vowel, add **-й** for the familiar-singular and **-йте** for the formal or plural.

(chiTAyut) **читают → чита +** they read	*(chiTAY)* **читай**	*(chiTAYtye)* **читайте**
(DUmayut) **думают → дума +** they think	*(DUmay)* **думай**	*(DUmaytye)* **думайте**

If you are left with two or more consonants after you drop the ending, add **-и, -ите**.

(KONchat) **кончат → конч +** they finish	*(KONchi)* **кончи**	*(KONchitye)* **кончите**

If you are left with a singular consonant you must determine if the stress or accent can fall on the ending. (Hint: Is the ending in the "I" form stressed?) If the ending can be stressed, add **-и, -ите**.

(iDUT) **идут → ид +** they go	*(iDI)* **иди**	*(iDItye)* **идите**
(gavaRYAT) **говорят → говор +** they speak/say	*(gavaRI)* **говори**	*(gavaRItye)* **говорите**

If there is a single consonant, and the ending is never stressed, form the imperative by adding **-ь, -ьте**.

(gaTOvyat) **готовят → готов +** they prepare	*(gaTOF')* **готовь**	*(gaTOF'tye)* **готовьте**

In the blanks below fill in the correct form of the formal imperative. (We have supplied the "they" form in parentheses).

1. Help me! **(помогут)** ____________ **мне!**
2. Check the oil. **(проверят)** ____________ **масло.**
3. Look here. **(смотрят)** ____________ **сюда.**
4. Go away! **(идут)** ____________ **вон!**
5. Don't forget! **(забудут)** **Не** ____________ **!**

Осторожно! (Be careful!) Driving in a foreign country means watching the road even when the sights and sounds are so fascinating. **Очень красиво!** Yes, it's very beautiful! Read the following passage and learn the phrases that might come in useful some day. At the end of the passage you will be asked to answer a few questions. So pay close attention.

ПЕРВЫЙ ВОДИТЕЛЬ (First Driver)	*(BOzhi)* *(astaROZHna)* **Боже мой! Осторожно.**	My goodness! Be careful.
	(uMYEitye) **Вы умеете читать?**	Do you know how to read?
	(VIditye) **Вы не видите, что**	Can't you see that
	(PRAva) *(MNOY)* **право за мной.**	I have the right of way?
ВТОРОЙ ВОДИТЕЛЬ (Second Driver)	**Я знаю. Но вы едете**	I know. But you're driving
	150 км в час,	150 km per hour,
	(agraniCHEniye) **где 60 км ограничение.**	where the speed limit is 60.
ТРЕТИЙ ВОДИТЕЛЬ (Third Driver)	*(paMOCH)* **Могу я вам помочь?**	May I help you?
ПЕРВЫЙ ВОДИТЕЛЬ	*(pazaVItye)* *(militsiaNYEra)* **Да. Позовите милиционера**	Yes. Call the policeman
	(pasmaTRYET') *(sluCHIlas')* **посмотреть что случилось.**	to see what happened.

ANSWERS

Imperative 1. Помогите **2.** Проверьте **3.** Смотрите **4.** Идите **5.** забудьте

МИЛИЦИОНЕР (Policeman)	*(praisKHOdit)* **Что происходит?**	What's going on?
ПЕРВЫЙ ВОДИТЕЛЬ	*(stalkNUlis')* **Наши машины столкнулись.**	Our cars collided.
	(vinaVAT) **Он виноват.**	He's to blame.
ВТОРОЙ ВОДИТЕЛЬ	**Это не правда.**	That's not true.
	(sumaSHETshi) **Он водит, как сумасшедший.**	He drives like a madman.
	(privySHAL) **И он превышал скорость.**	And he exceeded the speed limit.
МИЛИЦИОНЕР	*(niKTO)* *(RAnin)* **Никто не ранен? Хорошо.**	No one is injured? Good.
	(dakuMYENty) **Ваши документы, водительские права.**	Your documents, driver's licenses.
ВТОРОЙ ВОДИТЕЛЬ	*(paBLIzasti)* **Поблизости есть автосервис?**	Is there a repair shop nearby?
МИЛИЦИОНЕР	*(nidaliKO)* **Да. Недалеко по этой дороге. Два или три километра.**	Yes. Not far along this road. Two or three kilometers.

(В автосервисе)
(at the repair shop)

ВТОРОЙ ВОДИТЕЛЬ	*(pachiNIT')* **Вы можете машину починить?**	Can you repair the car?
МЕХАНИК (Mechanic)	*(pavizLO)* **Вам повезло. Нужно** *(smiNIT')* **будет сменить только бампер и фару.**	You're lucky. It will only be necessary to replace the bumper and a headlight.
ВТОРОЙ ВОДИТЕЛЬ	*(gaTOva)* **Когда машина будет готова?**	When will the car be ready?
МЕХАНИК	*(zapCHASti)* **У меня есть запчасти.**	I have the spare parts.
	(naVYERna) **Наверно, завтра днём.**	Probably tomorrow afternoon.

Try writing out the following phrases from the dialogue. They may come in handy.

1. May I help you? ______________________________

2. Is there a repair shop nearby? ______________________________

3. Can you repair a car? ______________________________

4. When will the car be ready? ______________________________

(YA) (khaCHU) *(YA) (maGU)* *(YA) (BUdu)*

я хочу, я могу, я буду

I want I can I will

These three little verbs can be of great assistance to you. Try to learn them by heart!

ХОТЕТЬ want	**МОЧЬ** can	**БЫТЬ** will
я хочу́	**я могу́**	**я бу́ду**
ты хо́чешь	**ты мо́жешь**	**ты бу́дешь**
она хо́чет	**он мо́жет**	**оно бу́дет**
мы хоти́м	**мы мо́жем**	**мы бу́дем**
вы хоти́те	**вы мо́жете**	**вы бу́дете**
они хотя́т	**они мо́гут**	**они бу́дут**

Now fill in the blanks with the new verbs.

1. ______________ **поехать в Москву?**
Do you want to go to Moscow?

2. ______________ **водить машину?**
Does he want to drive the car?

3. ______________ **пойти в Кремль.**
I can't go to the Kremlin.

4. **Когда оно** ______________ **готово?**
When will it be ready?

5. **Кто** ______________ **мне помочь?**
Who can help me?

6. ______________ **во Владимире.**
They will be in Vladimir.

ANSWERS

Helpful phrases **1.** Могу я вам помочь? **2.** Поблизости есть автосервис? **3.** Вы можете машину починить? **4.** Когда машина будет готова?
Fill in **1.** Вы хотите **2.** Он хочет **3.** Я не могу **4.** будет **5.** может **6.** Они будут

9 Как мы отдыхаем

(KAK) (MY) (adyKHAim)

How We Vacation

ВСЁ ЧТО НАМ НУЖНО

(FSYO) (SHTO) (NAM) (NUZHna)

Everything That We Need

(paLATka)
палатка
tent

(aDYEZHda)
одежда
clothes

(DYEriva)
дерево
tree

(SONtse)
солнце
sun

(SPAL'ny) (miSHOK)
спальный мешок
sleeping bag

(karMAny) (faNAR')
карманный фонарь
flashlight

(midVYET')
медведь
bear

(bayDARka)
байдарка
canoe

(adiYAla)
одеяло
blanket

(tuaLYETnaya) (buMAga)
туалетная бумага
toilet paper

(karZINka)
корзинка
basket

(BANki)
банки
cans

(sapaGI)
сапоги
boots

(Udachka)
удочка
fishing rod

(SHTOpar)
штопор
corkscrew

(kaSTRYUli)
кастрюли
pots

(viDRO)
ведро
bucket

(tuaLYETny) (priBOR)
туалетный прибор
toilet kit

(RAdio)
радио
radio

(SPICHki)
спички
matches

That's a lot of new words and expressions to remember! Let's play a little game. Look at the word maze below and see how many words associated with camping you can identify. Circle the words and then write them out in the spaces below. We have already found the first word for you.

а б в г д у е ё р а д и о с я
ф ш т в е д р о м б п ю п ь ю
я т ш я ш о е д т а у и а ы т
ю щ т а с ч ф е ч н ч ц л х б
з ж о ь к к ь я л к м н а н х
щ ю п ц б а н л и и и ы т ъ д
л о о у ы р с о в б н м к ъ п
ь ю р щ к а с т р ю л и а ц б
т у а л е т н ы й п р и б о р

(KYEMpink)

КЕМПИНГ

Camping

Russians love to spend time in the country. As travel restrictions on foreigners have been relaxed in the past few years, camping has become even easier and a more attractive option to see the vast expanses of Russia.

Mark and Caroline have already rented a car and are about to set off on their own. Let's see how they make out.

ANSWERS

Puzzle банки, ведро, кастрюли, одеяло, палатка, радио, спички, туалетный прибор, удочка, штопор

MARK	**Вы не скажете, где**	Could you tell me, where's
	(bliZHAYshi) **ближайший кемпинг?**	the nearest campground?
ДЕВУШКА (Young Woman)	**Почти 20 километров**	About twenty kilometers
	(atSYUda) **отсюда. Там будет**	from here. There will be
	(ZNAK) (paLATkay) **знак с палаткой**	a sign with a tent
	(siriDInye) **в середине.**	in the middle.
MARK	**Вы не знаете, там можно**	Do you know if you can
	(DUSH) **принимать душ?**	take a shower there?
ДЕВУШКА	*(paNYAtiya) (iMYEyu)* **Понятия не имею!**	I don't have the slightest idea.
	(spraSItye) (MYEStye) **Спросите на месте.**	Ask when you're there.

(v) (pradaVOL'STvinam) (magaZInye)

В ПРОДОВОЛЬСТВЕННОМ МАГАЗИНЕ

In the Grocery Store

MARK	**Доброе утро. Мне нужно**	Good morning. I need
	(polkiLO) (SYra) (GRAM) **полкило сыра, 300 грамм**	a half kilo of cheese, 300
	(vichiNY) **ветчины, и дайте**	grams of ham, and give me
	(baTON) (KHLYEba) **батон хлеба.**	a loaf of bread.
ХОЗЯЙКА	*(SHTO-nibut') (viNO)* **Ещё что-нибудь? Вино,**	Anything else? Wine,
	(limaNAT) (YAblaki) **лимонад? Яблоки**	soft drink? The apples are
	(FKUSny) **очень вкусны.**	very tasty.

MARK	**Спасибо. Это всё.**	Thank you. That's all.
	Сколько с меня?	How much do I owe you?
ХОЗЯЙКА	**Двенадцать рублей.**	Twelve rubles.
MARK	**Пожалуйста.**	Here you are.
	До свидания.	Goodbye.

(MOZHna)	*(NUZHna)*	*(nil'ZYA)*
можно	**нужно**	**нельзя**
It's possible	It's necessary	It's prohibited

Three more little words that can get you far. If you are asking for someone's permission or simply asking if it's possible, use **можно**.

If you need to do something or need a particular item, use **нужно**.

Please respect the sensitivities of your hosts. Remember that you are always a guest in a foreign country. If you hear **нельзя**, don't do it!

Let's see how successful you would be in locating a camping place and getting provisions for the night.

1. **Вы не скажете, где** ________________________ **?**
   nearest campground
2. **Вы не знаете,** ________________________ **?**
   can you take a shower there
3. ________________________ **полкило сыра.**
   I need
4. **Ещё что-нибудь?** ________________________ **?**
   Wine, soft drink?
5. ________________________ **?**
   How much do I owe you?

ANSWERS

Camping 1. ближайший кемпинг **2.** там можно принимать душ **3.** Мне нужно **4.** Вино, лимонад? **5.** Сколько с меня?

10 *(vrimiNA)* Времена *(GOda)* года, *(MYEsitsy)* Месяцы, *(paGOda)* Погода, *(DNI)* Дни *(niDYEli)* недели.

Seasons of the Year, Months, Weather, Days of the Week

(ziMA)
ЗИМА
winter

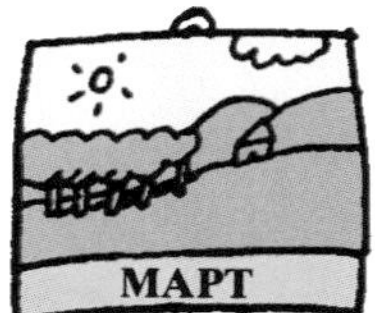

(viSNA)
ВЕСНА
spring

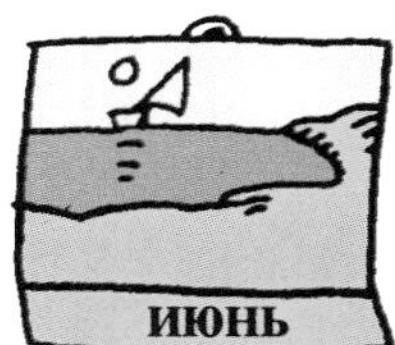

(LYEta)
ЛЕТО
summer

(Osin')
ОСЕНЬ
fall

Месяцы

The months

(yinVAR') **январь** January	*(aPRYEL')* **апрель** April	*(iYUL')* **июль** July	*(akTYABR')* **октябрь** October
(fiVRAL') **февраль** February	*(MAY)* **май** May	*(AVgust)* **август** August	*(naYABR')* **ноябрь** November
(MART) **март** March	*(iYUN')* **июнь** June	*(sinTYABR')* **сентябрь** September	*(diKABR')* **декабрь** December

Погода

The weather

Какая сегодня погода? — How is the weather today?

Сегодня погода ______________ **.** — The weather today is ______________ .

(khaROshaya)
хорошая
good

(plaKHAya)
плохая
bad

Какая прекрасная погода! — What splendid weather!

Сегодня ______________ **.** — Today it's ______________ .

(tiPLO)
тепло
warm

(ZHARka)
жарко
hot

(praKHLADna)
прохладно
cool

(KHOladna)
холодно
cold

(SVYEtit) (SONtse)
Светит солнце.
The sun is shining.

(DUyit) (VYEtir)
Дует ветер.
The wind is blowing.

(iDYOT) (DOSH)
Идёт дождь.
It's raining.

(iDYOT) (SNYEK)
Идёт снег.
It's snowing.

Can you describe the weather in the pictures below?

1. ______________________ **3.** ______________________

2. ______________________ **4.** ______________________

ANSWERS

Weather **1.** Идёт снег. **2.** Светит солнце. **3.** Идёт дождь. **4.** Дует ветер.

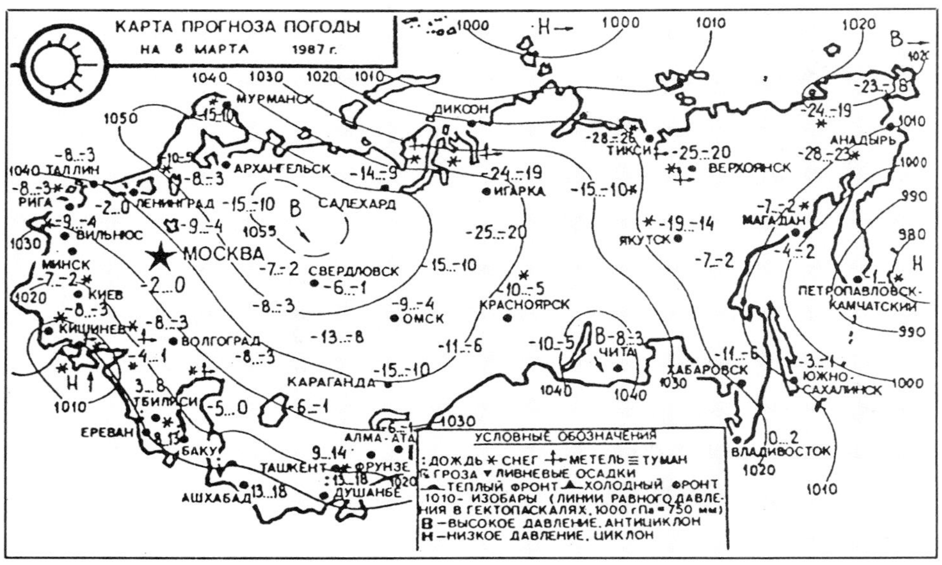

Сообщает Гидрометцентр СССР

На карте погоды над европейской частью страны видны две барические системы, которые в ближайшие дни будут определять здесь погоду. Над южной областью располагается циклон, поэтому значительные осадки ожидаются на Украине, Северном Кавказе и в Закавказье. В горных районах Кавказа увеличится лавинная опасность. В Центрально-Черноземном районе и на севере Украины из-за увеличения контрастов давления усилится ветер. В северной половине европейской части страны и на Урале характер погоды будет определяться областью высокого давления. Здесь будет морозно, в ночные часы в ряде пунктов морозы усилятся до 30-35 градусов.

В Москве 8 марта днем 0 — минус 2 градуса, без осадков.

Temperature conversions

To change degrees Fahrenheit to Centigrade subtract 32 and multiply by 5/9.

$$41°F - 32 = 9 \times 5/9 = 5°C$$

To convert from Centigrade to Fahrenheit, multiply by 9/5 and add 32:

$$10°C \times 9/5 = 18 + 32 = 50°F$$

A quick method to get an approximate temperature is to take the degrees Fahrenheit, subtract 30 and divide by 2. From Centigrade, multiply by 2 and add 30.

Most seasoned travelers know a few temperatures for reference.

ГРАДУСЫ
DEGREES

по Фаренгейту Fahrenheit	по Цельсию Celsius
212	100
98.6	37
86	30
77	25
68	20
50	10
32	0
14	−10
−04	−20
−22	−30
−40	−40

Термометр
Thermometer

It should be small consolation that at minus 40, degrees Fahrenheit and Centigrade are identical.

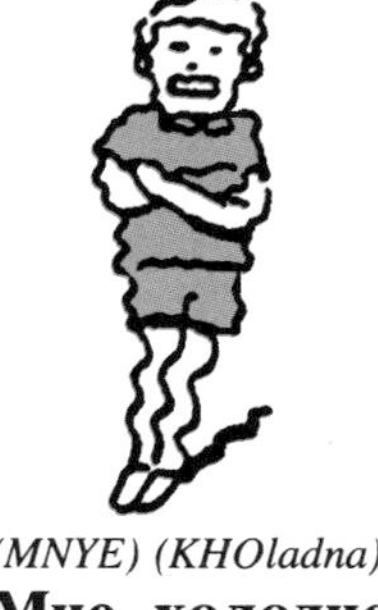

(MNYE) (KHOladna)
Мне холодно.
It is cold to me.

(MNYE) (tiPLO)
Мне тепло.
It is warm to me.

When Russians say "I am cold, she is warm," etc., they are actually saying, "It is cold to me, to her, to him," etc. The person "to whom" or "for whom" something is done is placed in the dative case. This construction can help us express many feelings, so it's important to learn it. Look at the examples below. Note that the dative case form of the pronoun is placed before the word describing the action or state.

Мне жарко.
I'm hot.

Тебе холодно?
Are you cold?

Ей/Ему плохо.
She's/He's not (feeling) well.

Нам интересно.
We are interested.

Вам скучно?
Are you bored?

Им легко.
They have it easy.

(imiNA) *(prilaGAtil'niye)*

Имена прилагательные

Adjectives

You have already noticed that Russian nouns can be masculine, feminine, and neuter, singular and plural. The adjectives and modifiers in Russian change their forms according to the noun they modify. You will need to know four basic forms of these words.

Masculine singular modifiers end most often in **ый**:

интересный, холодный
interesting cold

If the ending is stressed, they end in **ой**:

большой
large

After **к, г, х, ш, щ, ч,** and **ж**, they end in **ий**:

русский, американский
Russian American

Modifiers of feminine singular nouns end in **ая**:

интересная, большая, русская

Modifiers of neuter singular nouns end most often in **ое**:

интересное, холодное

After **ш, щ, ч, ц** and **ж**, if the ending is *not* stressed, they end in **ее**:

хорошее

Modifiers of most plural nouns end in **ые**:

интересные, холодные

After **к, г, х, ш, щ, ч,** and **ж**, they end in **ие**:

большие, русские, американские

Look at the pictures below and note how the adjectives combine with the nouns to form a phrase. For practice try writing the correct forms under the words.

Это

старый **человек.**

____________________ ____________________

молодая **девушка.**

____________________ ____________________

большое ______________ **зеркало.** ______________

маленькая ______________ **комната.** ______________

хорошая ______________ **гостиница.** ______________

высокая ______________ **девушка.** ______________

короткая ______________ **девушка.** ______________

интересные ______________ **люди.** ______________

11 *(samaLYOty)* Самолёты

Airplanes

(aeraPORT) Аэропорт

Airport

When you find the following useful words in the picture, write them out in the spaces provided.

(rigiSTRAtsiya) (biLYEtaf)
регистрация билетов ______________
check in (registration)

(aviakamPAniya)
авиакомпания ______________
airline

(baGASH)
багаж ______________
luggage

(chiSY)
часы ______________
clock

(PASpartny) (kanTROL')
паспортный контроль ______________
passport control

(taMOZHnya)
таможня ______________
customs

(LYOchik)
лётчик ______________
pilot

(styuarDYEsa)
стюардесса ______________
stewardess

(eskaLAtar)
эскалатор ______________
escalator

(VYkhat)
выход ______________
exit

(samaLYOT)

Самолёт

Airplane

Pronounce aloud the following items connected with airline flight as you search for some of them in the picture above. If you wish, you can write them out for practice.

(MYESta)
место
seat

____

(paSATka)
посадка
boarding

____

(zapaSNOY) (VYkhat)
запасной выход
emergency exit

____

(saLON)
салон
cabin

____

(kaBIna) (piLOta)
кабина пилота
cockpit

____

(VYlit)
вылет
takeoff

____

(riMYEN')
ремень
seat belt

____

(RYAT)
ряд
row

____

(RYEYS)
рейс
flight

____

(pasaZHYR)
пассажир
passenger

____

(ekiPASH)
экипаж
crew

____

(padNOS)
поднос
tray

____

(LYOTnaye) (POlye)
лётное поле
runway

(NYE) (kuRIT')
НЕ КУРИТЬ
NO SMOKING

______________________ ______________________

РАСПИСАНИЕ ДВИЖЕНИЯ ПАССАЖИРСКИХ САМОЛЕТОВ ИЗ МОСКВЫ
с 1 июня 1991 г.

Рейс	Аэропорт назначения	Дни отправления из Москвы	Время отправления из Москвы	Время прибытия в аэропорт назначения	Прибытие обратного рейса в Москву (четного)	Аэропорт отправления и прибытия рейса в Москву	Тип самолета	Тариф
1	2	3	4	5	6	7	8	9
161	АБАКАН с 30.06	2, 6, 7	0.20	2.30	19.20	ДМД	Ту-154	101
163	АБАКАН с 4.07	4	0.20	6.25	19.20	ДМД	Ту-154	101
167	АБАКАН с 30.06	ежд.	0.50	6.55	15.05	ДМД	Ту-154	101
169	АБАКАН по 28.06	1, 3, 5, 7	13.05	19.30	4.00	ДМД	Ту-154	101
169	АБАКАН с 30.06 по 30.08	1, 3, 5, 7	8.40	14.55	23.40	ДМД	Ту-154	101
23	АБАКАН с 2.07	ежд.	9.25	14.05	8.40	ВНК	Ил-86	101
45	АБАКАН с 10.06 по 28.06	ежд.	15.00	21.00	13.40	ДМД	Ту-154	101
45	АБАКАН с 30.06	ежд.	20.50	2.55	21.05	ДМД	Ту-154	101
525	АКТЮБИНСК по 29.06	1, 2, 4, 6	3.00	5.25	1.00	ДМД	Ил-86	62

Mark and his family are on their way back to Moscow and have decided to fly instead of taking the train.

ALEX — **Папа, где наши места?** *(miSTA)* — Papa, where are our seats?

СТЮАРДЕССА (Stewardess) — **Ваш посадочный талон.** *(paSAdochny) (taLON)* — Your boarding pass.

MARK — **Вы можете нам помочь? Мы все устали.** *(uSTAli)* — Can you help us? We are all tired.

СТЮАРДЕССА — **С удовольствием. Ряд 21, места А, Б, В, Г.** *(RYAT)* — With pleasure. Row 21, Seats A, B, V, G.

ALEX — **Вы будете нас кормить?** *(BUditye) (karMIT')* — Will you be feeding us?

СТЮАРДЕССА — **Я вам принесу обед после вылета.** *(priniSU)* — I will bring you dinner after takeoff.

ЛЕТЧИК (Pilot)	*(priVYETSTvuyim)* **Приветствуем вас на** *(barTU)* *(paLYOT)* **борту. Наш полёт в Москву длится 3 часа.** *(vysaTA)* **Высота полёта 10,000 метров. Скорость 750 км. в час.**	We welcome you on board. Our flight to Moscow takes 3 hours. Our altitude is 10,000 meters. The speed is 750 km per hour.
СТЮАРДЕССА	*(PROsim)* *(pristigNUT')* **Просим вас пристегнуть** *(rimNI)* *(kuRIT')* **ремни и не курить.**	We request you to fasten seat belts and not smoke.
MARK	**Нина, пристегни ремень.** *(vyliTAyim)* **Мы вылетаем.**	Nina, fasten your belt. We are taking off.
СТЮАРДЕССА	**Дорогие пассажиры, через несколько минут** *(prizimLIMsya)* **мы приземлимся в Москве. Температура плюс 5 градусов. Идёт дождь.**	Dear passengers, in a few minutes we will be landing in Moscow. The temperature is plus five degrees. It's raining.

ALEX	*(KHOchitsa)* **Девушка, мне хочется** *(paPIT')* **что-нибудь попить.**	Miss, I would like something to drink.
СТЮАРДЕССА	*(k) (sazhaLYEniyu)* **К сожалению, уже поздно. Я сейчас вам** *(kanFYETku)* **принесу конфетку.**	Unfortunately, it's already late. In just a minute I'll bring you a piece of candy.
MARK	**Смотри, Нина. Мы уже** *(ZDYES')* **здесь.**	Look, Nina. We're already here.

Try matching the important phrases in column one with those in column two. Write out the Russian for practice.

1. **Вы можете нам помочь?**	а. We are all tired.
2. **Мы все устали.**	б. No Smoking.
3. **Не курить.**	в. I would like something to drink.
4. **Мы приземлимся в Москве.**	г. Can you help us?
5. **Мне хочется что-нибудь попить.**	д. We will be landing in Moscow.

Будущее время

Future time

You may have already noticed that Russians have two ways to form the future tense, that we in English form with the help of the words "will" or "shall."

Just as in English, Russians can form a compound future consisting of two words. The first component is a form of the verb "to be."

я бу́ду	I will be
ты бу́дешь	you will be
он/она/оно бу́дет	he/she/it will be
мы бу́дем	we will be
вы бу́дете	you will be
они бу́дут	they will be

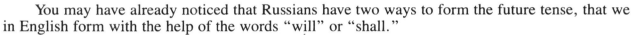

ANSWERS

Matching 1. г 2. а 3. б 4. д 5. в

You can form the future tense of the most verbs we have seen by combining the infinitive of these imperfective verbs with the proper form of **буду**.

I will listen.	**Я бу́ду слу́шать.**
You will read.	**Ты бу́дешь чита́ть.**
It will cost.	**Оно бу́дет сто́ить.**
We will hurry.	**Мы бу́дем спеши́ть.**
You will speak English.	**Вы бу́дете говори́ть по-русски.**
They will feed us.	**Они нас бу́дут корми́ть.**

Russians can also form a simple future from a "perfective" verb. In this instance, you already know all of the forms of the verbs because they are identical to those of the present tense. Look at the following example.

Present		Future	
I read	**я чита́ю**	I will read	**я почита́ю**
you speak	**ты говори́шь**	you will speak	**ты поговори́шь**
she is hurrying	**она спеши́т**	she will hurry	**она поспеши́т**

The examples show us one way in which a perfective verb can be formed from an imperfective verb by adding a prefix. The prefix **по** often means "just a little." Russians simply know which verbs are imperfective and perfective. For the moment, just concentrate on the meanings of verbs when you encounter them in our dialogues. We'll give you an easy way to check on the aspect of verbs at the end of the book in the Russian-English dictionary.

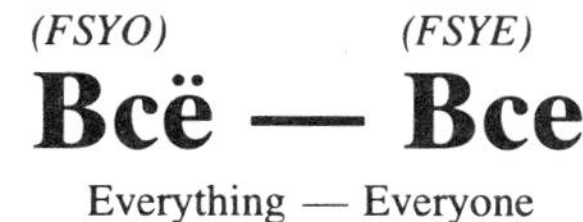

Everything — Everyone

In only a few word pairs is the difference between the letters **ё** and **е** as important as in **всё** meaning "everything" and **все** meaning "all the people" or "everyone."

Watch how they are used.

Всё в порядке.	Everything (all) is in order.
Все идут домой.	Everyone is (all are) going home.

Remember: in Russian **все** takes a plural verb, but in English "everyone" takes a singular verb. Watch how they are used in the next dialogue.

(ekSKURsiya) *(pa)* *(krimLYU)*
Экскурсия по Кремлю

An excursion around the Kremlin

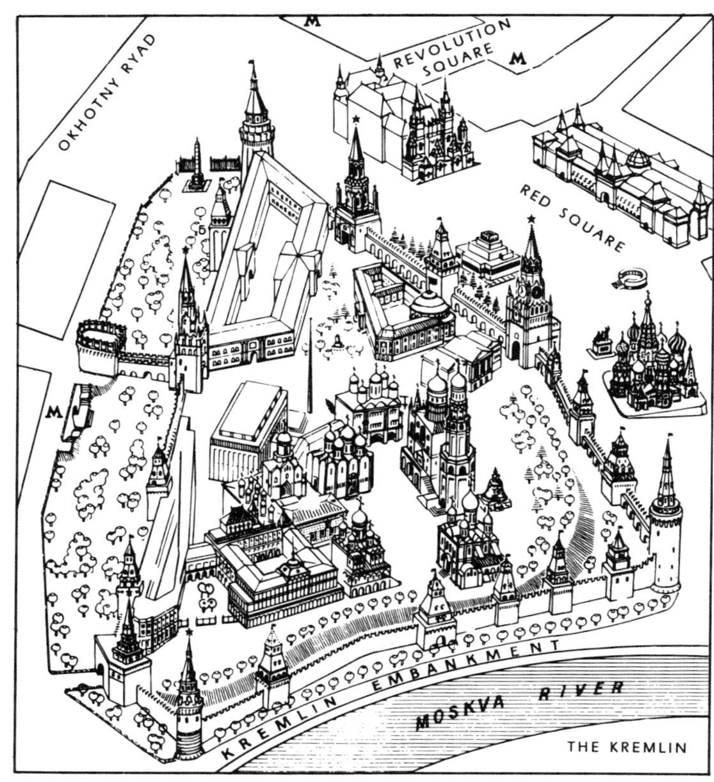

Caroline, Stephanie, and Alex have decided to take a tour of the Kremlin this afternoon.

ЭКСКУРСОВОД (Tour Guide)	*(naKHOdimsya)* **Мы теперь находимся на территории Московского Кремля.**	We are now located on the territory of the Moscow Kremlin.
CAROLINE	**Скажите, пожалуйста,** *(uSPYENski)* *(saBOR)* **где Успенский собор.**	Please tell us where the Cathedral of the Dormition is.
ЭКСКУРСОВОД	*(tuDA)* **Мы туда идём.** *(pakaZHU)* **Я вам покажу.**	We are going there. I'll show you.
ALEX	*(pakhaROniny)* **Там похоронены бывшие** *(tsaRI)* **цари.**	The former tsars are buried there.

ЭКСКУРСОВОД	*(druGIye)* **Вы видели другие достопримечательности?**	Have you seen the other sights?
STEPHANIE	**Я хочу посмотреть** *(TSAR'-KOlakal)* **Царь-колокол и** *(TSAR'-PUSHku)* **Царь-пушку.**	I want to look at the Tsar Bell and the Tsar Cannon.
ЭКСКУРСОВОД	**Конечно. Все хотят их посмотреть.**	Of course. Everyone wants to see them.
CAROLINE	*(dalzhNY)* **Мы должны спешить.** **На два часа у нас билеты** *(aruZHEYnuyu) (paLAtu)* **в Оружейную палату.**	We have to hurry. At two o'clock we have tickets to the Armory.
ЭКСКУРСОВОД	*(zaBUtye)* **Не забудьте посмотреть** *(KRASnuyu) (PLOschat')* **Красную площадь и смену караула.**	Don't forget to see Red Square and the changing of the guard.
ALEX	*(intiRYESna)* **Всё так интересно.**	Everything is so interesting.

ENTERTAINMENT

(razvliCHEniye)
Развлечение

12 *(tiATR)* Театр, *(kiNO)* Кино, *(PRAZniki)* Праздники
Theater, Movies, Holidays

(tiATR) ТЕАТР
Theater

Boris and Alexandra, a middle-aged couple from Omaha, Nebraska, are making their first visit to Russia. They both enjoy the theater. They are in Moscow on the second day of their stay. Being of Russian descent, they both speak some Russian. "Not one word of English during our vacation," they decide.

БОРИС	**Ты хочешь** *(payTI)* **пойти в театр сегодня вечером?**	Do you want to go to the theater this evening?
АЛЕКСАНДРА	*(zamiCHAtil'naya)* **Замечательная идея!**	A wonderful idea!
БОРИС	**В Большом театре балет «Лебединое озеро». Во Дворце съездов опера «Борис Годунов».**	In the Bolshoi Theater there's the ballet *Swan Lake*. In the Palace of Congresses there's the opera *Boris Godunov*.
АЛЕКСАНДРА	**Я люблю** *(Opiru)* **оперу, но четыре часа** *(SLISHkam)* **слишком долго.**	I love opera, but four hours is too long.
БОРИС	**Я** *(saGLAsin)* **согласен. Всё** *(ravNO)* **равно, я предпочитаю** *(baLYET)* **балет.**	I agree. All the same, I prefer the ballet.
АЛЕКСАНДРА	**Позвони в театральную кассу. Она** *(vniZU)* **внизу.**	Call the theater ticket desk. It's downstairs.

БОРИС	**Если есть билеты,** *(biLYEty)*	If there are tickets available,
	я закажу два на балконе. *(balKOnye)*	I'll order two in the balcony.
АЛЕКСАНДРА	**Пока. Я пойду в сауну.** *(SAUnu)*	See you later. I'm going to the sauna.

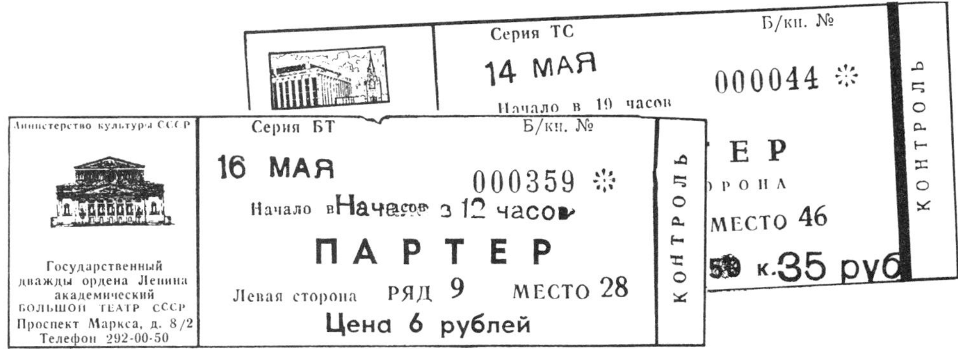

Many Russian and English words are similar. Always try to pronounce the Russian word aloud and you'll be pleasantly surprised with how many you can recognize. To help you remember them write out the words you will want to have **«на кончике языка»** ("on the tip of the tongue").

театр  theater ____________________

балкон  balcony ____________________

комедия  comedy ____________________

трагедия  tragedy ____________________

идея  idea ____________________

балет  ballet ____________________

опера ·  opera **мелодия**  melody

________________ ________________

(kiNO)

КИНО

Movies

Boris and Alexandra are discussing what movie they want to see.

АЛЕКСАНДРА	**Пойдём в кино!**	Let's go to the movies.
БОРИС	**В кинотеатре недалеко** *(nidaliKO)* **идёт современный** *(savriMYEny)* **русский фильм.**	In the movie theater not far away a contemporary Russian film is playing.
АЛЕКСАНДРА	**Фильм с титрами?** *(TItrami)*	A film with subtitles?
БОРИС	**Нет, без титров. Но ты будешь понимать почти всё.** *(pachTI)*	No. Without subtitles. But you will be able to understand almost everything.

В кассе (At the ticket office)

АЛЕКСАНДРА	**Два билета на вечерний сеанс.** *(viCHYERni) (siANS)*	Two tickets to the evening performance.
КАССИРША	**Поближе или подальше?** *(paBLIzhe) (paDAL'she)*	Closer or further away (from the screen)?

БОРИС	(BLISka) **Не слишком близко.**	Not too close.
	(zaBYL) (achKI) **Я забыл мои очки.**	I forgot my eyeglasses.
АЛЕКСАНДРА	(raskaZHU) **Ничего. Я тебе расскажу,**	Never mind. I'll tell you
	кто что делает.	who is doing what.
БОРИС	**Я так рад, что мы**	I'm so glad, that we
	(VMEStye) **всё делаем вместе.**	do everything together.
АЛЕКСАНДРА	**И я так рада.**	I'm so glad too.

(mistaiMYEniye) (i) (imiNA) (suschistVItil'niye)

Местоимение и Имена Существительные

Pronouns and nouns

Direct objects

We have already seen and heard several pronouns used in the dative cases: **Мне холодно, Вам скучно**. When some action is performed on someone or something, a direct object is required. Even in English the pronouns have different forms in the accusative case; for example, I see you, he hears me. Look at the examples below of Russian nouns and pronouns in the accusative case, and pay special attention to the forms you will most frequently use.

ACCUSATIVE CASE

Nouns

Feminine nouns. When the nominative case ends in **а**, the accusative case ends in **у**.

Эта книга. This is a book.	**Она понимает книгу.** She understands the book.

When the nominative case ends in **я**, the accusative case ends in **ю**.

Это моя тётя. This is my aunt.	**Я люблю тётю.** I love my aunt.

Neuter nouns have the same nominative and accusative case endings.

Где зеркало? Where is the mirror?	**Я вижу зеркало.** I see the mirror.

Continued on next page

Inanimate masculine nouns have identical nominative and accusative cases.

Это наш дом. This is our house.	**Я знаю ваш дом.** I know your house.

Animate masculine nouns end in **а** or **я** in the accusative case.

Это студент. This is a student.	**Она видит студента.** She sees the student.
Это Евгений. This is Yevgeny.	**Я знаю Евгения.** I know Yevgeny.

Pronouns

Nominative Case		Accusative Case	
I	**я**	me	**меня**
you	**ты**	you	**тебя**
she	**она**	her	**её**
he/it	**он/оно**	him/it	**его**
we	**мы**	us	**нас**
you	**вы**	you	**вас**
they	**они**	them	**их**

In many cases the object pronouns will come before the verb. Watch how they can be used to replace nouns.

I am reading a book.	**Я читаю книгу.**	I am reading it.	**Я её читаю.**
We love the theater.	**Мы любим театр.**	We love it.	**Мы его любим.**

Now try to replace the noun in italics with the proper form of the pronoun.

1. **Я понимаю этот *фильм*.** **Я** ______________________ **понимаю.**
2. **Я знаю эту *женщину*.** **Я** ______________________ **знаю.**
3. **Она любит *оперу*.** **Она** ______________________ **любит.**
4. **Они приносят *книги*.** **Они** ______________________ **приносят.**

ANSWERS

Fill in **1.** его **2.** её **3.** её **4.** их

(PRAZniki)
Праздники
Holidays

1 января	*(NOvy) (GOT)* **Новый год**	January 1—New Year's Day
8 марта	*(mizhdunaRODny)* **Международный** *(ZHENski) (DYEN')* **женский день**	March 8—International Women's Day
1 мая	*(PYERvaye) (MAya)* **Первое мая**	May 1—May Day Workers' Day
9 мая	*(DYEN') (paBYEdy)* **День победы**	May 9—Victory Day
7 октября	*(DYEN') (kanstiTUtsii)* **День конституции**	October 7—Constitution Day
7 ноября	*(gadafSCHIna)* **Годовщина** *(viLIkay) (okTYABR'skay)* **Великой Октябрьской** *(satsialiSTIchiskay) (rivaLYUtsii)* **Социалистической Революции**	November 7—Anniversary of the Great October Socialist Revolution

(z) (DNYOM) (razhDYEniya)
С днём рождения! — Happy Birthday!

(S) (PRAZnikam)
С праздником! — Happy holiday!

(s) (NOvym) (GOdam)
С Новым годом! — Happy New Year!

Russian Orthodox Churches still observe Christmas and Easter according to the old Julian calendar that was in use in Russia until the Gregorian calendar was adopted in 1918.

(s) (razhdistVOM) (khriSTOvym)
С Рождеством Христовым! — Merry Christmas! (With the Birth of Christ)

(khriSTOS) (vasKRYEsye)
Христос воскресе! — Happy Easter! (Christ is Risen)

Let's listen to **Василий** (Vasily) explain to Stefanie and Alexander about Russian holidays.

АЛЕКСАНДР	**Вася, какие у вас праздники?**	Vasya, which holidays do you have?
ВАСИЛИЙ	*(praSTOY) (vaPROS)* **Это не простой вопрос.**	That is not a simple question.
	(RAN'shi) **Раньше были**	Previously there were
	(kamuniSTIchiskiye) **коммунистические**	communist holidays
	праздники, как 7 ноября,	like November 7,
	Великая Октябрьская Революция.	Revolution Day.
СТЕФАНИ	**А Новый год?**	And New Year's?
ВАСИЛИЙ	**Да, 1 января.**	Yes, January 1.
	8 марта, Международный	March 8, International
	женский день тоже	Women's Day, is also
	(papuLYARny) **популярный праздник.**	a popular holiday.
АЛЕКСАНДР	*(fstriCHAitye)* **А как вы встречаете Рождество?**	And how do you celebrate Christmas?
ВАСИЛИЙ	**Мы встречаем Рождество**	We celebrate Christmas
	6 января. Это 25 декабря	January 6. That is December 25
	(STAramu) (kalindaRYU) **по старому календарю.**	on the old calendar.
СТЕФАНИ	*(YOLka)* **А ёлка?**	And the tree?
ВАСИЛИЙ	**И ёлка есть, и**	There's a tree, and
	(DYET) (maROS) **Дед Мороз.**	Father Frost [Russia's Santa Claus].

АЛЕКСАНДР	**Я знаю, что вы все страдали во время войны.**	I know that you all suffered during the time of the war.
ВАСИЛИЙ	**Да. Каждый год мы помним День победы 9 мая.**	Yes. Each year we remember Victory Day on May 9.
АЛЕКСАНДР	**Я знаю ещё один день. 1 мая.**	I know one more day. May Day, May 1.

Now see if you can connect the days on the right with the correct holidays.

1. 1 января	**а. День победы.**
2. 6 января	**б. Новый год.**
3. 8 марта	**в. Рождество.**
4. 9 мая	**г. Октябрьская революция.**
5. 7 ноября	**д. Международный женский день.**

ANSWERS

Holidays 1. б 2. в 3. д 4. а 5. г.

# 13 (SPORT) СПОРТ
Sport(s)

(khaDIT') (f) (paKHOdy) (i) (BYEgat')
ХОДИТЬ В ПОХОДЫ И БЕГАТЬ
Going on Hikes and Jogging

Caroline Smith is in great shape. She jogs every morning. Sometimes she is joined by her husband and children, but they can barely keep up. This morning she is approached by a newspaper reporter who is writing an article on sports.

КОРРЕСПОНДЕНТ (Reporter)	*(gaspaZHA)* **Доброе утро, госпожа. Я** *(karispanDYENT)* **корреспондент. Можно** *(zaDAT')* **вам задать несколько** **вопросов?**	Good morning, Miss. I am a reporter. May I ask you a few questions?
CAROLINE	**Пожалуйста. Только** *(MYEDlina)* **говорите медленно. Я** **американка и** **не понимаю всё.**	Please. Only speak slowly. I am an American and do not understand everything.
КОРРЕСПОНДЕНТ	*(CHASta)(BYEgaitye)* **Вы часто бегаете?**	Do you jog often?
CAROLINE	**Я бегаю каждое утро.** *(inagDA)* **Иногда мой муж** **и дети бегают** **со мной.**	I run every morning. Sometimes my husband and children run with me.

КОРРЕСПОНДЕНТ	**Что люди** *(NOsit)* **носят в Америке, когда они бегают?**	What do people wear in America when they jog?
CAROLINE	*(aBYCHna)* **Обычно мы носим** *(sparTIVny)* **спортивный костюм и** *(kraSOFki)* **кроссовки.**	Usually we wear a jogging suit and sneakers.
КОРРЕСПОНДЕНТ	**Какие другие виды спорта вы любите?**	What other types of sport do you like?
CAROLINE	**Моя семья очень любит ходить в походы.**	My family really likes to go on hikes.
КОРРЕСПОНДЕНТ	**Ваш муж любит смотреть спорт по** *(tiliVIzaru)* **телевизору?**	Does your husband like to watch sports on television?
CAROLINE	**И как ещё! Он смотрит** *(fudBOL)* **футбол или** *(baskidBOL)* **баскетбол каждую субботу.**	And how! He watches soccer or basketball every Saturday.
КОРРЕСПОНДЕНТ	**Спасибо за** *(intirV'YU)* **интервью.**	Thank you for the interview.

(gaspaDIN) *(gaspaZHA)*

господин, госпожа

Mr. Miss or Mrs.

In the days of the Soviet Union, a general means of address was **товарищ** (comrade). Today, Russians are likely to use the terms once reserved for foreigners: **господин** for Mr., **госпожа** for Miss or Mrs.

Another way to address someone is to say, **молодой человек** (young man) or **девушка** (Miss). Even for older people these expressions are a delightful compliment. Recently, Russians have begun using the term, **женщина** for Mrs. or any middle-aged woman.

(kuPAtsa) *(i)* *(PLAvat')*

КУПАТЬСЯ И ПЛАВАТЬ

Bathing and Swimming

(kuPAitsa)
Марк купается.
bathes
(PLAvait)
Каролина плавает.
swims
(PLAFki)
Он носит плавки.
swim trunks
(kuPAL'nik)
Она носит купальник.
bathing suit
(brass)
брасс
breaststroke
(KROL')
кроль
crawl
(PLAvaniye) (na) (spiNYE)
плавание на спине
backstroke
Марк отдыхает.
is resting
Каролина загорает.
is sunbathing

Verbs with -ся

Some Russian verbs have the particle **-ся** or **-сь** added after the required ending. Compare the conjugation of the verbs **плавать** (to swim) and **купаться** (to bathe).

плавать	**купаться**
я плаваю	**я купаюсь**
ты плаваешь	**ты купаешься**
она плавает	**он купается**
мы плаваем	**мы купаемся**
вы плаваете	**вы купаетесь**
они плавают	**они купаются**

Note that after consonants, including the soft sign **ь**, you add **ся**. After a vowel letter, you must add **сь**.

Now try your hand at adding the correct endings to some of the verbs below.

1. **Максим, где ты купа ____________ ?** (bathe, go swimming)
2. **Ирина и Сергей, вы всегда купа ____________ утром.** (bathes, goes swimming)
3. **Наши дети никогда не слуша ____________ .** (obey)
4. **Почему Марк улыба ____________ .** (smiling)
5. **Я умыва ____________ до завтрака.** (wash up)

Before we go out to do some exercise, let's try to answer a few simple questions.

а. **Что делает Каролина?** ________________________

б. **Что делает Марк?** ________________________

в. **Что это?** ________________________

г. **Что это?** ________________________

д. **Что это?** ________________________

ANSWERS

Verbs 1. купаешься **2.** купаетесь **3.** слушаются **4.** улыбается **5.** умываюсь.

Exercise а. Каролина бегает. **б.** Марк плавает. **в.** Это кроль. **г.** Это брасс. **д.** Это плавание на спине.

ORDERING A MEAL

(zakaZAT') *(aBYET)*
Заказать обед

14 *(ZAFtrak)* **Завтрак,** *(aBYET)* **Обед,** *(Uzhin)* **Ужин**

Breakfast Lunch/Dinner Supper

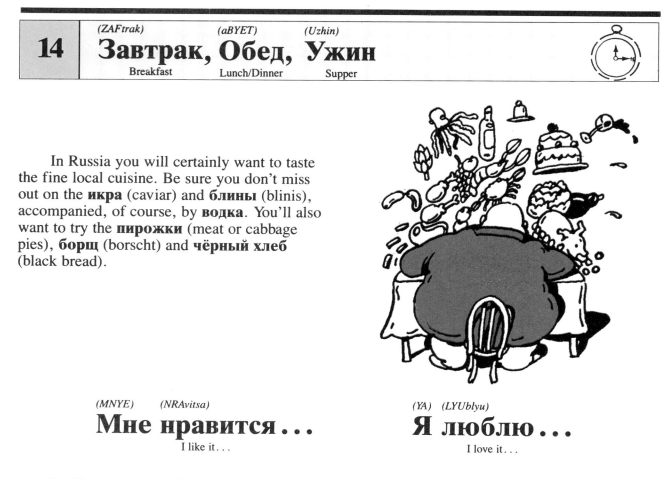

In Russia you will certainly want to taste the fine local cuisine. Be sure you don't miss out on the **икра** (caviar) and **блины** (blinis), accompanied, of course, by **водка**. You'll also want to try the **пирожки** (meat or cabbage pies), **борщ** (borscht) and **чёрный хлеб** (black bread).

(MNYE) *(NRAvitsa)*
Мне нравится . . .
I like it . . .

(YA) *(LYUblyu)*
Я люблю . . .
I love it . . .

You'll want to be able to distinguish between liking something or someone and loving it or her/him. When Russians say "I like it," they are actually saying, "It is pleasing to me." Note that the person or object liked will be the subject of the sentence in the nominative case — the form given in dictionaries and word lists. When Russians say, "I love him, her, it," they must use the direct object form in the accusative case.

Notice the difference in the following examples:

Мне нравится суп.  **Я люблю суп.**

Мне нравится молоко. **Я люблю молоко.**

Мне нравится водка.  **Я люблю водку.**

> Notice that the feminine noun for vodka **(водка)** changes the **«а»** to **«у»** in the accusative case.

Here are a few for you to try. Write in the answer for things you really love!

1. **Мне нравится чай.**  **Я люблю** ______________.

2. **Мне нравится масло.**  **Я люблю** ______________.

3. **Мне нравится рыба.**  **Я люблю** ______________.

4. **Мне нравится мясо.**  **Я люблю** ______________.

5. **Мне нравится сок.**  **Я люблю** ______________.

6. **Мне нравится курица.**  **Я люблю** ______________.

ANSWERS

Food **1.** чай **2.** масло **3.** рыбу **4.** мясо **5.** сок **6.** курицу

(ZAFtrak)
ЗАВТРАК
Breakfast

(buFYET)
буфет
snack bar

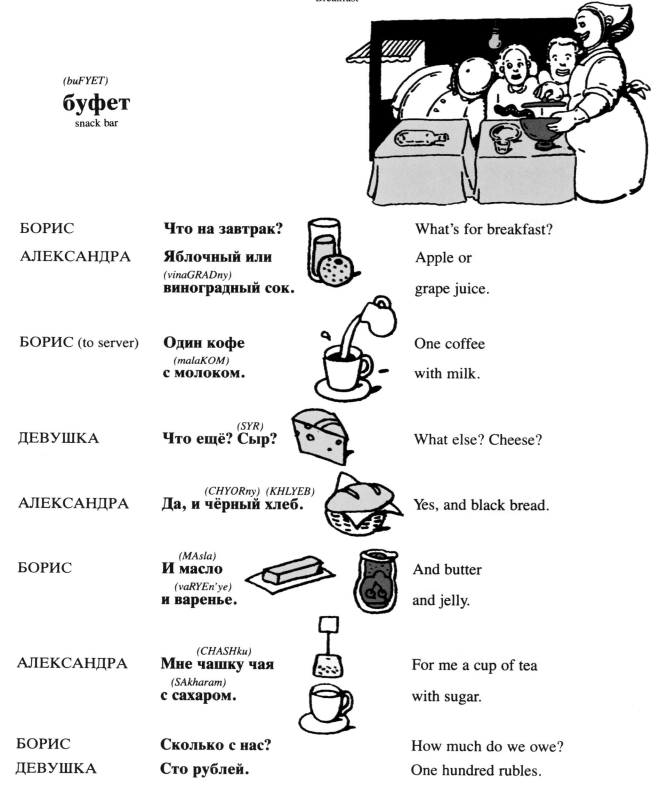

БОРИС	**Что на завтрак?**	What's for breakfast?
АЛЕКСАНДРА	**Яблочный или** *(vinaGRADny)* **виноградный сок.**	Apple or grape juice.
БОРИС (to server)	**Один кофе** *(malaKOM)* **с молоком.**	One coffee with milk.
ДЕВУШКА	**Что ещё?** *(SYR)* **Сыр?**	What else? Cheese?
АЛЕКСАНДРА	**Да, и** *(CHYORny)* **чёрный** *(KHLYEB)* **хлеб.**	Yes, and black bread.
БОРИС	*(MAsla)* **И масло** *(vaRYEn'ye)* **и варенье.**	And butter and jelly.
АЛЕКСАНДРА	*(CHASHku)* **Мне чашку чая** *(SAkharam)* **с сахаром.**	For me a cup of tea with sugar.
БОРИС	**Сколько с нас?**	How much do we owe?
ДЕВУШКА	**Сто рублей.**	One hundred rubles.

Fill in the blanks below and then repeat the sentences so that you will be able to order breakfast too.

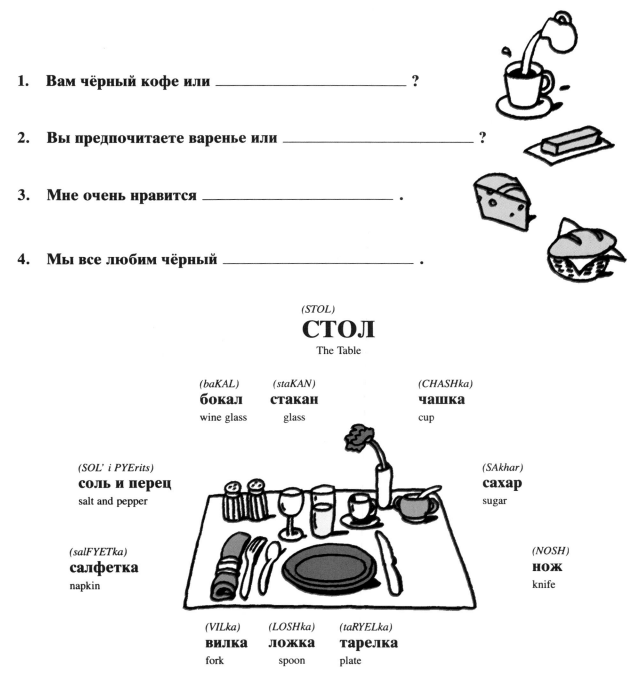

1. **Вам чёрный кофе или ____________________ ?**

2. **Вы предпочитаете варенье или ____________________ ?**

3. **Мне очень нравится ____________________ .**

4. **Мы все любим чёрный ____________________ .**

(STOL)

СТОЛ

The Table

ANSWERS

Breakfast **1.** кофе с молоком **2.** масло **3.** сыр **4.** хлеб

(aBYET)

ОБЕД

Lunch/Dinner

The main meal of the day for Russians is **обед**. It is likely to consist of appetizers or a salad, soup, a main course, and a light dessert. All of this is accompanied by plenty of bread, and perhaps a glass of wine, vodka or mineral water.

Look at the picture below and see if you can find the following items:

(YA) (vaz'MU)

Я возьму . . .

I'll take

я возьму	**мы возьмём**
ты возьмёшь	**вы возьмёте**
он/она возьмёт	**они возьмут**

At the snack bar or in the restaurant you will be asked what you want to order. Use the forms of the verb **взять** (take) to tell your hostess what you and your family want.

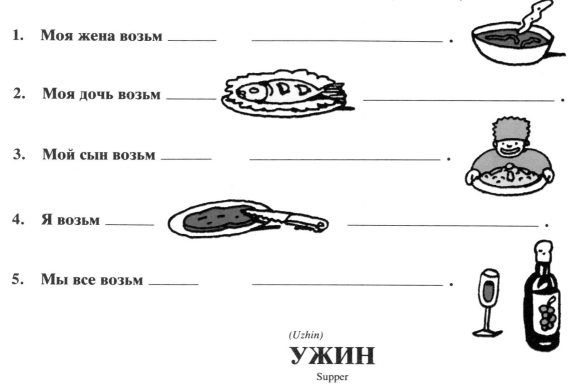

1. **Моя жена возьм** ______ ________________________ .

2. **Моя дочь возьм** ______ ________________________ .

3. **Мой сын возьм** ______ ________________________ .

4. **Я возьм** ______ ________________________ .

5. **Мы все возьм** ______ ________________________ .

(Uzhin)

УЖИН

Supper

If you have a full meal at midday, you will probably want only a light supper — **ужин**. This could be at a friend's house or at the theater buffet. One of the nicest buffet suppers is available before the performance at the Palace of Congresses **(Дворец съездов)**.

Дайте мне, пожалуйста Please, give me:

один бутерброд
one sandwich

два бутерброда
two sandwiches

три бутерброда
three sandwiches

четыре бутерброда
four sandwiches

(iKROY)
с икрой
with caviar

(SYram)
с сыром
with cheese

(vichiNOY)
с ветчиной
with ham

(kalbaSOY)
с колбасой
with salami

ANSWERS

Ordering **1.** возьмёт суп **2.** возьмёт рыбу **3.** возьмёт салат **4.** возьму мясо **5.** возьмём вино.

(asiTRInay)

пять бутербродов **с осетриной**
five sandwiches with sturgeon

(SYEMgay)

шесть бутербродов **с сёмгой**
six sandwiches with salmon

Что будем пить? What shall we drink?

(staKAN) *(shamPANskava)*
один стакан  **шампанского**

(buTYLku) *(limaNAda)*
одну бутылку  **лимонада**

(miniRAL'nay) *(vaDY)*
две бутылки  **минеральной воды**

А на сладкое? And for dessert?

(toRT)
торт
cake

(piROZHnaye)
пирожное
a pastry

(piCHYEn'ye)
печенье
cookie

(maROzhinaye)
мороженое
ice cream

Let's see if we can remember some of the more important words from our dining experiences.

1. What are the three meals of the day? ________, ________, ________.

2. Write three things you would like for breakfast:

________ ________ ________

ANSWERS

Food **1.** завтрак, обед, ужин **2.** сок, сыр, масло, хлеб, варенье, кофе, чай

3. Write down and pronounce aloud your choices for a full dinner.

______________________ ______________________ ______________________

______________________ ______________________ ______________________

______________________ ______________________ ______________________

4. Can you order supper for your guest at the theater buffet? She would like a sandwich with caviar, a glass of champagne, some pastry and a cup of tea.

______________________________ ______________________________

______________________________ ______________________________

Now match the words or expressions in the column on the right with the item most closely associated with it on the left.

1.	**чай**	а.	**ложка**
2.	**вилка**	б.	**соль**
3.	**хлеб**	в.	**с сахаром**
4.	**кофе**	г.	**с молоком**
5.	**перец**	д.	**белый и чёрный**

The following word puzzle contains several choices for the dinner menu. See if you can find all six:

а	б	с	а	л	а	т	ж
в	д	у	з	х	в	ш	ю
ш	и	п	ж	ц	и	м	я
р	ы	б	а	щ	н	я	т
я	ш	е	щ	т	о	с	у
в	с	л	а	д	к	о	е

ANSWERS

Food 3. закуски, суп, салат, овощи, мясо, рыба, фрукты, сладкое, вино
4. бутерброд с икрой, стакан шампанского, пирожное, чашка чая

Matching 1. в **2.** а **3.** д **4.** г **5.** б

Word puzzle салат, суп, рыба, вино, мясо, сладкое

15	*(ristaRAN)* **Ресторан** / *(chayiVIye)* **Чаевые**
	The Restaurant / Tips

(miNYU) *(paZHAluysta)*

Меню, пожалуйста

The menu, please

At the restaurant, remember the expressions for "bringing" and "taking":

(priniSItye) *(paZHAluysta)*
Принесите, пожалуйста... *Please bring...*

(YA) (siCHAS) (priniSU)
Я сейчас принесу. *I'll bring it right away.*

(YA) (vaz'MU)
Я возьму... *I'll take...*

МЕНЮ

закуски	appetizers
холодные	cold
горячие	hot
первое	first (course)
суп	soup
салат	salad
второе	second (course)
рыба	fish
мясо	meat
птица	poultry
овощи	vegetables
фрукты	fruits
третье	third (course)
сладкое	dessert (sweets)
напитки	beverages

Caroline and Mark have decided to have dinner in a fine Russian restaurant. After they have been seated and have studied the menu, the waiter approaches. They are ready to order.

ОФИЦИАНТ (Waiter)	**Добрый вечер. Я** *(SLUshayu)* **вас слушаю.**	Good evening. I'm at your service.

МАРК	**Что вы нам** (pasaVYEtuitye) **посоветуете?**	What can you recommend to us?
ОФИЦИАНТ	**Если вы любите** (iKRU) **икру, у нас и** (CHORnay) (KRASnaya) **чёрная и красная.**	If you like caviar, we have both black and red.
КАРОЛИНА	**Я возьму чёрную.**	I'll take the black.
МАРК	**А мне** (asarTI) (misNOye) **ассорти мясное.**	And for me the assorted meats.
ОФИЦИАНТ	**Кто хочет** (saLAT) **салат?**	Who would like salad?
МАРК	**Я возьму русский салат.**	I'll take the Russian salad.
ОФИЦИАНТ	**Вы будете суп?**	Will you be having soup?
КАРОЛИНА	**Я хочу** (paPRObavat') **попробовать русский борщ.**	I want to try the Russian borscht.
ОФИЦИАНТ	**А на второе?**	And for the main course?
МАРК	**Какие у вас** (FIRminiye) **фирменные** (BLYUda) **блюда?**	What are the house specialties?
ОФИЦИАНТ	**Я очень** (rikaminDUyu) **рекомендую** (asiTRInu) **осетрину.**	I highly recommend the sturgeon.
КАРОЛИНА	**Мне, пожалуйста,** (laSOsya) **лосося.**	For me, the salmon, please.
МАРК	**Я возьму** (tsyPLYONka) **цыплёнка.**	I'll take the chicken.
ОФИЦИАНТ	**Что вы будете пить?**	What will you be drinking?
КАРОЛИНА	**Красное вино, пожалуйста.**	Red wine, please.
МАРК	**Принесите** (buTYLku) **бутылку, и сто грамм водки.**	Bring a bottle, and 100 grams of vodka.
ОФИЦИАНТ	**Кофе или чай?**	Coffee or tea?

КАРОЛИНА	**Чай с лимоном, и мороженое.**	Tea with lemon, and ice cream.
МАРК	**Дайте мне кофе и пирожное.**	Give me some coffee and a pastry.
ОФИЦИАНТ	**Это всё?**	Is that all?
МАРК	**Я думаю, что да.**	I think so.
КАРОЛИНА	**А! Чёрный хлеб и масло.**	Ah! Black bread and butter.
ОФИЦИАНТ	**Сейчас принесу.**	I'll bring it right away.

(tuaLYEty)

Туалеты

Restrooms

After their meal, Mark and Caroline both want to freshen up.

(ZHENski)
женский
ladies'

(muSHKOY)
мужской
men's

Да или Нет?

Read back over the dialogue between the waiter and Caroline and Mark. Then examine the statements and fill in the blanks with **Да** or **Нет** (True or False).

1. **Каролина возьмёт чёрную икру.** ____________
2. **Марк хочет попробовать русский борщ.** ____________
3. **Официант рекомендует цыплёнка.** ____________
4. **Марк и Каролина любят красное вино.** ____________
5. **Каролина хочет белый хлеб.** ____________
6. **Марк будет пить кофе.** ____________
7. **Каролина возьмёт мороженое.** ____________

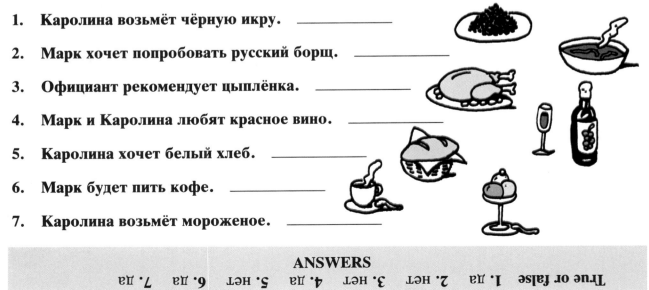

ANSWERS

True or false **1.** да **2.** нет **3.** нет **4.** да **5.** нет **6.** да **7.** да

It's finally time for Caroline and Mark to pay for their meal.

МАРК	**Дайте нам, пожалуйста, счёт.**	Please, give us the bill.
ОФИЦИАНТ	**Пожалуйста.**	Here it is.
МАРК	**Всё было очень вкусно. Обслуживание входит в счёт?**	Everything was delicious. Is service included in the bill?
ОФИЦИАНТ	**Да. 10 процентов.**	Yes. Ten percent.
КАРОЛИНА	**Сколько стоило?**	How much did it cost?
МАРК	**4000 рублей. И я оставил ещё 100 рублей на чай.**	4000 rubles. And I left another 100 rubles for a tip.
ОФИЦИАНТ	**Благодарю вас.**	I thank you.

In most restaurants, a service charge of ten to twenty percent is included in the bill. You might want to round off the final charge as a tip, or as Russians say **на чай** ("for tea").

(priYATnava) (apiTIta)

Приятного аппетита!

Bon appetit!

You have just returned from Russia and all of your friends are coming for dinner tonight. You have promised them a real Russian meal with all the trimmings. Draw up a menu of what you plan to serve them.

закуски	______________________	**второе**	______________________
	______________________	**овощи**	______________________
салат	______________________	**сладкое**	______________________
суп	______________________	**напитки**	______________________
	______________________		______________________
	______________________		______________________

HOW ARE WE DOING?

(KAK) (MY) (DYElaim)
Как мы делаем?

You're already half-way through and you have certainly learned a lot. Now you might want to go back over the first fifteen chapters and do a careful review of all the material we have covered.

In the next few pages you'll find some exercises designed to show you how much you can already accomplish in Russian.

Давайте начнём! Now let's begin!

Can you read the following Russian signs? Look at them carefully and then write the meaning for each sign in the space next to it.

1. **РЕСТОРАН** ____________________
2. **АЭРОПОРТ** ____________________
3. **ЖЕНСКИЙ** ____________________
4. **НЕ КУРИТЬ** ____________________
5. **ЦЕНТР** ____________________

Respond to the following questions and courtesy expressions by matching the forms in column **A** with those in column **B**.

<u>A</u>	<u>B</u>
1. **Как вас зовут?**	а. **Пожалуйста.**
2. **Спасибо.**	б. **Книга стоит пять рублей.**
3. **Сколько стоит эта книга?**	в. **Сейчас уже десять часов.**
4. **Который сейчас час?**	г. **Сегодня тепло.**
5. **Какая сегодня погода?**	д. **Меня зовут Иван Попов.**

ANSWERS

Signs 1. RESTAURANT 2. AIRPORT 3. LADIES' 4. NO SMOKING 5. CENTER

Matching 1. д 2. а 3. б 4. в 5. г

Can you recognize the gender of nouns and replace them with the proper pronouns? Read the first sentence carefully and then fill in the blank space with the correct form of the pronouns **он, она, оно, они**.

1. **Это моя книга.** ________________ **новая.**
2. **Где наш автобус?** **Вот** ________________ **идёт.**
3. **Это ваша газета?** **Нет,** ________________ **не моя.**
4. **Наши стюардессы — русские?** **Да,** ________________ **живут в Москве.**
5. **Где моё письмо?** **Я не знаю, где** ________________ **.**

Do you know all of the words with the letter **«а»** in our word puzzle? Look at the pictures and then fill in the blanks.

ANSWERS

Pronouns **1.** Она **2.** он **3.** она **4.** они **5.** оно

Puzzle рыба, туалет, магазин, паспорт, банк

Let's see how well you know your numbers in Russian. Do the following simple mathematical equations and fill in the blanks with the written forms of the numerals.

а. 10 ____________ – 8 ____________ = ______ (____________)

б. 3 ____________ + 4 ____________ = ______ (____________)

в. 6 ____________ – 5 ____________ = ______ (____________)

Now let's tell time in Russian. Examine the clocks and fill in the blanks below.

Который сейчас час?

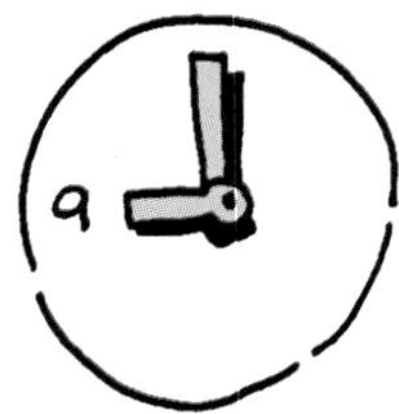

Сейчас ____________________ ____________________ ____________________

How well do you know how to form the present tense forms of verbs? Can you construct correct Russian sentences? Fill in the blanks below with the correct endings of the verbs. Remember that the verb form is determined by the subject of the sentence.

1. **Наш отец работа ____________ в Москве.**
2. **Нина и Борис жив ____________ в Санкт-Петербурге.**
3. **Мы завтрака ____________ в шесть часов.**
4. **Я отдыха ____________ вечером и в субботу.**
5. **Как вы ед ____________ ? На Красной Стреле?**

ANSWERS

Equations 1. десять – восемь = 2 (два) **2.** три + четыре = 7 (семь) **3.** шесть – пять = 1 (один).

Telling time девять часов, восемь часов, три часа.

Verbs 1. работает **2.** живут **3.** завтракаем **4.** отдыхаю **5.** едете

How good are you at recognizing flags and nationalities? It's not as hard as it seems. Look at the names below and check the flag to identify the proper nation.

1. **Я украинец.** 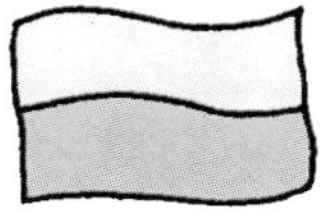 **Моя страна** __________________

2. **Каролина американка.**  **Её страна** __________________

3. **Мы русские.** 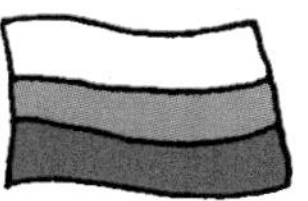 **Наша страна** __________________

4. **Он англичанин.**  **Его страна** __________________

5. **Они беларусы.** 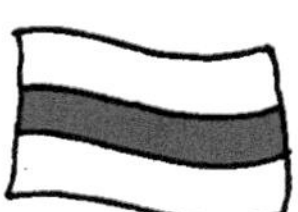 **Их страна** __________________

Can you tell what the weather will be like in **Москва** and the surrounding areas? Look at the questions first and then find the answers in the weather report below from the newspaper **Правда** (PRAVDA) and answer the questions below:

1. What kind of weather is expected on December 13?
   а. bitter cold **б.** rainy **в.** sunshine
2. What is the high temperature (in Centrigrade, of course) for December 13?
   а. 0° **б.** +3° **в.** +5°
3. How cold will it get during the night of December 14?
   а. 0° **б.** −5° **в.** −8°
4. It will be chilly on December 15. What is the daytime high?
   а. 0° **б.** −2° **в.** −5°
5. What can you tell your friends about the weather on December 15?
   а. snow flurries **б.** rain **в.** sunshine

В Москве 13 декабря сохранится тёплая погода. Ночью температура от −2 до 0 градусов, днём максимальная температура от +3 до +5, дождь. 14 декабря ночью от −8 до −5 градусов, 15 декабря днём от −5 до −2 градусов. 14 и 15 декабря небольшой снег.

ANSWERS

Flags 1. Украина **2.** США **3.** Россия **4.** Англия **5.** Беларусь

Weather 1. б **2.** в **3.** в **4.** б **5.** а

Do you recognize what our friends are doing for recreation? Choose from the following list to fill in the blanks with the correct form of the verb corresponding to the scenes below. **(обедать, любить, купаться, отдыхать, бегать)**

1. Каролина ____________________ .

2. Вечером они всегда ____________________ в ресторане.

3. Марк ____________________ .

4. Мы очень ____________________ русскую оперу.

5. Где и как ты ____________________ ?

Could you order a meal in a Russian restaurant? Fill in the blanks with the correct word from the list below.

(икра, борщ, рыба, кофе, мороженое, вино, курица)

1. Вы возьмёте суп? Да, я очень люблю

русский ______________ .

2. Вам нравится ______________ ? У нас и чёрная и красная.

3. На второе я возьму ______________ ,

а мой муж возьмёт ______________ .

ANSWERS

Recreation 1. бегает **2.** обедают **3.** купается **4.** любим **5.** отдыхаешь

Food 1. борщ **2.** икра **3.** рыбу, мясо

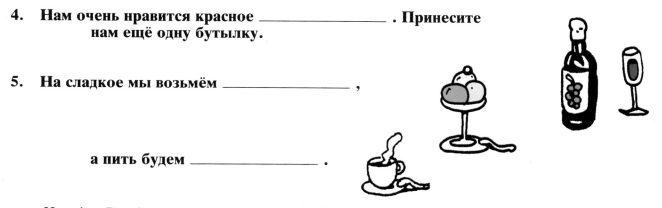

4. **Нам очень нравится красное ________________ . Принесите нам ещё одну бутылку.**

5. **На сладкое мы возьмём ________________ ,**

а пить будем ________________ .

Here is a Russian **кроссворд** with words chosen from the chapters on transportation and eating. See how many you can get.

Кроссворд

Crossword puzzle

										4		5			
1		2				3									
										8					
	6					7									
				9							10				
									11					12	
				13		14	15								
			16												

По горизонтали
ACROSS

1. bus
4. fork
6. caviar
7. subway
8. knife
9. salt
14. trolley bus
16. vodka

По вертикали
DOWN

2. taxi
3. airplane
4. wine
5. spoon
10. train
11. bread
12. soup
13. meat
15. fish

ANSWERS

Food 4. вино **5.** мороженое, кофе

Crossword puzzle

ACROSS 1. автобус **4.** вилка **6.** икра **7.** метро **8.** нож **9.** соль **14.** троллейбус **16.** водка

DOWN 2. такси **3.** самолёт **4.** вино **5.** ложка **10.** поезд **11.** хлеб **12.** суп **13.** мясо **15.** рыба

AT THE STORE

(v) (magaZInye)
В магазине

16 *(aDYEZHda)* Одежда, *(razMYEry)* Размеры, *(tsviTA)* Цвета

Clothing, Sizes, Colors

(ON) (adiVAitsya)
Он одевается.
He is getting dressed.

(oNA) (razdiVAitsya)
Она раздевается.
She is undressing.

(ON) (nadiVAit) (ruBASHku)
Он надевает рубашку.
He is putting on his shirt.

(oNA) (sniMAit) (kambiNAtsiyu)
Она снимает комбинацию.
She is taking off her slip.

(SHTO) (NUZHna) (ZNAT')
Что нужно знать.
What you need to know.

In most Russian shops you will first want to examine the articles with the help of the salesperson behind the counter. You may want to ask them to show you an item — **Покажите, пожалуйста** (Show me, please). You may want to try something on — **Можно примерить?** (May I try it on?) When you have finally decided on your purchase you will need to find out the total price — **Сколько стоит?** (How much does it cost?) Then you must go to the cashier and tell him or her the total cost and in which section of the store the item is found. After paying you will receive a receipt (**чек**) which you bring back to the original counter where your purchase will be waiting for you. If you feel unsure of the Russian number system, you might want to have the salesperson write down the price for you. If you smile and show courtesy and good humor, you are likely to be helped through the process.

(muSHKAya) *(aDYEZHda)*

МУЖСКАЯ ОДЕЖДА

Men's Clothing

(naSKI)
носки
socks

(ruBASHka)
рубашка
shirt

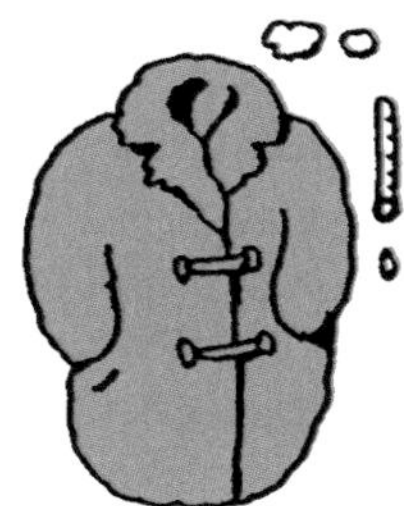

(pal'TO)
пальто
overcoat

(GALstuk)
галстук
necktie

(nasaVOY) *(plaTOK)*
носовой платок
handkerchief

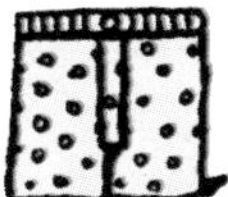

(truSY)
трусы
underpants

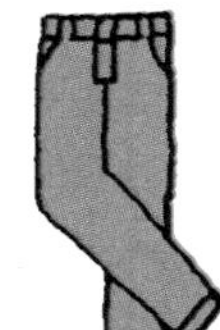

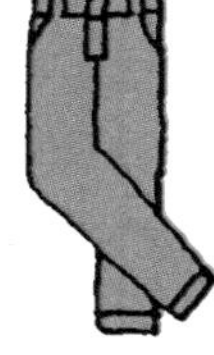

(BRYUki)
брюки
slacks

(SVItir)
свитер
sweater

(MAYka)
майка
undershirt

(pidZHAK)
пиджак
sport coat

(ZONT)
зонт
umbrella

(kaSTYUM)
костюм
suit

(SHLYApa)
шляпа
hat

(sapaGI)
сапоги
boots

(riMYEN')
ремень
belt

(pirCHATki)
перчатки
gloves

(SHTO) (MNYE) (NUZHna)

Что мне нужно?

What do I need?

When you need something (or someone) in Russian, you must use a form of **нужно**. Literally, the Russians are saying: *Something is necessary to me*. The form of **нужно** will change according to the subject, which is the thing needed. Look at the following examples.

(MNYE) (NUzhin) (NOvy) (kaSTYUM) **Мне нужен новый костюм.**	I need a new suit.
(MNYE) (nuzhNA) (NOvaya) (SHLYApa) **Мне нужна новая шляпа.**	I need a new hat.
(MNYE) (NUZHna) (NOvaye) (pal'TO) **Мне нужно новое пальто.**	I need a new coat.
(MNYE) (nuzhNY) (NOviye) (BRYUki) **Мне нужны новые брюки.**	I need new pants.

Now try to tell the salesperson what you need.

1. **Здравствуйте. Мне ______________ новый зонт.**
2. **Извините, пожалуйста. Мне ______________ новая рубашка.**
3. **Скажите, пожалуйста, где здесь сапоги. Нам ______________ сапоги.**
4. **Покажите нам ваши галстуки. Мне ______________ модный галстук.**
5. **Как вы думаете, мне ______________ новое пальто?**

When you shop for clothes in the Soviet Union you must be aware that there are great variations in sizes. It is helpful if you know your height (**рост** *(ROST)*), chest (**обхват груди** *(abKHVAT)(GRUdi)*) and waist (**обхват талии** *(abKHVAT)(TAlii)*) measurements in centimeters in order to use the conversion charts found in many department and clothing stores. In any case, you should be sure to try on the item. Ask for the changing booths — **примерочные кабины** *(priMYErachniye) (kaBIny)*.

ANSWERS

Need 1. нужен **2.** нужна **3.** нужны **4.** нужен **5.** нужно

Mark's suitcase has been misplaced on the flight to Moscow. He needs a complete set of clothes for his business meetings. Let's see how he does at the *(univirSAL'ny)* **универсальный** *(magaZIN)* **магазин** (department store).

ПРОДАВЩИЦА (Salesclerk)	**Как можно вам помочь?**	How may I help you?
MARK	**Мне нужно всё — новый костюм, рубашка, и галстук.**	I need everything — a new suit, shirt, and tie.
ПРОДАВЩИЦА	**Хорошо. А что ещё? Носки, трусы, майки?**	Fine. And what else? Socks, underpants, undershirts?
MARK	**Да. Можно примерить брюки и пиджак?**	Yes. May I try on the pants and the jacket?
ПРОДАВЩИЦА	**Конечно. Примерочная кабина вон там.**	Certainly. The changing room is over there.
MARK	**Это не мой размер, и** *(tSVYET)* **цвет мне не нравится.**	This isn't my size, and I don't like the color.
ПРОДАВЩИЦА	**Может быть, этот** *(siDIT)* **сидит лучше?**	Maybe this one fits better?
MARK	**Да. Вы** *(PRAvy)* **правы.**	Yes. You're right.
ПРОДАВЩИЦА	**Нет. Вы правы.** *(pakuPAtil')* **Покупатель всегда прав.**	No. You're right. The customer is always right.
MARK	**Я возьму всё.** *(paschiTAYtye)* **Подсчитайте, пожалуйста, сколько это стоит.**	I'll take everything. Please, figure up how much it costs.

ПРОДАВЩИЦА	**С удовольствием.**	With pleasure.
	(zavirNUT') **Вам завернуть?**	Should it be wrapped for you?
MARK	*(naDYEnu)* **Нет. Я всё надену на себя. Спасибо и до свидания.**	No. I'll wear it all. Thank you and goodbye.

(Obuf')

ОБУВЬ

Shoes

(tiSNY)
Они мне тесны.
They are too narrow.

(ZHMUT)
Они мне жмут.
They pinch me.

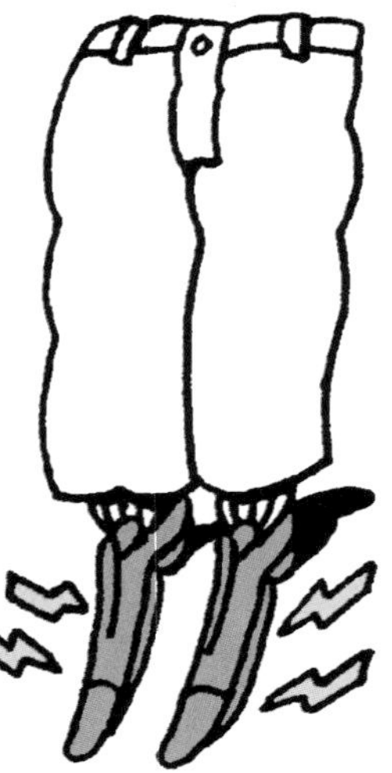

(viliKI)
Они мне велики.
They are too large.

(shiraKI)
Они мне широки.
They're too wide for me.

(sapaGI)
сапоги

(TUfli)
туфли

(baTINki)
ботинки

(ZHENskaya) *(aDYEZHda)*

ЖЕНСКАЯ ОДЕЖДА

Women's Clothing

(asnavNIye) *(tsviTA)*

Основные цвета

Basic colors

(ZHOLty) (byustGAL'tir)
жёлтый бюстгальтер
yellow bra

(CHORnaya) (SUMka)
чёрная сумка
black handbag

(galuBOye) (PLAt'ye)
голубое платье
light blue dress

(SIni) (SHARF)
синий шарф
dark blue scarf

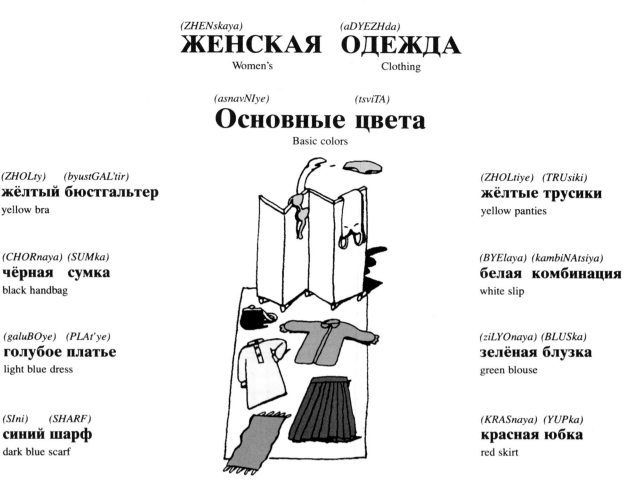

(ZHOLtiye) (TRUsiki)
жёлтые трусики
yellow panties

(BYElaya) (kambiNAtsiya)
белая комбинация
white slip

(ziLYOnaya) (BLUSka)
зелёная блузка
green blouse

(KRASnaya) (YUPka)
красная юбка
red skirt

You and a friend are going to a masquerade ball and want some clothes that really stand out. Write out your order beforehand and then tell the shopkeeper exactly what you need.

Здравствуйте. Мы идём на маскарад, и нам нужны следующие вещи:
following items

1. a yellow blouse ______________________
2. a green tie ______________________
3. a light blue jacket ______________________
4. dark blue pants ______________________
5. red boots ______________________
6. a black shirt ______________________

ANSWERS

Clothes 1. жёлтая блузка **2.** зелёный галстук **3.** голубой пиджак **4.** синие брюки **5.** красные сапоги **6.** чёрная рубашка

17	*(gastraNOM)* **Гастроном** The Supermarket

The local **гастроном** (supermarket) may have all or at least some of your needs. You may also see signs for individual shops. Learning them now will help you recognize the stores you'll want to visit.

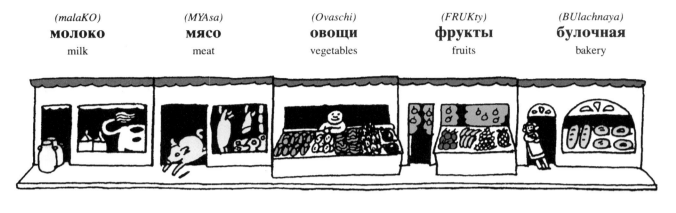

(malaKO)	*(MYAsa)*	*(Ovaschi)*	*(FRUKty)*	*(BUlachnaya)*
молоко	**мясо**	**овощи**	**фрукты**	**булочная**
milk	meat	vegetables	fruits	bakery

(RYba)	*(kanFYEty)*	*(kanDItirskaya)*	*(maROzhinaye)*	*(vino)*
рыба	**конфеты**	**кондитерская**	**мороженое**	**вино**
fish market	candy store	pastry shop	ice cream shop	wine store

(SLISHkam) (MNOga) (vaPROsaf)

Слишком много вопросов

Too many questions

Mark and Caroline approach a **милиционер** (policeman).

MARK	**Можно вам задать вопрос?**	May I ask you a question?
МИЛИЦИОНЕР	**Слушаю вас.**	I'm listening.
MARK	**Где можно купить хлеб?**	Where can I buy bread?

МИЛИЦИОНЕР	**Булочная на этой улице.**	The bakery is on this street.
CAROLINE	**Где можно купить шампанское?**	Where can I buy champagne?
МИЛИЦИОНЕР	**В магазине «ВИНО»**	In the liquor store.
CAROLINE	**А где можно купить масло и кефир?**	Where can one buy butter and kefir?
МИЛИЦИОНЕР	**В магазине «МОЛОКО».**	In the dairy store.
MARK	**Где овощи и фрукты?**	Where are the vegetables and fruits?
МИЛИЦИОНЕР	**В магазине «ОВОЩИ» и «ФРУКТЫ», или на рынке.** *(RYNkye)*	In the vegetable and fruit store, or at the market.
CAROLINE	**А где можно найти** *(nayTI)* **говядину** *(gaVYAdinu)* **и свинину?** *(sviNInu)*	Where can one find beef and pork?
МИЛИЦИОНЕР	**В магазине «МЯСО».**	In the meat store.
MARK	**Я люблю торт. Где . . . ?**	I love cake. Where is . . . ?
МИЛИЦИОНЕР	**В кондитерской.**	In the pastry shop.
CAROLINE	**А где кофе, и чай, и лимонад, и вино?**	And where is the coffee, and the tea, and the soda, and the wine?
МИЛИЦИОНЕР	**Хватит!** *(KHVAtit)* **Вы задаёте** *(zadaYOtye)* **слишком много вопросов.**	That's enough! You're asking too many questions.
MARK	**Какой несимпатичный милиционер!**	What an unfriendly policeman!
CAROLINE	**Нет, Марк, он прав. Это было действительно** *(diystVItil'na)* **много вопросов.**	No, Mark, he's right. That was really a lot of questions.

Read the following statements about Mark and Caroline's conversation and write **правда** (true) or **неправда** (false) in the blanks.

1. **Хлеб можно найти в булочной.** ______________________
2. **Масло можно купить в магазине «ВИНО».** ______________________
3. **Шампанское можно найти в магазине «ФРУКТЫ».** ______________________
4. **Говядину можно купить в магазине «МЯСО».** ______________________
5. **Торт можно найти в кондитерской.** ______________________

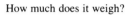

(SKOL'ka) *(VYEsit)*

Сколько весит?

How much does it weigh?

Although the metric system is widely used for measurements in Russia and in other countries and has become increasingly more familiar to Americans, it is still useful to examine how Russians order items in their shops.

100 грамм	100 grams = 3.5 ounces
200 грамм	200 grams = 7 ounces (almost 1/2 pound)
500 грамм, полкило	500 grams, half a kilo = 17.5 ounces (one pound + 1.5 ounces)
1000 грамм, 1 килограмм	1000 grams, one kilogram = 2.205 pounds
1 литр	1 liter = 1.06 quarts

ANSWERS

True or false **1.** правда **2.** неправда **3.** неправда **4.** правда **5.** правда

(SKOL'ka) (STOit)

Сколько стоит?

How much does it cost?

Read aloud the names of the different sorts of containers that food can come in. Then ask the clerk how much the items cost.

(kuSOK) (MYla)
кусок мыла
bar of soap

(BANka) (KOfye)
банка кофе
jar of coffee

(diSYAtak) (yaITS)
десяток яиц
ten eggs

(LITR) (malaKA)
литр молока
a liter of milk

(paKYET)(muKI)
пакет муки
package of flour

(STO) (GRAM) (SYra)
сто грамм сыра
100 grams of cheese

(kaROPka) (kanFYET)
коробка конфет
a box of candy

(ruLON) (tuaLYETnay) (buMAgi)
рулон туалетной бумаги
a roll of toilet paper

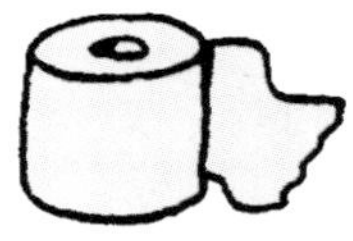

(baTON) (BYElava) (KHLYEba)
батон белого хлеба
a loaf of white bread

(PACHka) (SAkhara)
пачка сахара
a bag of sugar

(buTYLka) (viNA)
бутылка вина
a bottle of wine

(kilaGRAM) (karTOSHki)
килограмм картошки
a kilogram of potatoes

THE GENITIVE CASE

We have seen several instances where Russians use the genitive case when they describe a container or measure of something: a liter of, a package of, a box of, a bottle of, etc. The item contained in the package is rendered in Russian in the genitive case. Look at the way the genitive case is formed.

For masculine nouns that end in a hard consonant, and neuter nouns ending in **o**, the genitive case is formed by the addition of the ending **a**.

Nominative	Genitive
хлеб	loaf of bread **батон хлеба**
молоко	bottle of milk **бутылка молока**

If there is a soft consonant, such as **й**, or a soft sign **ь** ending for masculine nouns, or the ending **е** for neuter nouns, change the ending to **я**.

чай	package of tea **пачка чая**

For feminine nouns ending in **а**, change the **а** to **ы**.

рыба	kilogram of fish **килограмм рыбы**

If the noun ends in **я**, it changes to **и**. Also observe the spelling rule that requires us to write **и**, not **ы** after the letters **к, г, х, ш, щ, ж, ч**.

бумага	roll of paper **рулон бумаги**

Let's see if you can ask the clerk for the following items. Be sure to put the item in the genitive case.

Дайте мне, пожалуйста . . . (Please give me a . . .)

1. (a bottle of beer) **пиво** — **бутылку** ________________ .
2. (a can of soup) **суп** — **банку** ________________ .
3. (100 grams of vodka) **водка** — **сто грамм** ________________ .
4. (a kilogram of fish) **рыба** — **килограмм** ________________ .
5. (a package of tea) **чай** — **пачку** ________________ .

(RYnak)

РЫНОК

The Market

One place you should not overlook in your shopping is the **рынок**. These marketplaces are almost always better stocked than the stores, and they offer a feast of sights and smells. The local farmers are eager to sell their wares and will enter into lively conversations as they let you sample their goods. Be sure to bring a plastic or net bag to carry home your purchases. Russians even have a special word for this bag you take along "just in case" — **авоська** *(aVOS'ka)*.

ANSWERS

Genitive case **1.** бутылку пива **2.** банку супа **3.** сто грамм водки **4.** килограмм рыбы **5.** пачку чая.

(kuDA) (NAda) (iTI)

Куда надо идти?

Where must I go?

It's your turn to do the shopping. Which way must you go to get all of the items at the right? Do you remember the words for directions?

прямо	straight ahead
направо	to the right
налево	to the left

You are standing near the ice cream shop. Fill in the blanks as you move from one shop to the next.

Сперва я иду ________________ купить мороженое. Потом мне надо купить рыбу и я иду ________________ . Мои дети хотят конфеты, поэтому я иду ________________ . Потом я иду ________________ , где я всегда покупаю овощи и фрукты. Чтобы купить молоко, мне надо идти ________________ и ________________ . Уже поздно, но нам ещё нужен хлеб. Я иду прямо и ________________ в булочную. Это всё? Нет! Где можно купить вино? Идите ________________ . Теперь я могу идти ________________ домой.

ANSWERS

Food shopping прямо, налево, прямо, направо, налево, направо, налево, направо, прямо.

18 *(parfyuMYEriya)* Парфюмерия / *(apTYEka)* Аптека

Drugstore / Pharmacy

If you are looking for toiletries, cosmetics or simple personal needs, you might find them in the hotel lobby at a **киоск** or in a special section of the store called **парфюмерия**. If you have a prescription to be filled you will have to take it to the pharmacy — **аптека**. Let's take a look at some of the names for frequently needed items.

(zubNAya) (SCHOTka)
зубная щётка
toothbrush

(SCHOTka)
щётка
hairbrush

(ZYERkala)
зеркало
mirror

(zubNAya) (PASta)
зубная паста
toothpaste

(rasCHOSka)
расчёска
comb

(salFYETki)
салфетки
tissues

(LAK) (dlya) (vaLOS)
лак для волос
hairspray

(ruMYAna)
румяна
rouge

(TUSH) (dlya) (risNITS)
тушь для ресниц
mascara

(atsiTON)
ацетон
nail polish remover

ОТДЕЛ «ПАРФЮМЕРИЯ»

The Toiletries Section

ИРИНА (Irina)	*(KRYEM) (liTSA)* **Мне нужен крем для лица.**	I need some face cream.
МАША (Masha)	*(meyk-UP)* **Ты купила мэйк-ап вчера.**	You purchased makeup yesterday.
ИРИНА	**Я знаю, но он мне не** *(paNRAvilsya)* **понравился.**	I know, but I did not like it.
МАША	**Да. И я забыла купить** *(buMAZHniye) (pilYONki) (TAL'K)* **бумажные пелёнки и тальк.**	Yes. And I forgot to buy disposable diapers and talcum.
КАССИРША (Cashier)	**Могу ли я вам помочь?**	May I help you?
МАША	**У вас есть бумажные пелёнки?**	Do you have disposable diapers?
КАССИРША	**К сожалению, я продала последний пакет час назад.**	Unfortunately, I sold the last package an hour ago.
МАША	*(duKHI)* **Ничего. А духи у вас** *(daraGIye)* **дорогие?**	That's all right. Are your perfumes expensive?
КАССИРША	**Не очень. Вы попробовали наши новые русские духи?**	Not very. Have you tried our new Russian perfume?
ИРИНА	**Я их возьму, и также** *(gubNUyu) (paMAdu) (TYEni)* **губную помаду, тени и крем для рук.**	I'll take it, and also lipstick, eyeshadow and hand cream.

(praSHEDsheye) *(VRYEmya)*

Прошедшее время

The past tense

купить to buy	**купи + ла**	**Ирина купила мэйк-ап.** Irina bought makeup.
забыть to forget	**забы + л**	**Я забыл зубную щётку.** I forgot the toothbrush.
продать to sell	**прода + ли**	**Они продали все духи.** They sold all the perfume.
понравиться to like	**понрави + ло + сь**	**Это нам не понравилось.** We did not like this.

To form the past tense of a Russian verb, you drop the **ть** or **ти** ending of the infinitive and in the singular you add **л** for masculine subjects, **ла** for feminine subjects, and **ло** for neuter subjects. For all plurals you add **ли**. When the verb ends in **ся**, form the past tense first and then add **ся** after **л**, and **сь** after **ла, ло, ли**.

Now let's see how well you can recognize the past tense in practice. Fill in the blanks with the Russian words **правда** or **неправда**.

1. **Ирина купила мэйк-ап вчера?** ________________
2. **Мэйк-ап Маше понравился?** ________________
3. **Маша купила бумажные пелёнки?** ________________
4. **Кассирша продала последний пакет час назад?** ________________
5. **Ирина взяла крем для рук?** ________________

ANSWERS

Past tense **1.** правда **2.** неправда **3.** неправда **4.** правда **5.** правда

(NUZHniye) *(VYEschi)*
Нужные вещи

Necessary items

Write the names of these important items in the blanks provided.

(dizadaRANT)
дезодорант
deodorant

____

(elikTRIchiskaya) *(BRITva)*
электрическая бритва
electric shaver

____

(LYEZviya)
лезвия
razor blades

____

(BRITva)
бритва
razor

____

When his electric shaver breaks, Alexander discovers that he too has a few items to pick up.

АЛЕКСАНДР	**Моя электрическая бритва не работает.**	My electric shaver doesn't work.
КАССИР	**Купите бритву и лезвия.**	Buy a razor and blades.
АЛЕКСАНДР	**Это слишком много** *(raBOty)* **работы.**	That's too much work.
	Крем для *(brit'YA)* **бритья,**	Shaving cream,
	(las'YON) **лосьон после бритья.**	aftershave lotion.
КАССИР	**Да. Но она** *(vizDYE)* **везде работает.**	Yes. But it works everywhere.
АЛЕКСАНДР	**Вы правы. И я всегда беру** *(MYla)* **мыло и** *(shamPUN')* **шампунь.**	You're right. And I always take soap and shampoo.
КАССИР	**Не забудьте** *(adikaLON)* **одеколон!**	Don't forget the cologne!

В АПТЕКЕ

At the Pharmacy

If you are given a prescription you will need to go to a pharmacy — **Аптека**. Here you can also find non-prescription remedies for what ails you. There is also a *(riTSEPTny)* *(aDYEL)* **Рецептный отдел** (prescription section). You should ask **Нужен рецепт?** (Is a prescription necessary?) To find out if they have the proper medicine ask: **У вас есть лекарство по этому рецепту?** Or you may simply ask for *(bizriTSEPTniye)* **безрецептные** *(liKARSTva)* **лекарства** (the non-prescription medicines).

We hope you won't need to use the following words and phrases, but just in case:

Мне нужно что-нибудь от ________ .
I need something for ________ .

(NASmarka)
насморка
a cold

(zaPOra)
запора
constipation

(KASHlya)
кашля
cough

(paNOsa)
поноса
diarrhea

(ZHAra)
жара
a fever

(galavNOY) (BOli)
головной боли
a headache

(tashnaTY)
тошноты
nausea

(SOLnichnava) (aZHOga)
солнечного ожога
sunburn

(zubNOY) (BOli)
зубной боли
a toothache

(zhiLUdachnava) (raSTROYSTva)
желудочного расстройства
upset stomach

У вас есть ________ ?
Do you have ________ ?

(PLAStyr')
пластырь
adhesive tape

(SCHOlach)
щёлочь
an antacid

(SPIRT)
спирт
alcohol

(antiSYEPtik)
антисептик
an antiseptic

(aspiRIN)
аспирин
aspirin

(BINT)
бинт
bandages

(VAta)
вата
cotton

(glazNIye) (KApli)
глазные капли
eyedrops

(YOT)
йод
iodine

(tirMOmitr)
термометр
a thermometer

Let's make sure that we can get some of the essentials.

Match items in column A with associated words or phrases in column B.

A	B
1. аспирин	**а. от желудочного расстройства**
2. мэйк-ап	**б. лезвия**
3. бритва	**в. губная помада**
4. щёлочь	**г. от головной боли**

Here is your shopping list. Can you translate the items into Russian for the cashier?

а. shampoo ____________________

б. deodorant ____________________

в. face cream ____________________

г. toothpaste ____________________

д. rouge ____________________

ANSWERS

Matching 1. г **2.** в **3.** б **4.** а.

Shopping list а. шампунь **б.** дезодорант **в.** крем для лица **г.** зубная паста **д.** румяна

19 *(STIRka)* Стирка / *(khimCHISTka)* Химчистка

Laundry / Dry Cleaner's

(pastiRAT')	(paCHIStit')	(pasuSHYT')	(paGLAdit')
постирать	**почистить**	**посушить**	**погладить**
to wash	to clean	to dry	to iron

You may be able to have your shirts, blouses, and underwear washed at the hotel for a modest price. There will also probably be an ironing board and iron on your floor. Simply ask the key lady (**дежурная**). Otherwise, you may want to try out the laundromat and dry cleaner's.

(PRAchichnaya) (samaapSLUzhivaniya)
прачечная самообслуживания
laundromat

(khimCHISTka)
химчистка
dry cleaner's

(paraSHOk) (dlya) (STIRki)
порошок для стирки
soap powder

(glaDIL'naya) (daSKA)
гладильная доска
ironing board

(uTYUK)
утюг
iron

(stiRAL'naya) (maSHYna)
стиральная машина
washing machine

(STIRka) (i) (CHISTka) (v) (gaSTInitse)

СТИРКА И ЧИСТКА В ГОСТИНИЦЕ

Laundry and Dry Cleaning in the Hotel

(GORnichnaya)

The **горничная** (maid) in your hotel will be happy to do your laundry. Here are some useful expressions.

(biL'YO) **Вы можете постирать моё бельё?**	Can you wash my underwear?
(priSHEYtye) (PUgavitsu) **Пришейте, пожалуйста, пуговицу.**	Please sew on the button.
(ruKAF) **Вы можете починить этот рукав?**	Can you mend this sleeve?
Вы можете погладить рубашку?	Can you iron the shirt?
(nakraKHMAL'tye) **Накрахмальте только немножко.**	Just a little starch.
(kaSTYUM) **Вы можете сдать костюм в чистку?**	Can you take my suit to the cleaner's?
(VYvisti) (pitNO) **Вы можете вывести это пятно?**	Can you remove this stain?

Now fill in the blanks using the words and expressions found above.

1. **У вас есть** ______________ (an iron) **и** ______________ (an ironing board) .
2. **Вы можете** ______________ (wash) **моё** ______________ (my underwear) .
3. **Вы можете** ______________ (an iron) **мою** ______________ (shirt) .
4. **Вы можете сдать** ______________ (suit) **в** ______________ (the cleaner's) .
5. **Вы можете** ______________ (remove) **это** ______________ (stain) .

ANSWERS

Fill in **1.** утюг, гладильная доска **2.** постирать, бельё **3.** погладить, рубашку **4.** костюм, чистку **5.** вывести, пятно

(ZHAlaby)

ЖАЛОБЫ

Complaints

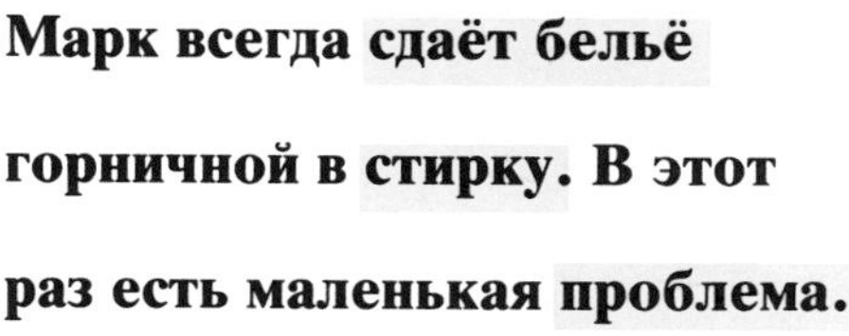

Марк всегда сдаёт бельё горничной в стирку. В этот раз есть маленькая проблема. Он получил не своё бельё. Марк жалуется горничной. Он не носит женское бельё. В рубашках слишком много крахмала, двух носков не хватает, один красный носок, и один зелёный. И наконец, в одной рубашке есть дырка. Марк очень сердит. Как вы думаете? У него есть на что жаловаться?

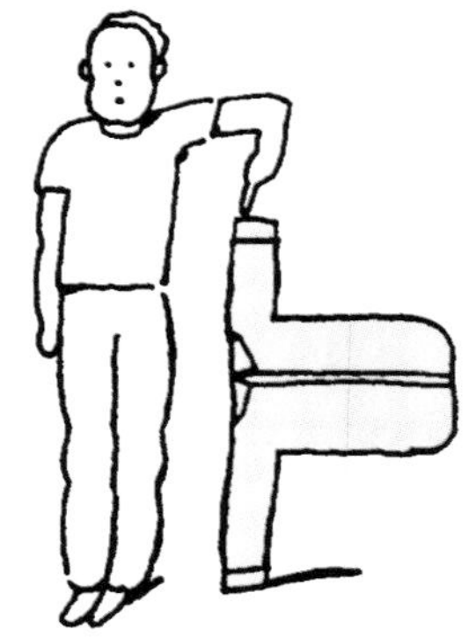

Mark always gives his clothes to the maid to be washed. This time there is a small problem. He received someone else's underwear. Mark complains to the maid. He doesn't wear women's underwear. The shirts have too much starch. Two socks are missing, one red sock, and one green one. And finally, in one shirt there's a hole. Mark is very angry. What do you think? Does he have something to complain about?

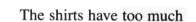

Here are some useful phrases if you have a complaint.

(YA) (BUdu) (ZHAlavatsa)
Я буду жаловаться.
I'm going to complain.

(NYE) (khvaTAit) (PUgavitsy)
Не хватает пуговицы.
A button is missing.

(VY) (NYE) (slaZHYli) (ruBASHki)
Вы не сложили рубашки.
You didn't fold the shirts.

(Eta) (NYE) (maYO) (biL'YO)
Это не моё бельё.
This is not my laundry.

(NYE) (khvaTAit) (MAYki)
Не хватает майки.
An undershirt is missing.

(VY) (NYE) (paGLAdili) (YUPku)
Вы не погладили юбку.
You didn't iron the skirt.

Can you fill in the blanks corresponding to the pictures?

1. **Мне надо погладить_____________________ .**

2. **Мне надо сдать в стирку _____________________ .**

3. **Вы можете мне пришить _____________________ ?**

4. **Вы можете сдать в чистку _____________________ .**

5. **Мне надо постирать _____________________ .**

ANSWERS

Fill in 1. костюм **2.** бельё **3.** пуговицу **4.** платье **5.** носки

20 (parikMAkhirskaya) Парикмахерская

Beauty Salon / Barber Shop

(ZHENski) (ZAL) ЖЕНСКИЙ ЗАЛ

Ladies' Salon

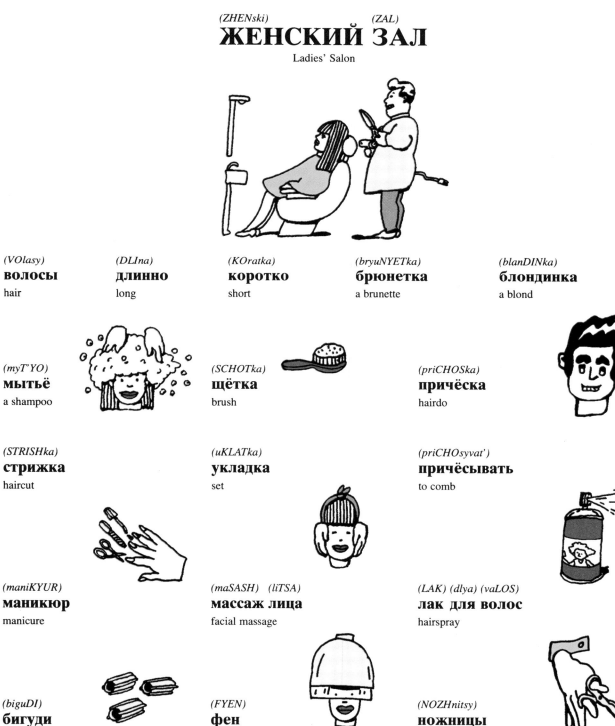

(VOlasy)
волосы
hair

(DLIna)
длинно
long

(KOratka)
коротко
short

(bryuNYETka)
брюнетка
a brunette

(blanDINka)
блондинка
a blond

(myT'YO)
мытьё
a shampoo

(SCHOTka)
щётка
brush

(priCHOSka)
причёска
hairdo

(STRISHka)
стрижка
haircut

(uKLATka)
укладка
set

(priCHOsyvat')
причёсывать
to comb

(maniKYUR)
маникюр
manicure

(maSASH) (liTSA)
массаж лица
facial massage

(LAK) (dlya) (vaLOS)
лак для волос
hairspray

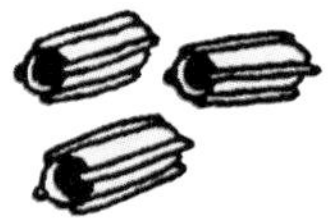

(biguDI)
бигуди
rollers

(FYEN)
фен
hair dryer

(NOZHnitsy)
ножницы
scissors

Two women, Dorothy and Joan, decide to go to the beauty shop.

ПАРИКМАХЕР (Hairdresser)	**Что вам сделать?**	What can I do for you?
JOAN	*(VYmayte)* *(GOlavu)* **Вымойте мне голову, и сделайте стрижку и укладку.**	I'd like a shampoo, and a cut and set.
ПАРИКМАХЕР	**А вам, госпожа?**	And for you, Miss?
DOROTHY	**Вымойте мне голову, сделайте укладку и маникюр.**	I'd like a shampoo, and a set and a manicure.
ПАРИКМАХЕР	*(paKRAsit')* **Вам покрасить** *(VOlasy)* **волосы?**	Would you like a color rinse?
DOROTHY	**Нет. Не сегодня.**	No. Not today, thank you.
ПАРИКМАХЕР	**Только поправить?**	Just a touch-up?
DOROTHY	**Хорошо, но без лака, пожалуйста.**	All right, but no hairspray, please.
ПАРИКМАХЕР	**Можно феном?** *(vzgliNItye)* **Теперь взгляните в зеркало.**	May I use the hair dryer? Now look in the mirror.
DOROTHY	**Прекрасно. Спасибо.**	Marvelous. Thank you.

Here are some useful expressions for the beauty parlor. Repeat them aloud as you write them out.

Можно записаться на завтра? May I make an appointment for tomorrow?

____

Сделайте мне модную причёску. Give me a modern (new) hairdo.

____

Что-нибудь с кудрями. Something with curls.

____

Мне нужно покрасить волосы. I need a color rinse.

____

Мытьё и укладку, пожалуйста.	A wash and set, please.
Химическую завивку и тон.	A permanent (wave) and a tint.
Совсем немного лака.	Just a little hairspray.

FOR WOMEN ONLY: You are off to the beauty salon. Do you know what you want? Make a list in Russian just in case.

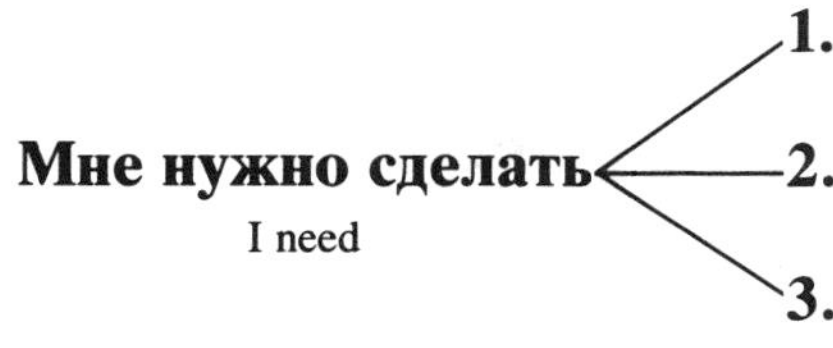

Мне нужно сделать
I need

1. (a wash) ____________
2. (a set) ____________
3. (a cut) ____________

Мне нужно 4. (a color rinse) ____________

(muSHKOY) *(ZAL)*

МУЖСКОЙ ЗАЛ

The Barber Shop

(parikMAkhir)
парикмахер
barber

(paBRIT')
побрить
shave

(BRITva)
бритва
razor

(paBRItsa)
побриться
shave oneself

ANSWERS

Beauty salon **1.** мытьё **2.** укладку **3.** стрижку **4.** покрасить волосы

(baraDA) (i) (viSOCHki)
борода и височки
beard and sideburns

(uSY)
усы
moustache

(priCHOsyvat')
причёсывать
to comb/brush

(STRISHka)
стрижка
cut

(priCHOsyvatsa)
причёсываться
to comb/brush one's own hair

MARK	**Где хорошая парикмахерская?**	Where is there a good barber shop?
HOTEL CLERK	**Есть парикмахерская в гостинице.**	There's a barber shop in the hotel.
MARK	**Мне долго ждать?**	Do I have to wait long?
ПАРИКМАХЕР (Barber)	**Нет, вы следующий.**	No, you're next.
MARK	**Я хочу постричься и побриться.**	I want a haircut and a shave.
ПАРИКМАХЕР	**Как вас постричь?**	How do you want it cut?
MARK	**Сзади коротко, спереди длинно.**	Short in the back, long in the front.
ПАРИКМАХЕР	**Вам голову помыть?**	Would you like a shampoo?
MARK	**Нет, не надо.**	No, that's not necessary.

ПАРИКМАХЕР	**Так хорошо?**	Is that all right?
MARK	**Можно покороче по бокам.**	A little shorter on the sides.
ПАРИКМАХЕР	**Вы причёсываете волосы прямо назад?**	Do you comb your hair straight back?
MARK	**Нет, у меня пробор налево.**	No, I have a part on the left.
ПАРИКМАХЕР	**Вам одеколон?**	Would you like some cologne?
MARK	**Пожалуйста.**	Please.
	Сколько с меня?	How much do I owe you?

The following expressions will come in handy if you need a haircut and shave in Russia. In many hotels there is a barber shop, and it can be a pleasant and relaxing half-hour out of your busy day. Repeat aloud the important expressions below as you write them out.

Где хорошая парикмахерская? — Where is there a good barber shop?

____

Мне долго ждать? — Do I have long to wait?

____

Я хочу постричься. — I would like a haircut.

____

Я хочу побриться. — I would like a shave.

____

Подстригите немножко сверху. — Cut a little off the top.

____

Подправьте, пожалуйста, усы. — Please trim the moustache.

____

Ножницами, или только бритвой? — With the scissors or a razor cut?

____

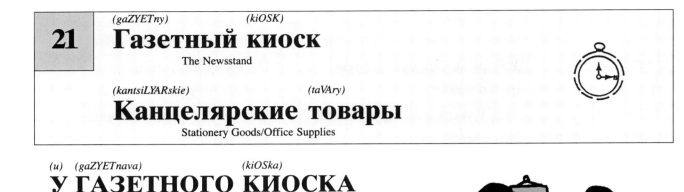

21 Газетный киоск

(gaZYETny) (kiOSK)

The Newsstand

Канцелярские товары

(kantsiLYARskie) (taVAry)

Stationery Goods/Office Supplies

У ГАЗЕТНОГО КИОСКА

(u) (gaZYETnava) (kiOSka)

At the Newsstand

English-language newspapers and magazines may be available at the hotel newsstand. At these and other stands throughout the cities you can also purchase stamps, postcards, envelopes, maps of the city, and the little lapel pins — **значки** — that make fine souvenirs.

(zhurNAL)
журнал
magazine

(gaZYEta)
газета
newspaper

(atKRYTki)
открытки
postcards

(MARki)
марки
stamps

(sigaRYEty)
сигареты
cigarettes

CAROLINE	**У вас есть газеты** (anGLIYskam) (yizyKYE) **на английском языке?**	Do you have newspapers in English?
SALESCLERK	**Да. И вот ещё журналы на английском.**	Yes. And here are some magazines in English.
CAROLINE	**Я хочу** (kuPIT') **купить эти открытки.**	I would like to buy these postcards.
SALESCLERK	**Вам нужны марки?**	Do you need stamps?
CAROLINE	**Нет. У меня есть.**	No. I have some.
	Сколько стоит этот (znaCHOK) **значок?**	How much does that pin cost?

SALESCLERK	**Один рубль. А здесь**	One ruble. But here is
	(naBOR) **красивый набор наших**	a beautiful set of our
	(FLAgof) **флагов за 10 рублей.**	flags for ten rubles.
CAROLINE	**Хорошо. Я возьму**	Fine. I'll take
	один набор.	one set.
SALESCLERK	**Ещё что-нибудь?**	Anything else?
CAROLINE	**Спасибо. Это всё.**	Thank you. That's everything.
	Я почти забыла.	I almost forgot.
	У вас есть	Do you have any
	американские сигареты?	American cigarettes?
SALESCLERK	**К сожалению,**	Unfortunately,
	(rasPROdany) **все распроданы.**	they were all sold out.

Read through the conversation several times and review the new words you will need. Then see if you can write down the necessary words in Russian for your friend who is going out for a few items. He has written them down in English. Can you provide the Russian?

1. stamps ____________________

2. postcards ____________________

3. cigarettes ____________________

4. a lapel pin ____________________

(f) *(kantsiLYARskam)* *(aDYElye)*

В КАНЦЕЛЯРСКОМ ОТДЕЛЕ

At the Stationery Store

Here are some of the items you might want to purchase at the stationery store. Say them aloud and then write out the words in the spaces provided.

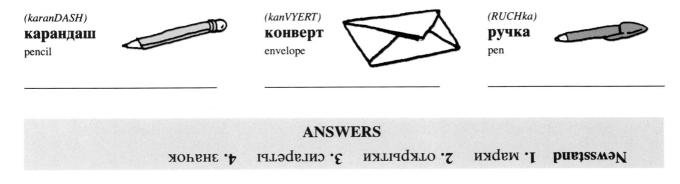

(karanDASH)
карандаш
pencil

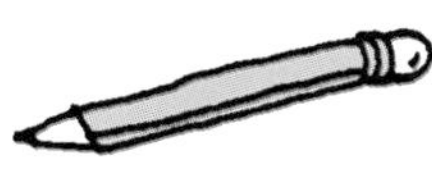

____

(kanVYERT)
конверт
envelope

____

(RUCHka)
ручка
pen

____

ANSWERS

Newsstand **1.** марки **2.** открытки **3.** сигареты **4.** значок

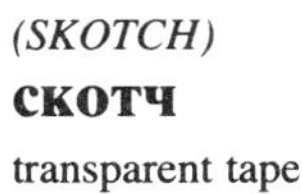

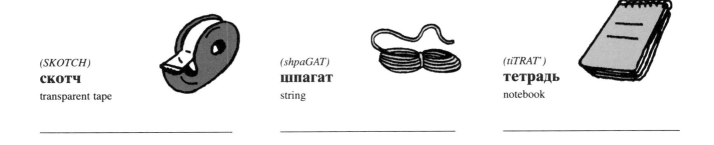

(SKOTCH)
скотч
transparent tape

____

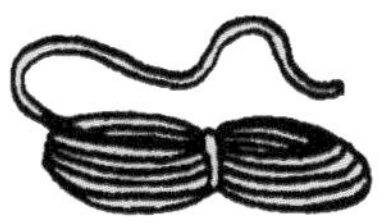

(shpaGAT)
шпагат
string

____

(tiTRAT')
тетрадь
notebook

____

(blakNOT)
блокнот
writing pad

____

(buMAga) (dlya) (PIsim)
бумага для писем
writing paper

____

Here is a short paragraph to study about Oleg's trip to the newsstand.

Вчера вечером я хотел писать	Last evening I wanted to write
письмо сыну и дочке. Сперва я	a letter to my son and daughter. First I
пошёл в магазин «Канцелярские	went to the stationery store
товары», где я купил блокнот и	where I purchased a writing pad and
конверты. После того как я	envelopes. After I had written
написал письма, я пошёл в киоск.	the letters, I went to the newsstand.
Там я купил марки, несколько	There I purchased stamps, several
открыток, и пачку сигарет.	postcards, and a pack of cigarettes.
По пути домой я съел	On the way home I ate
мороженое и купил хлеб	some ice cream and bought bread
и молоко.	and milk.

Now read through the Russian text again aloud without looking at the English. Can you trace Oleg's route from start to finish on the map below?

Now let's end with a word search. Find and circle the Russian equivalents for the following words: envelope, postcard, stamps, pencil, pen, newspaper, writing pad. When you have found all of the words, write them in the spaces below.

а	б	р	г	а	з	е	т	а	д
з	л	у	к	о	н	в	е	р	т
м	о	о	а	т	р	с	ы	ф	х
а	к	а	р	а	н	д	а	ш	щ
р	н	х	д	з	п	н	м	л	к
к	о	т	к	р	ы	т	к	а	ю
и	т	я	щ	р	у	ч	к	а	щ

ANSWERS

Word search газета, конверт, карандаш, открытка, ручка, марки, блокнот

22 Ювелирные изделия

(yuviLIRniye) *(izDYEliya)*

Ювелирные изделия
Jewelry Articles

(chiSY)

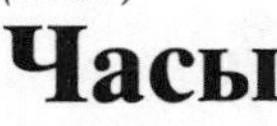

Часы
Watches

(yuviLIRny) *(magaZIN)*

Ювелирный магазин
The Jewelry Store

(braSLYET)
браслет
bracelet

(BROSH)
брошь
brooch

(azhiRYEl'e)
ожерелье
necklace

(tsiPOCHka)
цепочка
chain

(kal'TSO)
кольцо
ring

(SYER'gi)
серьги
earrings

(kal'TSO) *(s)* *(KAMnim)*
кольцо с камнем
ring with precious stone

Mark goes to a jewelry store to buy a gift for his wife.

SALESCLERK	**Как вам помочь?**	How may I help you?
MARK	**Я хочу купить жене что-нибудь.**	I would like to buy something for my wife.
SALESCLERK	**Браслет, или может** *(MOzhit)* **быть** *(BYT')* **серебряное** *(siRYEbrinaye)* **кольцо?**	A bracelet, or perhaps a silver ring?

MARK	**Нет. Она предпочитает** *(ZOlata)* **золото.**	No. She prefers gold.
SALESCLERK	**Как вам нравится эта** *(PAlikha)* **брошь из Палеха?**	How do you like this brooch from Palekh?
MARK	**Она очень красива.** *(yintaRYOM)* **И эти серьги с янтарём тоже очень красивы.**	It's beautiful. And these amber earrings are lovely too.
SALESCLERK	**Да. И у нас есть** *(padkhaDYAscheye)* **подходящее ожерелье.**	Yes. And we have a matching necklace.
MARK	**Прекрасно. Сколько** *(VMYEStye)* **они стоят вместе?**	Fine. How much do they cost together?
SALESCLERK	**Две тысячи рублей.**	Two thousand rubles.
MARK	**Вы думаете, что я** *(baGATy)* **богатый американец?**	What do you think, that I am a rich American?
SALESCLERK	**Нет. Но вы совсем не** *(BYEDny)* **бедный русский!**	No. But you are certainly not a poor Russian either!
MARK	**Тогда я их возьму. Они дорогие, но** *(paDYElaish)* **что поделаешь?**	In that case I'll take them. They're expensive, but what can you do?

Some of your relatives back home have expensive tastes and want you to bring them a piece of jewelry from Russia. Can you make out your list in Russian?

1. Aunt Dottie would like a brooch. ______________________
2. Grandma wants some earrings. ______________________
3. Your daughter-in-law wants a ring. ______________________
4. Grandpa wants a bracelet for his new girlfriend. ______________________
5. You only need a chain for your watch. ______________________

ANSWERS

Jewelry **1.** брошь **2.** серьги **3.** кольцо **4.** браслет **5.** цепочка *(dragaTSEnye)* *(KAMni)*

Драгоценные камни

Precious stones

Pronounce the words below aloud and write them out in the spaces provided.

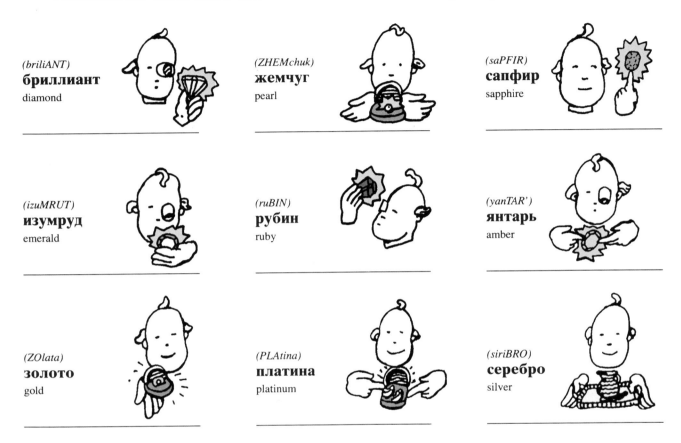

(briliANT)
бриллиант
diamond

____

(ZHEMchuk)
жемчуг
pearl

____

(saPFIR)
сапфир
sapphire

____

(izuMRUT)
изумруд
emerald

____

(ruBIN)
рубин
ruby

____

(yanTAR')
янтарь
amber

____

(ZOlata)
золото
gold

____

(PLAtina)
платина
platinum

____

(siriBRO)
серебро
silver

____

Do you remember the adjectives for colors in Russian? See if you can match the following color adjectives with the names of the precious stones that they modify.

1. **зелёный**	а. **сапфир**
2. **белый**	б. **изумруд**
3. **красный**	в. **жемчуг**
4. **жёлтый**	г. **рубин**
5. **синий**	д. **янтарь**

ANSWERS

Matching 1. б 2. в 3. г 4. д 5. а

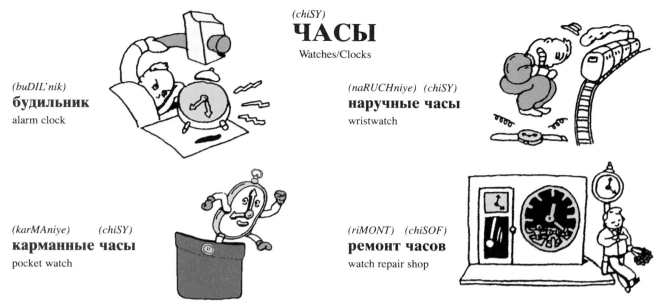

(chiSY)

ЧАСЫ

Watches/Clocks

(buDIL'nik)
будильник
alarm clock

(naRUCHniye) (chiSY)
наручные часы
wristwatch

(karMAniye) (chiSY)
карманные часы
pocket watch

(riMONT) (chiSOF)
ремонт часов
watch repair shop

Practice saying aloud and writing the words from the sentences below. Read them over again until you feel comfortable with the expressions you will need to get your watch repaired.

Can you repair this watch?
Вы можете починить эти часы?

____

Can you clean it?
Можно их почистить?

____

My watch is fast.
Мои часы спешат.

____

My watch is slow.
Мои часы отстают.

____

My watch has stopped running.
Мои часы стоят.

____

My watch doesn't run well.
Мои часы плохо идут.

____

I wind it every day.
Я завожу их каждый день.

____

Can you put in a new battery?
Можно поставить новую батарейку?

____

Note that the Russian word for watch or clock is **часы** (hours) and is plural. Therefore it requires a plural form of the verb.

Try to select the correct word(s) to fill in the blanks below.

Ремонт часов, спешат, плохо идут, отстают, батарейку.

1. **Когда мои часы ____________________ , я прихожу рано.** (I arrive early.)
2. **Когда мои часы ____________________ , я опаздываю.** (I am late.)
3. **Когда мои часы стоят, я иду в магазин ____________________**
4. **Когда мои часы ____________________ ,**
5. **можно поставить новую ____________________ .**

ANSWERS

Fill in **1.** спешат **2.** отстают **3.** ремонт часов **4.** плохо идут **5.** батарейку

23

(paDARki) **Подарки,** Gifts *(suviNIry)* **Сувениры,** Souvenirs *(plaSTINki)* **Пластинки,** Records *(fotaapaRAty)* **Фотоаппараты** Cameras

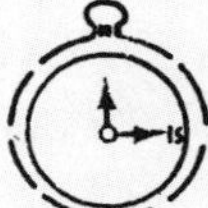

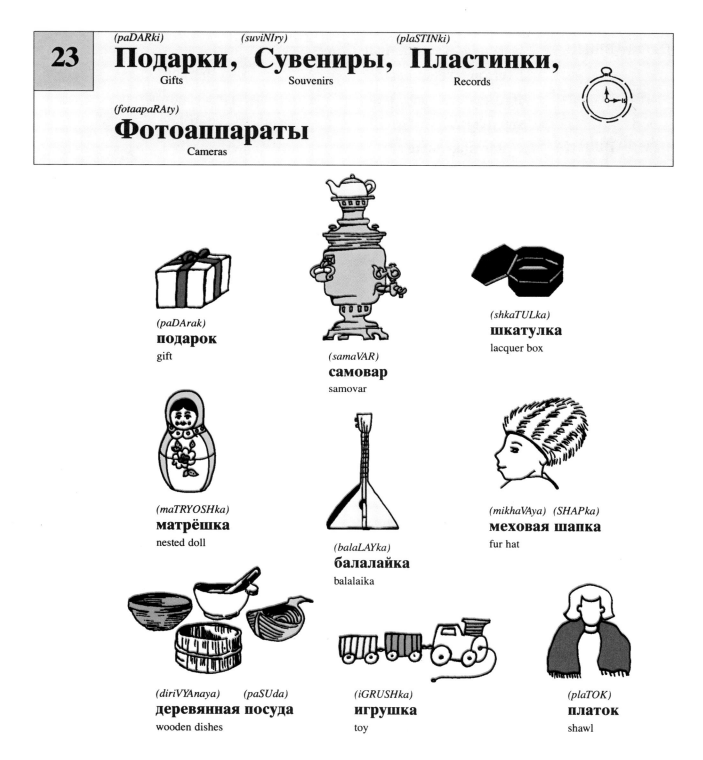

(paDArak)
подарок
gift

(samaVAR)
самовар
samovar

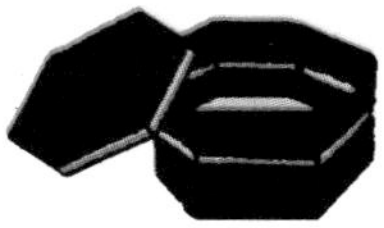

(shkaTULka)
шкатулка
lacquer box

(maTRYOSHka)
матрёшка
nested doll

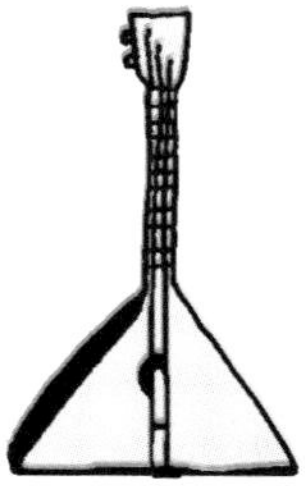

(balaLAYka)
балалайка
balalaika

(mikhaVAya) (SHAPka)
меховая шапка
fur hat

(diriVYAnaya) (paSUda)
деревянная посуда
wooden dishes

(iGRUSHka)
игрушка
toy

(plaTOK)
платок
shawl

Make sure you visit the gift shop before you leave. Read carefully how Mark goes shopping for his friends and family back home.

MARK	**Я хотел бы купить** *(NYEskal'ka)* **несколько сувениров.**	I would like to purchase some souvenirs.

ПРОДАВЩИЦА	**Вам нужны типичные** *(tiPICHniye)* **русские сувениры?**	You need real Russian souvenirs.
MARK	**Да, как самовар, или матрёшка.**	Yes, like a samovar, or a nested doll.
ПРОДАВЩИЦА	**У нас красивые балалайки, и деревянные ложки.** *(LOSHki)*	We have lovely balalaikas, and wooden spoons.
MARK	**Сколько стоит эта меховая шапка?**	How much does this fur hat cost?
ПРОДАВЩИЦА	**Она дорогая.** *(daraGAya)* **Это настоящая норка.** *(NORka)*	It is expensive. It is real mink.
MARK	**Может быть я возьму эту палехскую** *(PAlikhskuyu)* **шкатулку?**	Maybe I'll take this Palekh lacquer box.
ПРОДАВЩИЦА	**Хорошо. Она хотя не дешёвая,** *(diSHOvaya)* **но и не слишком дорогая.**	Good. Although it is not inexpensive, it is not too expensive.
MARK	**Можно платить кредитной** *(kriDITnay)* **карточкой?** *(KARtachkay)*	May I pay with a credit card?
ПРОДАВЩИЦА	**Конечно. Вам завернуть?** *(zavirNUT')*	Of course. Should I wrap it for you?

Read through the following questions and write in the answer **правда** or **неправда**.

1. **Марк хочет купить русские сувениры.** ______________________

2. **Меховая шапка не очень дорогая.** ______________________

3. **Самовар настоящий русский сувенир.** ______________________

4. **Палехская шкатулка слишком дешёвая.** ______________________

5. **Марк хочет платить кредитной карточкой.** ______________________

(magaZIN) (gramplaSTINki)

МАГАЗИН-«ГРАМПЛАСТИНКИ»

The Record Store

(kaSYEta)
кассета
cassette tape

(kamPAKTny) (DISK)
компактный диск
CD (compact disc)

(plaSTINka)
пластинка
record

(videokaSYEta)
видеокассета
videocassette

(naRODnaya) (MUzyka)
народная музыка
folk music

(klaSIchiskaya) (MUzyka)
классическая музыка
classical music

(savriMYEnaya) (MUzyka)
современная музыка
pop (contemporary) music

(RAdio)
радио
radio

(tiliVIzar)
телевизор
television

(praIgryvatil')
проигрыватель
record player

ANSWERS

True or false **1.** правда **2.** неправда **3.** правда **4.** неправда **5.** правда

(magnitaFON)
магнитофон
tape recorder

(videomagnitaFON)
видеомагнитофон
VCR (videocassette recorder)

(mikraFON)
микрофон
microphone

Try to read aloud the following paragraph that will come in handy if you enjoy listening to music.

Мама и папа очень любят музыку.	Mom and Dad like music very much.
Когда они были в Москве, они	When they were in Moscow, they
ходили в магазин «Грампластинки».	went to the record store.
Там мама хотела купить	There Mom wanted to buy
классическую музыку, Чайковский,	classical music, Tchaikovsky,
Римский-Корсаков, Бородин.	Rimsky-Korsakov, Borodin.
Она купила пластинки. У неё	She bought some records. She has
есть проигрыватель. Папа любит	a record player. Dad likes
русскую народную музыку, и он	Russian folk music, and he
купил кассеты. Ведь у него	bought cassettes. After all he has a
есть магнитофон. Теперь	tape recorder. Now in our
в нашем доме можно всё	house you can listen all the
время слушать русскую музыку.	time to Russian music.

Read over the dialogue one more time and then try to write out the words in the missing blanks.

1. **Мама хотела купить ______________________ музыку.**
2. **Она купила ______________________ .**
3. **Папа любит русскую ______________________ музыку.**
4. **Он купил ______________________ .**
5. **Теперь в нашем доме можно слушать ______________________ музыку.**

ANSWERS

Fill in **1.** классическую **2.** пластинки **3.** народную **4.** кассеты **5.** русскую

(fotataVAry)

ФОТОТОВАРЫ

Photographic Supplies

(fotaKARtachka)
фотокарточка
print

(fotaapaRAT)
фотоаппарат
camera

(batiREYka)
батарейка
battery

(SLAYdy) (diapaziTIvy)
слайды (диапозитивы)
slides

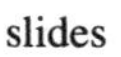

(PLYONka)
плёнка
film

(videoKAmira)
видеокамера
video camera

At the photo counter Caroline tries to get her film developed.

CAROLINE	*(prayiVLYAitye)* **Вы проявляете плёнку?**	Do you develop film?
CLERK	*(napiCHAtat')* **Да. Вам напечатать все?**	Yes. Should I print them all?
CAROLINE	**Да, тридцать шесть кадров.**	Yes, thirty-six exposures.
CLERK	*(CHORna- BYEliye) (tsvitNIye)* **Чёрно-белые или цветные?**	Black-and-white or color?
CAROLINE	*(uviLIchit')* **Цветные, и можно увеличить.**	Color, and you can enlarge them.
CLERK	*(GLYANtsiviye) (MAtaviye)* **Глянцевые или матовые?**	Glossy or matte finish?
CAROLINE	**Мне всё равно.**	I don't care.
CLERK	**Они будут готовые в пятницу.**	They will be ready on Friday.

CAROLINE	**Вы продаёте плёнку?**	Do you sell film?
CLERK	**Да. Что вам нужно?**	Yes. What do you need?
CAROLINE	*(tsvitNUyu)* **Цветную плёнку,**	Color film,
	двадцать кадров,	twenty exposures,
	ГОСТ 100. И мне нужна	ASA 100. And I need
	батарейка для вспышки. *(FSPYSHki)*	a battery for my flash.
CLERK	**Вот вам, девушка.**	Here you are, Miss.

Find the Russian words for the corresponding pictures in the word puzzle and then write them out in the spaces below.

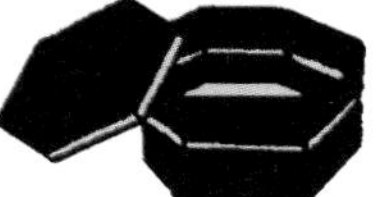

щ ш а б в г д б ф

м а т р ё ш к а э

д р ъ ь б х я л н

ш к а т у л к а з

я е т б ъ и ю л ь

ж с ц з г х щ а м

м н о п д ы ч й ё

а ц в п л ё н к а

щ к а с с е т а я

_______________________________ _______________________________

_______________________________ _______________________________

____

ANSWERS

Puzzle матрёшка, шкатулка, плёнка, кассета, балалайка

24 Ремонт: очков, обуви

(riMONT) (achKOF) (Obuvi)

Repair Services Eyeglasses Shoes

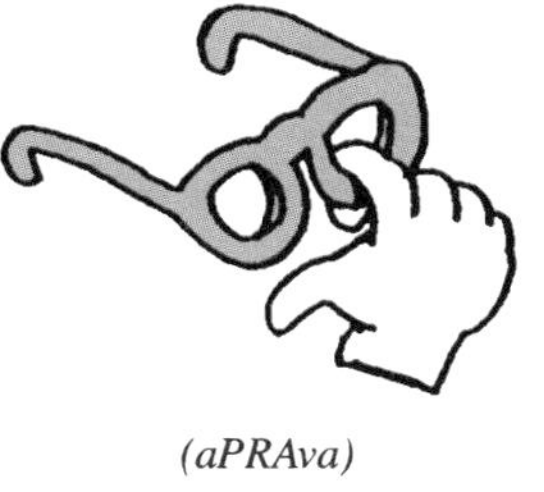

(OPtik)
оптик
optician

(achKI)
очки
glasses

(aPRAva)
оправа
frame

(kanTAKTniye) (LINzy)
контактные линзы
contact lenses

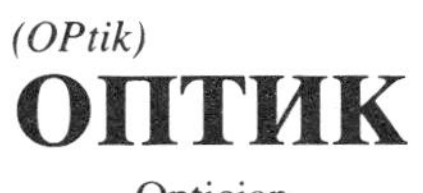

(OPtik)

ОПТИК

Optician

We hope that you will not need the following phrases, but better safe than sorry.

ТУРИСТ (Tourist)	(pachiNIT') (achKI) **Вы можете починить эти очки?**	Can you repair these glasses?
	(razBIL) (stiKLO) **Я разбил стекло и** (aPRAvu) **оправу.**	I've broken a lens and the frame.
ОПТИК	**Нет ли у вас запасных очков?**	Don't you have an extra pair?

ТУРИСТ	Да, есть. Но сломан *(SLOman)* заушник. *(zaUSHnik)*	Yes, I have. But the earpiece is broken.
ОПТИК	Легче найти новый заушник, чем вставить новое стекло.	It's easier to find a new earpiece, than put in a new lens.
ТУРИСТ	У меня есть контактные линзы, но я оставил их в гостинице.	I do have contact lenses, but I left them in the hotel.
ОПТИК	Ничего. У меня есть солнечные *(SOLnichniye)* очки. Среди *(sriDI)* них мы найдём *(nayDYOM)* заушник.	No problem. I have some sunglasses. Among them we'll find an earpiece.
ТУРИСТ	Спасибо большое. Не забудьте *(zaBUt'ye)* подвернуть *(padvirNUT')* винтик *(VINtik)*.	Thank you very much. Don't forget to tighten the screw.

(riMONT) РЕМОНТ *(Obuvi)* ОБУВИ

Shoe Repairs

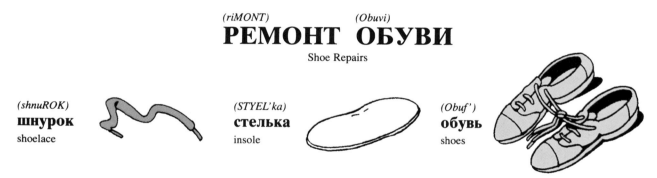

(shnuROK)
шнурок
shoelace

(STYEL'ka)
стелька
insole

(Obuf')
обувь
shoes

All around town you are likely to see tiny shoeshine and shoe repair booths. Why not step inside and treat yourself to a shine? At the booths you can have minor repairs performed. For major repairs you can bring your shoes or boots to the shoe repair shops.

ТУРИСТКА (Tourist)	Почистите *(paCHIStitye)*, пожалуйста.	I'd like a shoeshine, please.
МАСТЕР (Repairman)	Вам нужны шнурки *(shnurKI)* или стельки?	Do you need any laces or insoles?

ТУРИСТКА	**Спасибо, но не надо.**	Thank you, but it's not necessary.
	Вы можете починить	Can you repair
	(sapaGI) **мои сапоги?**	my boots?
МАСТЕР	*(kabluKI)* **Только каблуки?**	Only the heels?
ТУРИСТКА	*(padMYOTki)* **И подмётки, если вы**	And the soles, too, if you
	можете сейчас.	can do it now.

Go over the material for the optician and shoe repair shops. Then see if you can fill in the blanks provided for the following emergency situations.

1. You have broken your eyeglasses. Ask if they can be repaired.

Вы можете ________________________________ **?**

2. Explain that you have broken a lens and the frame.

Я разбил ________________________________ **.**

3. Tell your friend that you left your contact lenses at the hotel.

Я оставил ________________________________ **в гостинице.**

4. You have broken your heel. Tell the shoemaker what you need.

Мне нужны новые ________________________________ **.**

5. An important business meeting is approaching. Can you get your shoes shined?

________________________________ **.**

ANSWERS

Fill in **1.** починить эти очки **2.** стекло и оправу **3.** контактные линзы **4.** каблуки **5.** Почистите, пожалуйста.

ESSENTIAL SERVICES

(bytaVIye) (uSLUgi)
Бытовые услуги

25 Банк / Сберегательная касса

(BANK) (zbiriGAtil'naya) (KAsa)
Банк / Сберегательная касса
Bank / Savings Bank

МОНЕТЫ И КУПЮРЫ

(maNYEty) (i) (kuPYUry)
Coins and Bills

Even after the fall of the Soviet Union in 1991, the basic unit of currency in Russia remained the **рубль** (ruble), which was divided into 100 **копейка** (kopecks). Older currency may still bear the hammer and sickle and the letters for the USSR — **СССР**.

In 1992 the **Банк России** (Bank of Russia) began issuing ten and twenty ruble coins. Since these coins are similar in size to the old kopeck pieces, be sure to examine your change very carefully.

As you repeat aloud the following denominations of bills and small change **(мелочь)**, notice that the form of the word is determined by the number.

БАНКОВСКИЕ БИЛЕТЫ Bank Notes	
один рубль 1 р.	**сто рублей 100 р.**
три рубля 3 р.	**двести рублей 200 р.**
пять рублей 5 р.	**пятьсот рублей 500 р.**
десять рублей 10 р.	**тысяча рублей 1000 р.**
двадцать пять рублей 25 р.	

МОНЕТЫ Coins	
одна копейка 1 к.	**пятнадцать копеек 15 к.**
две копейки 2 к.	**двадцать копеек 20 к.**
три копейки 3 к.	**пятьдесят копеек 50 к.**
пять копеек 5 к.	**один рубль 1 р.**
десять копеек 10 к.	

(LYUdi) *(VYEschi)*

Люди и вещи

People and things

(DYEN'gi)
деньги
money

(BANK)
банк
bank

(naLICHnye)
наличные
cash

(vaLYUta)
валюта
hard currency

(diRYEKtar)
директор
manager

(KAsa)
касса
teller's window

(daROZHniye) (CHEki)
дорожные чеки
travelers' checks

(SCHOT)
счёт
account

(zaYOM)
заём
loan

(priKHODny) (ORdir)
приходный ордер
deposit slip

(kriDITnaya) (KARtachka)
кредитная карточка
credit card

(rasKHODny) (ORdir)
расходный ордер
withdrawal slip

Как

How to

(abmiNYAT')
обменять
exchange

(abMYEny) (KURS)
обменный курс
rate of exchange

(plaTIT')
платить
pay

(atKRYT') *(SCHOT)*
открыть счёт
open an account

(VYdat') *(FKLAT)*
выдать вклад
make a deposit

(priNYAT') *(FKLAT)*
принять вклад
make a withdrawal

(raspiSAtsa)
расписаться
sign

Mark and Caroline have to exchange dollars for rubles. They go the bank office at their hotel. Unfortunately, Mark has left his customs declaration form in his room.

MARK	*(abmiNYAT')* **Я хочу обменять**	I want to exchange some
	(DOlary) **американские доллары.**	American dollars.
КАССИРША (Teller)	**Сколько вы хотите обменять?**	How much do you want to exchange?
MARK	**Если можно, 100 долларов, дорожные чеки?**	If possible, 100 dollars, in travelers' checks.
КАССИРША	*(diklaRAtsiyu)* **Дайте мне вашу декларацию и паспорт, пожалуйста.**	Give me your declaration and passport, please.

MARK	**Я оставил декларацию в номере.**	I left my declaration in the room.
КАССИРША	**Без неё я ничего** *(nichiVO)* **не могу делать.**	Without it I can do nothing.
CAROLINE	**Вот моя декларация, и я хочу обменять 500 долларов.**	Here is my declaration, and I wish to exchange 500 dollars.
КАССИРША	**Всё вместе это будет 600 долларов.**	All together that will be 600 dollars.
CAROLINE	**Если можно, мелкими** *(MYELkimi)* **купюрами.**	If possible, small bills.
КАССИРША	**Распишитесь, пожалуйста, вот здесь.**	Please sign here.
	Вот квитанция *(kviTANtsiya)*. **Держите** *(dirZHYtye)* **её.**	Here's a receipt. Hold onto it.
MARK	**Спасибо.**	Thank you.
КАССИРША	**В следующий** *(SLYEduyuschi)* **раз, не забудьте декларацию. Она важный документ.**	Next time, please don't forget your declaration. It's an important document.

Now look at the pictures and say the words aloud. Then write them in the blanks provided.

1. ______________________________

2. ______________________________

3. ______________________________

4. ______________________________

ANSWERS

Fill in **1.** паспорт **2.** мелочь **3.** дорожные чеки **4.** наличные

6. ______________________________

5. ______________________________

(YA) (maGU) (YA) (khaCHU)

Я могу / Я хочу

I can / I want

Do you remember the Russian verbs meaning "can" and "want"?

МОЧЬ can	**ХОТЕ́ТЬ** want
я могу́	**я хочу́**
ты мо́жешь	**ты хо́чешь**
она мо́жет	**он хо́чет**
мы мо́жем	**мы хоти́м**
вы мо́жете	**вы хоти́те**
они мо́гут	**они хотя́т**

Now fill in the blanks of the following text with the correct forms of **мочь** and **хотеть**.

Марк ______________________ (wants) **обменять деньги в банке, но он не** ______________________ (able) **быть там** (be there) **в 10 часов утра. Его жена говорит** (says)**, я тоже** ______________________ (want) **обменять дорожные чеки, и я** ______________________ (can) **пойти** (go) **в банк. Сколько долларов ты** ______________________ (want) **обменять? Марк отвечает** (answers)**, что я** ______________________ (want)**, и что я** ______________________ (can) **— это две разные вещи.** (those are two different things)

ANSWERS

Fill in хочет, может, хочу, могу, хочешь, хочу, могу

Fill in **5.** расписаться **6.** деньги

26

(POCHta)

Почта

Mail/Post Office

Most post offices — **Почта** — are open from 9 A.M. to 9 P.M. with an hour break for lunch. The **Главпочтамт** (main post office) also has **телеграф** (telegraph) and **телефон** (telephone) service and is open around the clock. Mailboxes are painted bright blue. You can purchase stamps at many newsstands and kiosks in addition to post office windows.

Read the following story about our amateur postman. Some of the words you will need are on the following pages.

Раиса говорит с Сашей, её маленьким сыном.

Raisa is speaking with Sasha, her little son.

— Саша, что ты делаешь так рано?

"Sasha, what are you doing so early?"

— Я играю в почтальона.

"I'm playing postman."

(pachtaLYON)
— Какой ты почтальон? Где твои (PIS'ma) **письма?**

"You are some mailman. Where are your letters?"

— У меня есть письма, мама.

"I have letters, Mom."

— Откуда?

"Where from?"

(POMnish)
— Помнишь письма в твоём (shkaFU) **шкафу?**

"Do you remember the letters in your closet?"

(kanVYERty)
— Те конверты с розовой лентой?

"Those envelopes with the pink ribbon?

(razdaVAL)
— Да, мама. Я их раздавал (saSYEdyam) **соседям.**

"Yes, Mom. I gave them out to the neighbors."

— Боже мой. Любовные письма от папы!

My goodness. The love letters from Papa!

(pachTOvy) (YAschik)
почтовый ящик
mailbox

(tiliGRAma)
телеграмма
telegram

(MARki)
марки
stamps

(pis'MO)
письмо
letter

(atKRYTka)
открытка
postcard

(pachtaL'YON)
почтальон
mailman

(paSYLka)
посылка
package

Ваня и Надя идут на почту.

Steven discusses the post office with Nina.

STEVEN	*(atPRAvit')* **Я хочу отправить** *(aviapis'MO)* **авиаписьмо в США.**	I want to send an airmail letter to the USA.
NINA	**Я не знаю, сколько оно стоит. Пойдём на почту.**	I don't know how much it costs. Let's go to the post office.
STEVEN	*(paSLAT')* **Тогда я могу послать посылку сыну и дочке.**	Then I can send a package to my son and daughter.
NINA	*(sabiRAyut)* **Если они собирают марки, вы можете купить очень красивые наборы.**	If they collect stamps, you can purchase some very lovely sets.

STEVEN	**Где можно послать телеграмму или телефакс?** *(tiliFAKS)*	Where can I send a telegram or fax?
NINA	**Тоже на почте. Ещё что-нибудь?**	Also at the post office. Anything else?
STEVEN	**Я обещал** *(abiSCHAL)* **позвонить моему начальнику** *(naCHAL'niku)* **из России.**	I promised to telephone my boss from Russia.
NINA	**И это вы можете сделать на почте.**	You can do that at the post office, too.
STEVEN	**Всё ли можно сделать на почте?**	Can you do everything at the post office?
NINA	**Нет, не всё, но почти всё!**	No, not everything, but almost everything!

На почте

At the post office

STEVEN	**Я хочу отправить важное** *(VAZHnaye)* **письмо в США.**	I want to send an important letter to the USA.
СЛУЖАЩИЙ (Postal Clerk)	**Можно послать авиапочтой и заказным** *(zakazNYM)* **письмом.**	It can be sent via airmail, and as a registered letter.
STEVEN	**Мне нужно 3 марки по 5 р. и 10 марок по 25 р.**	I need 3 stamps for 5 rubles and 10 stamps for 25 rubles.
СЛУЖАЩИЙ	**Вам нужны конверты или открытки?**	Do you need any envelopes or postcards?
STEVEN	**Спасибо, но они у меня уже есть.**	Thank you, but I already have them.

(kanVYERT)

Конверт

The envelope

To address a Russian envelope you begin on the line **Куда** (where to) with the country, followed by the city, then the street address. On the line with **Кому** (to whom) write the person's last name followed by the initials for the first name and patronymic. The name goes in the dative case. Then provide your own address in the same order under the recipient's address.

Let's look at an example of an address:

Куда Россия

Москва 117932

ул. Пушкина д.2 кв1

Кому Ерофееву В.В.

От Россия

Москва 117432

гостиница „Космос"

Смит Р.

THE DATIVE CASE

To send something to someone or call someone on the telephone, Russians place that person in the dative case. To form the dative case of masculine nouns, add **у** or **ю**. For most feminine nouns replace the **а** or **я** with **е**. With feminine nouns that end in **ия**, like **Мария**, the dative ending is **ии**. Feminine last names end in **ой**.

Иван → Ивану   **Юрий → Юрию**   **Пушкин → Пушкину**

Ирина → Ирине   **Катя → Кате**   **Вера → Вере**

Мария → Марии   **Евгения → Евгении**   **Виктория → Виктории**

Иванова → Ивановой   **Каренина → Карениной**   **Толстая → Толстой**

You will want to review the dative case of the following pronouns:

мне to me   **тебе** to you   **ему** to him   **ей** to her

нам to us   **вам** to you   **им** to them

Now using the envelope below, fill in your own address and the address of a business associate in Russia. Notice how Russians are trying to encourage the use of the zip code **(индекс)** written in the boxes in the lower left according to the examples given on the flap.

Choose your own correspondent, or this actual Russian address:

Россия, Москва 117423, ул. Чехова, д. 3, кв. 7, Иванову, В.И.

Внимание!
Образец написания цифр индекса:

0 1 2 3 4 5 6 7 8 9

СПОНСОР — АВТОБАНК

ВСЕРОССИЙСКАЯ ФИЛАТЕЛИСТИЧЕСКАЯ ВЫСТАВКА

«АВТОФИЛЭКС 92»

МОСКВА

РОССИЯ 80 ROSSIJA 1992

Куда ______________________

Кому ______________________

Индекс предприятия связи | и адрес отправителя

Пишите индекс предприятия связи места назначения

Try to address the Russian telegram and let your host know that you are “alive and well” — **жив, здоров** — and staying in: **Москва, гостиница «Метрополь», комната 452.**

ф. ТГ-4а

Слов	Плата руб. / коп.

Принял ____

МИНИСТЕРСТВО СВЯЗИ СССР

МЕЖДУНАРОДНАЯ ТЕЛЕГРАММА

№ ____

Место подачи и страна (в именительном падеже) ____

____ сл. ____ го ____ ч. ____ м.

Передача

____ го ____ ч ____ м

Номер рабочего места

Автоответ пункта приема

Передал ____

Служебные отметки

Категория и отметки особого вида

Фамилия адресата (в именительном падеже)

Адрес

Город, страна

Фамилия и адрес отправителя не оплачивается и по связям не передается

КВИТАНЦИЯ В ПРИЕМЕ ТЕЛЕГРАММ

____ ч. ____ м.

Куда ____

Претензии принимаются в теч. 4 мес. со дня подачи

Before we leave the post office, write in the Russian words for the following important items in the spaces provided.

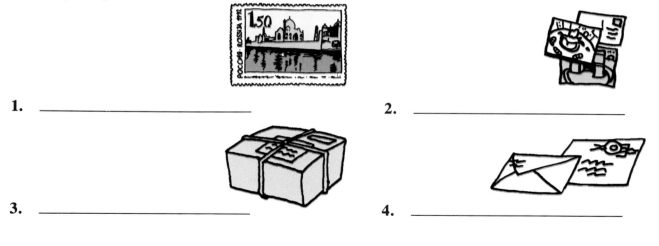

1. ____________________

2. ____________________

3. ____________________

4. ____________________

ANSWERS

Post office **1.** марка **2.** открытка **3.** посылка **4.** письмо

27 *(tiliFON)* Телефон

Telephone

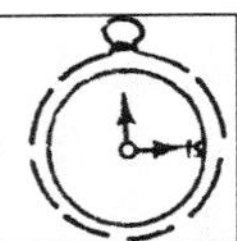

(aLYO) (aLYO)

АЛЛО! АЛЛО!

Hello! Hello!

You can usually place local calls from your hotel room, either by dialing directly or by dialing a single number for an outside line. For international calls you may have to place an order through the international operator.

Here are some useful expressions for making telephone calls in Russia.

(MOZHna) (at) (VAS) (pazvaNIT')
Можно от вас позвонить?
Can I use your phone?

(kaKOY) (u)(VAS) (NOmir) (tiliFOna)
Какой у вас номер телефона?
What is your telephone number?

(YA) (khaCHU) (zakaZAT')
Я хочу заказать ______.
I want to order a ______ .

(VOT) (NOmir)
Вот номер.
Here is the number.

(I) (KOT) (GOrada)
И код города?
And the area code?

(mizhdugaRODny) (razgaVOR)
междугородный разговор
long-distance call

(na) (chilaVYEka)
на человека
a person-to-person call

(mizhdunaRODny) (razgaVOR)
международный разговор
international call

(na) (NOmir)
на номер
station-to-station

(DYEvushka) (nabiRAYtye) (paZHAlusta) (Etat) (NOmir)
Девушка, набирайте, пожалуйста, этот номер!
Operator, would you please dial this number for me!

(PLOkha) (SLYSHna)
Плохо слышно.
I can barely hear you.

(ZAnyata)
Занято.
The line is busy.

(MOZHna) (gavaRIT') (s)
Можно говорить с ______ ?
May I speak with ______ ?

(tiliFON) (aftaMAT)
телефон-автомат
pay telephone

(padniMAT') (TRUPku)
поднимать трубку
lift the receiver

(miNYA) (razyidiNIli)
Меня разъединили.
I've been disconnected.

(NYE) (klaDItye) (TRUPku)
Не кладите трубку!
Don't hang up!

(piriDAYtye) (yiMU) (paZHAlusta)
Передайте ему, пожалуйста.
Please give him a message.

(tiliFOnaya) (KNISHka)
телефонная книжка
telephone book

(nabiRAT') (NOmir)
набирать номер
dial a number

THE INSTRUMENTAL CASE

When Russians speak with someone, they use the preposition **c** and the instrumental case. For masculine (and neuter) nouns, the instrumental ending is **ом (ем)** and **ым** in last names. For most feminine nouns the ending is **ой (ей)**.

Иван → с Иваном	**Василий → с Василием**	**Иванов → с Ивановым**
Анна → с Анной	**Варя → с Варей**	**Каренина → с Карениной**

You will also want to remember the following pronouns:

со мной	with me	**с тобой**	with you	**с ним**	with him	**с ней**	with her
с нами	with us	**с вами**	with you			**с ними**	with them

(tiliFOnaya) *(kaBIna)*

ТЕЛЕФОННАЯ КАБИНА

Telephone Booth

ТОМ	*(padniMAyu)* **Да. (себе) Сперва я поднимаю трубку, потом опускаю монету.** *(apuSKAyu)* *(guDIT)* *(nabiRAyu)* **Гудит. Хорошо! Я набираю номер 234-09-58. Алло! Алло! Это говорит господин Буш.**	Yes. (to himself) First I lift the receiver, then I drop the coin. It's ringing. That's good. I dial the number 234-09-58. Hello! Hello! This is Mr. Bush speaking.
ГОЛОС (A voice)	**Плохо слышно. Говорите** *(GROmche)* **громче.**	I can't hear you. Speak louder.
ТОМ	*(papraSItye)* **Попросите Бориса Николаевича к телефону.**	Please ask Boris Nikolaevich to come to the telephone.
ГОЛОС	**Вы не туда попали.**	You have the wrong number.
ТОМ	*(bispaKOYSTva)* **Извините за беспокойство. (Он кладёт трубку и идёт обратно в гостиницу).**	Excuse me for bothering you. (He puts down the receiver and goes back to his hotel.)

EMERGENCY TELEPHONE NUMBERS		
Fire	**Пожарная охрана**	01
Police	**Милиция**	02
Medical Care	**Скорая помощь**	03
Gas Leaks	**Газ**	04

Here is a word search for you. Find the Russian equivalents for the following words, circle them,and then write them out for practice in the spaces below: telephone, hello, receiver, dial, busy, number, area code, to call

а	б	в	т	е	л	е	ф	о	н
л	д	е	р	р	т	ы	и	п	а
л	щ	ч	у	г	з	ф	ь	ж	б
о	з	х	б	ц	а	б	н	м	и
а	с	ф	к	д	н	о	м	е	р
я	ч	ы	а	ш	я	ф	г	у	а
к	о	д	и	ё	т	ю	ъ	щ	т
ф	п	о	з	в	о	н	и	т	ь

ANSWERS

Word search телефон, алло, трубка, набирать, занято, номер, код, позвонить

28 Врач, Зубной врач, Больница

(VRACH) (zubNOY) (VRACH) (bal'NItsa)

Doctor, Dentist, Hospital

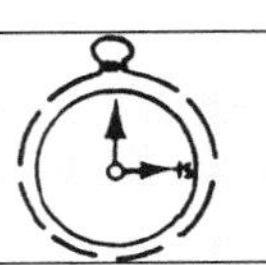

(paftaRYEniye) (MAT') (uCHEniya)

ПОВТОРЕНИЕ МАТЬ УЧЕНИЯ

Repetition Is the Mother of Learning

Нина and **Александр** are studying the parts of the body. See if you can learn the words along with them.

НИНА	**Ну, кто начинает** (nachiNAit) **— ты или я?**	Well, who should begin — you or I?
АЛЕКСАНДР	**Ты начинаешь спрашивать,** (SPRAshivat') **и я буду отвечать** (atviCHAT') **на вопросы.**	You begin the questioning, and I'll answer the questions.
НИНА	**Хорошо, что у тебя вот здесь?**	Okay, what do you have right here?
АЛЕКСАНДР	**Волосы.** (VOlasy)	Hair.
НИНА	**А что это?**	And what is this?
АЛЕКСАНДР	**Один глаз,** (GLAS) **но у тебя два глаза.** (GLAza)	One eye, but you have two eyes.
НИНА	**А между глазами?**	And between the eyes?
АЛЕКСАНДР	**Это мой нос.** (NOS)	That's my nose.

НИНА **Это твой рот, а что это над ртом?** (ROT) (RTOM)

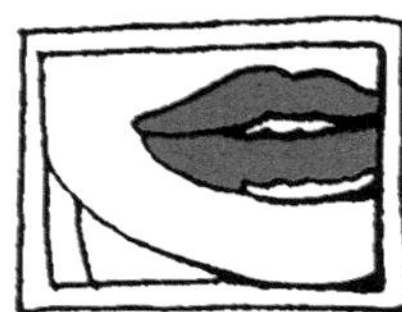

This is your mouth, but what is above the mouth?

АЛЕКСАНДР **Ты имеешь ввиду усы?** (uSY)

Do you mean my moustache?

НИНА **Да. У тебя одно ухо?** (Ukha)

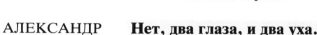

Yes. Do you have one ear?

АЛЕКСАНДР **Нет, два глаза, и два уха.**

No, two eyes, and two ears.

НИНА **А это моя щека.** (schiKA)

And this is my cheek.

АЛЕКСАНДР **А это твоё лицо,** (liTSO)

And this is your face,

и твоя голова. (galaVA)

and your head.

НИНА **Когда ты улыбаешься, я вижу . . .**

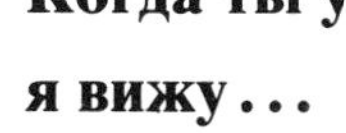

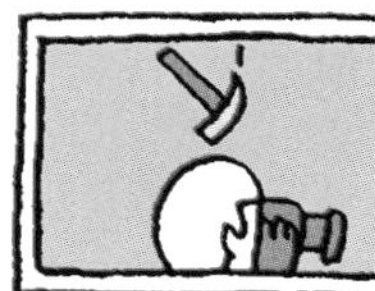

When you smile, I see . . .

АЛЕКСАНДР **Мои зубы. У врача я показываю . . .**

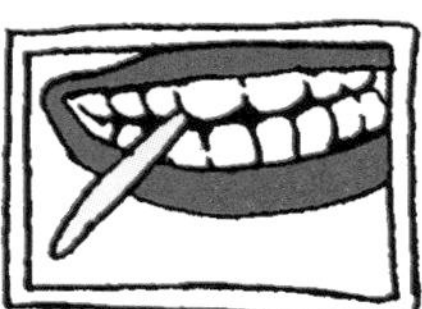

My teeth. At the doctor's I put out my . . .

НИНА **Язык.** (yiZYK)

Tongue.

Это подбородок. (padbaROdak)

This is a chin.

АЛЕКСАНДР	**А это, конечно,** *(SHEya)* **шея.**		And this is, of course, the neck.
НИНА	**Вот одно** *(pliCHO)* **плечо,**	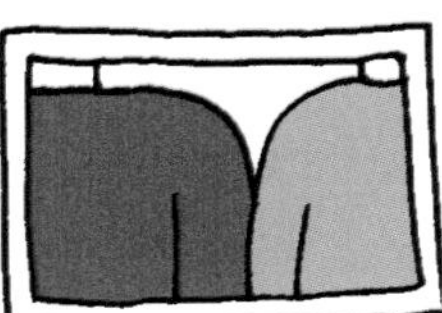	Here is one shoulder,
АЛЕКСАНДР	**Плюс моё плечо,** *(pliCHA)* **два плеча.**		Plus my shoulder, is two shoulders.
НИНА	**Одна** *(ruKA)* **рука, а две** *(ruKI)* **руки...**	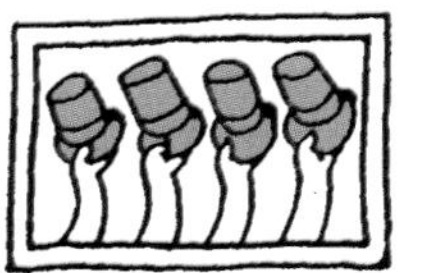	One arm, two arms . . .
АЛЕКСАНДР	**Но мы говорим «все руки».**		But we say "all the arms."
НИНА	**Один** *(LOkat')* **локоть или два** *(LOKtya)* **локтя.**		One elbow or two elbows.
АЛЕКСАНДР	**Мы говорим «все наши локти».**		We say "all our elbows."
НИНА	**Сколько** *(PAL'tsif)* **пальцев на** *(ruKYE)* **руке?**		How many fingers on a hand?
АЛЕКСАНДР	**Один** *(PAlits)* **палец, два** *(PAL'tsa)* **пальца, три пальца, четыре пальца, пять пальцев.**		One finger, two fingers, three fingers, four fingers, five fingers.
НИНА	**А у меня и десять пальцев.**		And I have ten fingers, too.
АЛЕКСАНДР	**Да, но не все пальцы на одной руке!**		Yes, but not all ten fingers on one hand!
НИНА	**Как всегда, ты прав.**		As always, you're right.
АЛЕКСАНДР	**Теперь я** *(zadaYU)* **задаю вопросы. Это**		Now I'll ask the questions. This is the
НИНА	*(spiNA)* **спина.**		back.
АЛЕКСАНДР	**Впереди находится**		In front is the
НИНА	*(GRUT')* **грудь.**		breast.
АЛЕКСАНДР	**Когда ты слишком много** *(YESH)* **ешь, что у тебя** *(baLIT)* **болит?**		When you eat too much, what hurts?
НИНА	*(zhiLUdak)* **Желудок.**		My stomach.
АЛЕКСАНДР	**Правильно. А ещё ниже мы находим**		That's correct. And even lower we find

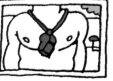

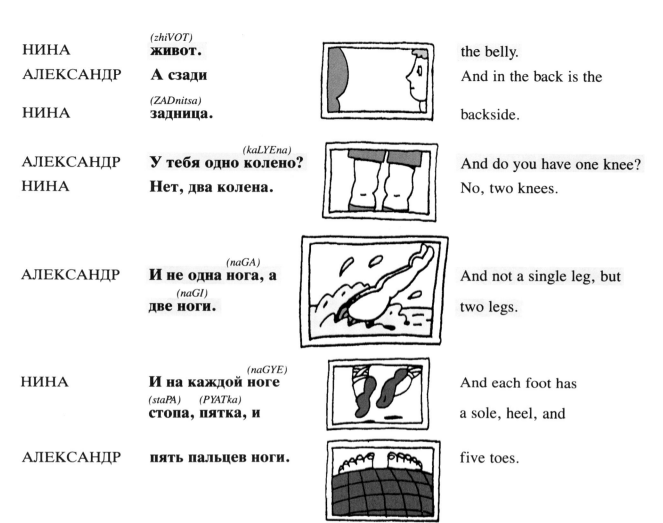

НИНА	*(zhiVOT)* **живот.**		the belly.
АЛЕКСАНДР	**А сзади**		And in the back is the
НИНА	*(ZADnitsa)* **задница.**		backside.
АЛЕКСАНДР	*(kaLYEna)* **У тебя одно колено?**		And do you have one knee?
НИНА	**Нет, два колена.**		No, two knees.
АЛЕКСАНДР	*(naGA)* **И не одна нога, а** *(naGI)* **две ноги.**		And not a single leg, but two legs.
НИНА	*(naGYE)* **И на каждой ноге** *(staPA) (PYATka)* **стопа, пятка, и**		And each foot has a sole, heel, and
АЛЕКСАНДР	**пять пальцев ноги.**	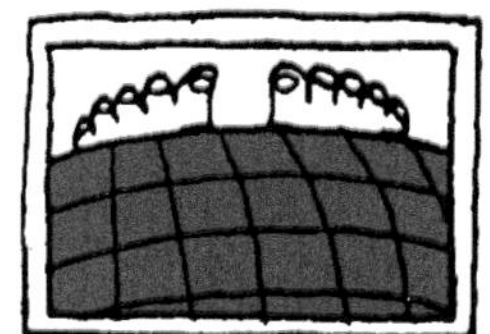	five toes.

That was certainly a lot of new words to learn. Try repeating them to yourself several times and then see if you can draw lines matching the Russian words with their English equivalents.

1.	**голова**	**а.**	leg/foot
2.	**рот**	**б.**	ear
3.	**нога**	**в.**	elbow
4.	**рука**	**г.**	finger
5.	**плечо**	**д.**	arm/hand
6.	**живот**	**е.**	head
7.	**колено**	**ж.**	mouth
8.	**локоть**	**з.**	knee
9.	**палец**	**и.**	shoulder
10.	**ухо**	**к.**	belly

ANSWERS

Matching **1.** е **2.** ж **3.** а **4.** д **5.** и **6.** к **7.** з **8.** в **9.** г **10.** б

(SHTO) (u) (VAS) (baLIT)

Что у вас болит?

What hurts?

To say in Russian that you are ill or something hurts, you need the expression **у меня, у вас**, etc. Literally, this means I have, you have [something that aches]. We use the genitive case of the pronouns after the preposition **у**.

у кого — who has

у меня	— I have	**у нас**	— we have
у тебя	— you have	**у вас**	— you have
у него	— he has	**у них**	— they have
у неё	— she has		

We hope you won't need to use them, but the following expressions for basic aches and pains are good ones to learn, **на всякий случай** (just in case). In an emergency you will want to call the number for immediate care—**Скорая помощь**. The number in Moscow and St. Petersburg is **03**. When you identify yourself as a foreigner and describe the problem, a physican will be at your hotel within minutes to see you. In non-emergency situations you should call your embassy or ask your hosts or the hotel personnel for the location of the nearest polyclinic.

(u) *(vraCHA)*

У ВРАЧА

At the Doctor's

If you become ill on your trip, the following list of expressions will come in handy to communicate with the doctor.

Я чувствую себя плохо.	I don't feel well.
Я заболел.	I feel sick.
У меня высокая температура.	I have a high temperature.
Болит здесь.	It hurts here.
У меня болит ________ .	My ________ hurts.
голова	head
бедро	hip
горло	throat
ребро	rib
У меня ________ .	I have ________ .
перелом	a broken bone
ушиб	a bruise
ожог	a burn
насморк	a head cold
кашель	a cough
понос	diarrhea
температура	a fever
Откройте рот!	Open your mouth!
Покажите язык!	Stick out your tongue!
Разденьтесь (до пояса)!	Undress (to the waist)!
Ложитесь!	Lie down!

Вы мне выпишете лекарство?	Are you going to give me a prescription?
Как часто принимать лекарство?	How often should I take the medicine?

(zubNOY) ЗУБНОЙ (VRACH) ВРАЧ: (atKROYtye) ОТКРОЙТЕ (ROT) РОТ!

The Dentist: Open Your Mouth

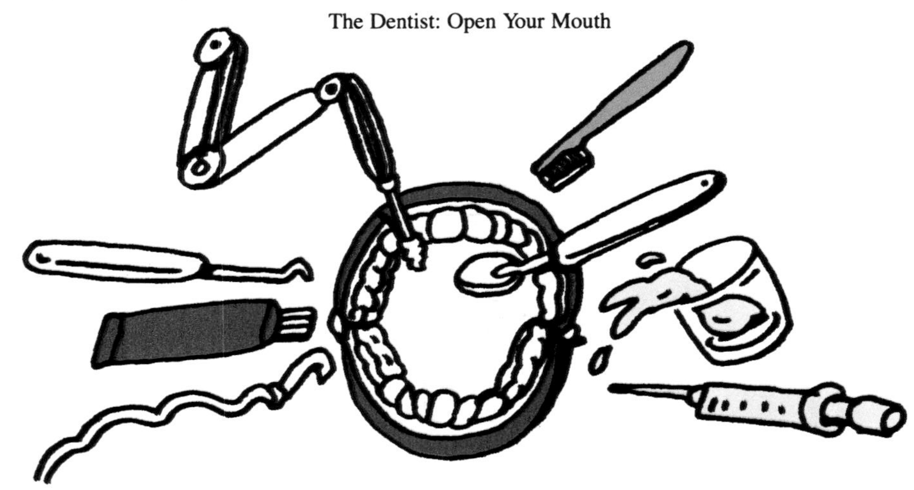

It hasn't been a happy day for Stefanie who goes to visit the dentist with a toothache.

STEFANIE	**У меня страшно болит зуб.**	I have a terrible toothache.
ЗУБНОЙ ВРАЧ	**Вы потеряли** (PLOMbu) **пломбу.**	You've lost a filling.
STEFANIE	**Можете поставить новую пломбу?**	Can you put in a new filling?
ЗУБНОЙ ВРАЧ	**Да, если нет** (inFYEKtsii) **инфекции.**	Yes, if there's no infection.
STEFANIE	**Вы поставите** (amal'GAmu) **амальгаму?**	Will you put in an amalgam filling?
ЗУБНОЙ ВРАЧ	**Нет, только** (VRYEminuyu) **временную. Когда вы вернётесь домой, обратитесь к вашему зубному врачу.**	No, just a temporary one. When you return home, go to your own dentist.
STEFANIE	**Спасибо. Кстати, сколько стоит новая** (kaRONka) **коронка?**	Thank you. By the way, how much does a new crown cost?
ЗУБНОЙ ВРАЧ	**Не думайте об этом!**	Don't even think about that!
STEFANIE	**А не надо удалить этот зуб?**	And you don't have to pull this tooth?

ЗУБНОЙ ВРАЧ	**Нет, всё в порядке.**	No, everything is in order.
STEFANIE	**Хорошо! Всего доброго.**	Okay! Have a nice day.

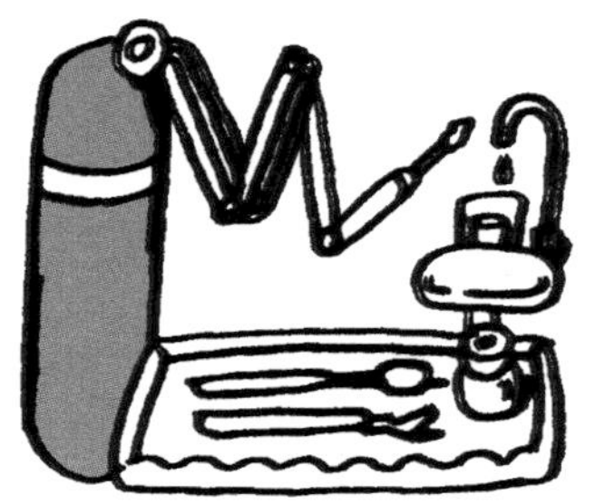

(v) (bal'NItse)

В БОЛЬНИЦЕ

At the Hospital

Now read along as Mark describes his visit to a Russian hospital.

Сегодня утром я вдруг почувствовал себя плохо. Вызвали врача, который осмотрел меня, и потом посоветовал мне лечь в больницу.	This morning I suddenly felt ill. They summoned a doctor, who examined me and then recommended that I go to a hospital.
В больнице медсестра измерила моё давление и температуру.	At the hospital a nurse measured my blood pressure and temperature.
Потом сделали анализ крови.	Then they did a blood analysis.
Врач слушал пульс, сердце и лёгкие. Он решил не делать операцию, а сделал укол, и выписал рецепт на лекарство.	The doctor listened to my pulse, heart and lungs. He decided not to perform an operation, but gave me a shot, and wrote out a prescription for some medicine.

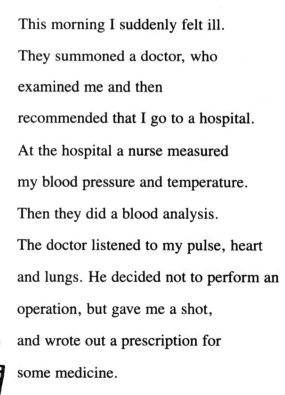

Have fun with the crossword puzzle using expressions you've learned and might need in a medical emergency. We've given you a start with the word for "patient" — **больной**.

Кроссворд

по горизонтали
ACROSS

4. nurse
5. prescription
7. patient
9. tooth
10. eye

по вертикали
DOWN

1. temperature
2. nose
3. doctor
6. pulse
8. mouth

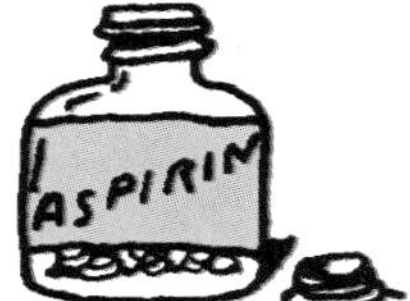

ANSWERS

Puzzle 1. температура **2.** нос **3.** врач **4.** медсестра **5.** рецепт **6.** пульс **7.** больной **8.** рот **9.** зуб **10.** глаз

(pamaGItye)

29 Помогите!

Help!

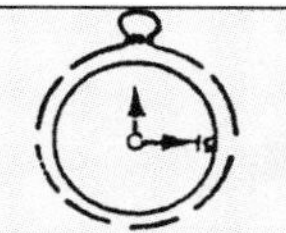

(KRAYnyaya) (niabkhaDImast')

КРАЙНЯЯ НЕОБХОДИМОСТЬ

An Emergency

Russia has traditionally been a safe country for tourists. While most people are honest, friendly and helpful, hard economic times have given rise to more street crime.

We hope you don't find yourself in a medical or other emergency situation, but it is a good idea to know some useful words and phrases.

First, here are the vital phone numbers:

(miLItsiya)
Милиция **02**
Police

(SKOraya) (POmasch)
Скорая помощь **03**
Emergency First Aid

(maSHYna)

МАШИНА СКОРОЙ ПОМОЩИ И

(midiTSYNskaya) (POmasch)

МЕДИЦИНСКАЯ ПОМОЩЬ

Ambulance and Medical Help

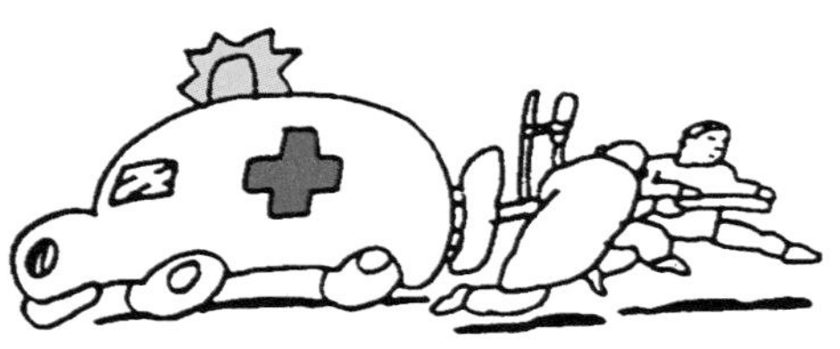

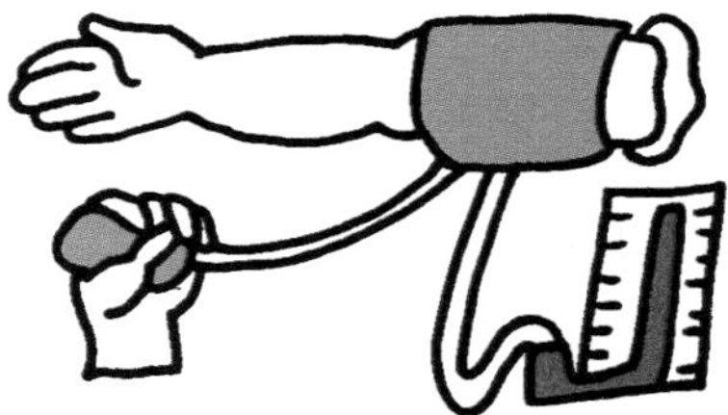

To get emergency medical aid from your hotel notify the key lady on your floor or the front desk staff. They can call for an ambulance with trained medical personnel to assist you on the spot or to transport you to the hospital. Here are a few expressions for you to learn.

машина скорой помощи
ambulance

крайняя необходимость
emergency

больница
hospital

(pamaGItye) **Помогите!**	Help!
(VYzavitye) (vraCHA) **Вызовите врача!**	Call for a doctor!
Вызовите скорую помощь!	Call an ambulance!
Отвезите меня в больницу!	Take me to a hospital!
(uPAL) **Я упал.**	I fell.
(SBIla) **Меня сбила машина.**	I was hit by a car.
(sirDYECHny) (PRIstup) **У меня сердечный приступ.**	I'm having a heart attack.
Я обварился.	I burned myself.
Я порезалась.	I cut myself.
(kravatiCHEniye) **У меня кровотечение.**	I'm bleeding.
(patiRYAla) (KROvi) **Я потеряла много крови.**	I've lost a lot of blood.
(piriLOM) **Я думаю, у меня перелом.**	I think the bone is broken.
Нога вздута.	The leg is swollen.
Запястье растянуто.	The wrist is twisted.
(laDYSHKa) (VYvykhnuta) **Лодыжка вывихнута.**	My ankle is dislocated.

(miLItsiya)
МИЛИЦИЯ
The Police (Militia)

(miLItsianir)
милиционер
policeman

(miliTSEYski) *(uCHAStak)*
милицейский участок
police (militia) station

In most Russian cities you can find police officers directing traffic and patroling the streets. If you have problems, the police can probably help you — from finding your way to finding lost items. Items that you have lost often turn up. If you do leave something in a restaurant, museum or hotel, don't assume it's gone forever. Check first with the local staff, or with the police. You might want to ask for the Lost and Found Bureau **(Бюро находок)**.

Here are some expressions you should know in case you need to call the police.

(miLItsiyu) **Вызовите милицию!**	Call the police!
(bliZHAYschi) **Где ближайший милицейский участок?**	Where is the nearest police station?

(patiRYAla) **Я потеряла мой паспорт.**	I've lost my passport.
Я потерялся.	I'm lost.
(uKRAli) *(buMAZHnik)* **Украли мой бумажник.**	My wallet has been stolen.

BEFORE YOU LEAVE

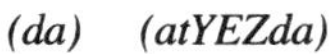

(da) (atYEZda)

До отъезда

You've learned a lot of Russian by now — probably much more than you realize. This section is a very important step in the learning process — a step in which you can review and solidify your understanding of the new language.

We've organized the section around basic situations you might encounter. For each situation there are a number of questions about appropriate Russian expressions. If you have difficulty remembering what to say in a particular situation, review the relevant unit in this book.

Good luck and have a good trip!

Счастливого пути!

Situation 1: Давайте познакомимся!

Let's get acquainted!

1. When you meet a Russian, how do you start up a conversation?

- **а. Хорошо, спасибо.**
- **б. Не волнуйтесь.**
- **в. Здравствуйте.**

2. You hear the question **«Как вас зовут?»** You should reply:

- **а. До свидания.**
- **б. Меня зовут ____________ .**
- **в. Я из США.**

3. Someone asks how are things (**«Как дела?»**). How should you reply?

- **а. Хорошо, спасибо.**
- **б. Вы правы.**
- **в. Что нам делать?**

4. If someone does you a favor, you might want to say "thank you."

- **а. Вот моя жена.**
- **б. Спасибо.**
- **в. Здравствуйте.**

5. When you part, you say "goodbye" to your new acquaintance.

- **а. Как вам помочь?**
- **б. Извините, пожалуйста.**
- **в. До свидания.**

ANSWERS

Situation 1 **1.** в **2.** б **3.** а **4.** б **5.** в

Situation 2: Приезд

Arrival

1. To reserve a hotel room you tell the room clerk:
   - а. **Идите прямо.**
   - б. **Я хочу забронировать номер.**
   - в. **Окно не открывается.**
2. If you need a room with a shower you ask for:
   - а. **номер с душем.**
   - б. **ключ в номер.**
   - в. **завтрак в буфете.**
3. What do you want to say if the television doesn't work?
   - а. **Погода неплохая.**
   - б. **Телевизор не работает.**
   - в. **Туалет не работает.**
4. How do you find where the snack bar is located?
   - а. **Вы не скажете, где здесь буфет?**
   - б. **Как насчёт завтрака?**
   - в. **А где лифт?**

Situation 3: Достопримечательности

Places of interest

1. Suggest to your companion that you go by subway.
   - а. **Поедем на такси.**
   - б. **Давайте поедем на автобусе.**
   - в. **Поедем на метро.**

2. Can you tell your next appointment that you'll be there at 11 o'clock?
   - а. **Я приду в одиннадцать часов.**
   - б. **Билет стоит десять рублей.**
   - в. **Шестой этаж.**

ANSWERS

Situation 2 1. б 2. а 3. б 4. а **Situation 3** 1. в 2. а

3. Please communicate to the clerk that you are working on Saturday.
   а. **Я иду в пятницу.**
   б. **Иван завтракает в семь часов.**
   в. **Я работаю в субботу.**

4. Can you ask the price of a ticket to **Новгород**?
   а. **Сколько стоит билет в Новгород?**
   б. **Нам нужно два купе?**
   в. **Когда отправляется поезд в Санкт-Петербург?**

5. Try to tell your hosts that you are an American, but you understand Russian.
   а. **Я армянин, но говорю по-английски.**
   б. **Я американка, но я понимаю по-русски.**
   в. **Я украинка, но читаю по-русски.**

6. Which of the following persons is likely to have difficulty getting around?
   а. **Мария живёт в Англии, и она хорошо говорит по-английски.**
   б. **Роберт работает в Москве, но не понимает по-русски.**
   в. **Ваня поедет в Токио, и он понимает по-японски.**

7. What do you need to know to rent a small car?
   а. **Я хотел бы взять напрокат маленькую машину.**
   б. **Мне нужен микроавтобус.**
   в. **Можно купить большую машину у вас?**

8. At the service station you ask the attendant to check the water and oil.
   а. **Как проехать в Кремль?**
   б. **У вас есть автодорожная карта?**
   в. **Проверьте, пожалуйста, воду и масло.**

9. Can you choose the most unlikely weather report?
   а. **В Москве в феврале идёт снег.**
   б. **В Санкт-Петербурге в июне хорошая погода.**
   в. **В Одессе в августе очень холодно.**

10. What can you assume when your guide tells you **«Сегодня пятница.»**
   а. **Вчера был четверг.**
   б. **Завтра будет понедельник.**
   в. **Завтра будет среда.**

11. Where must you go when you arrive at the **Аэропорт**?
   а. **Вокзал.**
   б. **Паспортный контроль.**
   в. **Сентябрь.**

ANSWERS

Situation 3 **3.** в **4.** а **5.** б **6.** б **7.** а **8.** в **9.** в **10.** а **11.** б

12. How would you ask the length of the flight?
   а. Сколько времени длится наш полёт?
   б. Где наши места?
   в. Когда вы будете нас кормить?

Situation 4: Развлечение

Entertainment

1. Can you invite your business acquaintance to the ballet this evening?
   а. Хотите пойти в кинотеатр сегодня?
   б. У меня два билета на оперу завтра.
   в. Хотите пойти в Большой театр на балет сегодня вечером?

2. Tell the hotel clerk that you like to jog in the morning.
   а. Моя жена плавает каждый вечер.
   б. Я бегаю каждое утро.
   в. Я смотрю футбол и баскетбол по телевизору.

Situation 5: Заказать обед

Ordering a meal

1. Find out what's for breakfast.

   а. Где мы будем обедать?
   б. Что сегодня на завтрак?
   в. Вам нравится суп?

2. Tell the waiter that you'll take the fish course.
   а. Мы предпочитаем салат.
   б. Они ужинают вечером.
   в. Я возьму рыбу.

3. Ask for a copy of the menu to look at.
   а. Принесите, пожалуйста, меню.
   б. Я сейчас принесу закуски.
   в. Вы любите икру?

ANSWERS

Situation 3 12. а   Situation 4 1. в 2. б   Situation 5 1. б 2. в 3. а

4. Ask the waitress for her suggestions.
- **а. Что вы нам советуете?**
- **б. Я возьму русский салат.**
- **в. Принесите, пожалуйста, борщ.**

5. What dish might you choose for an appetizer?
- **а. Соль и перец.**
- **б. Чай с сахаром.**
- **в. Ассорти мясное.**

6. Choose a main course.
- **а. На сладкое я люблю мороженое.**
- **б. На второе я возьму сёмгу.**
- **в. Принесите, пожалуйста, бутылку шампанского.**

7. You forgot to ask for some famous Russian black bread.
- **а. И чёрный хлеб и масло.**
- **б. И кофе и пирожное.**
- **в. Нам красное вино, пожалуйста.**

8. Try to find out what's for dessert.
- **а. Что мы будем пить?**
- **б. Что на сладкое?**
- **в. Я сейчас принесу салфетку.**

Situation 6: В магазине

At the store

1. You've made your way to the store with the sign **ОДЕЖДА**. What items will you **not** find there?
- **а. носки, рубашки, свитер**
- **б. платье, юбка, блузка**
- **в. бритва, лезвия, духи**

2. Ask the salesperson if your companion can try on the suit.
- **а. Можно примерить костюм?**
- **б. Покажите нам, пожалуйста, сапоги.**
- **в. Сколько стоит этот модный галстук?**

ANSWERS

Situation 5 **4.** а **5.** в **6.** б **7.** а **8.** б **Situation 6** **1.** в **2.** а

3. Now you're off to the **ГАСТРОНОМ**. Which list will you need for your shopping?
   - **а. зубная щётка, расчёска, зеркало**
   - **б. ботинки, шляпа, перчатки**
   - **в. молоко, овощи, фрукты, мясо**

4. You're still at the **ГАСТРОНОМ**. Which item won't you find there?
   - **а. десять литров бензина**
   - **б. банка кофе**
   - **в. десяток яиц**

5. Which of the following do you still need to purchase at the **РЫНОК**?
   - **а. телевизор и радио**
   - **б. юбка и блузка**
   - **в. рыба и мороженое**

6. At the big department store you see **Отдел ПАРФЮМЕРИЯ**. What might you purchase there?
   - **а. Дайте мне, пожалуйста, десяток яиц и пачку сахара.**
   - **б. Я возьму кусок мыла, шампунь и лак для волос.**
   - **в. Покажите мне, пожалуйста, коробку конфет.**

7. Oh! Oh! You've come down with a headache. Quick! Off to the **АПТЕКА**.
   - **а. У вас есть что-нибудь от зубной боли?**
   - **б. Я возьму глазные капли.**
   - **в. Мне нужен аспирин.**

8. You ask the **Горничная** to do your laundry and iron your shirts.
   - **а. Пришейте, пожалуйста, пуговицу.**
   - **б. Вы можете постирать бельё и погладить рубашки?**
   - **в. Это не мои носки, один красный, другой зелёный.**

9. Before you do any more shopping you sit down for a quick haircut. What do you **not** want to have done at the **Парикмахерская**?
   - **а. Я хочу постричься.**
   - **б. Вымойте мне голову.**
   - **в. Вы можете мой костюм сдать в чистку?**

ANSWERS

Situation 6 **3.** в **4.** а **5.** в **6.** б **7.** в **8.** б **9.** в

Match up your needs with the shops and stores.

1.	**Мы хотим купить русский самовар.**	**а.**	**Женский зал**
2.	**Я люблю слушать классическую музыку.**	**б.**	**Газетный киоск**
3.	**Вы продаёте цветную плёнку?**	**в.**	**Канцелярские товары**
4.	**Мне нужны подмётки и каблуки.**	**г.**	**Ювелирные изделия**
5.	**Я сегодня купил блокнот и конверты.**	**д.**	**Ремонт часов**
6.	**Вы можете починить эти очки?**	**е.**	**Подарки**
7.	**Мне надо купить жене кольцо или серьги.**	**ж.**	**Фототовары**
8.	**Где можно купить газеты и журналы?**	**з.**	**Ремонт обуви**
9.	**Мои часы спешат. Что делать?**	**и.**	**Ремонт очков**
10.	**Сделайте мне стрижку и укладку.**	**к.**	**Грампластинки**

ANSWERS

Matching 1. е 2. к 3. ж 4. з 5. в 6. и 7. г 8. б 9. д 10. а

Situation 7: Бытовые услуги

Essential services

1. You need some more money for souvenir shopping. You go to the **БАНК**.
   а. **Я хочу обменять сто долларов, дорожные чеки.**
   б. **Вы продаёте марки?**
   в. **Извините. Вы не знаете, где почта?**

2. Can you find out today's exchange rate?
   а. **Можно открыть счёт?**
   б. **Какой сегодня обменный курс?**
   в. **Можно платить кредитной карточкой?**

3. Let's drop into the local **ПОЧТА** and send a fax back home.
   а. **Мы хотим послать телефакс. Вы можете нам помочь?**
   б. **Сколько стоит телеграмма?**
   в. **Я хочу отправить письмо в США.**

4. Ask your new friend for his telephone number in **Москва**.
   а. **Я хочу заказать международный разговор.**
   б. **Можно от вас позвонить?**
   в. **Какой у вас номер телефона?**

5. You've just dialed the emergency number. What do you hope to hear?
   а. **Погода плохая!**
   б. **Скорая помощь!**
   в. **Извините за беспокойство!**

6. Tell the doctor that your throat hurts.
   а. **У меня болит горло.**
   б. **У меня понос.**
   в. **Разденьтесь!**

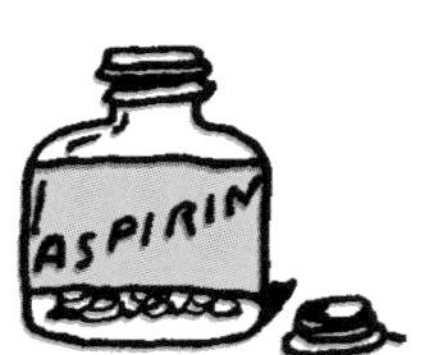

ANSWERS

Situation 7 **1.** а **2.** б **3.** а **4.** в **5.** б **6.** а

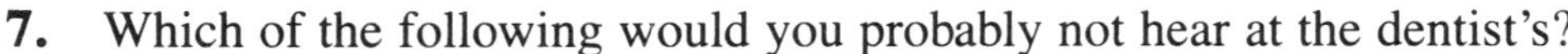

7. Which of the following would you probably not hear at the dentist's?
   а. **Он поставит пломбу.**
   б. **Мы сделаем анализ крови.**
   в. **Сколько стоит новая коронка?**

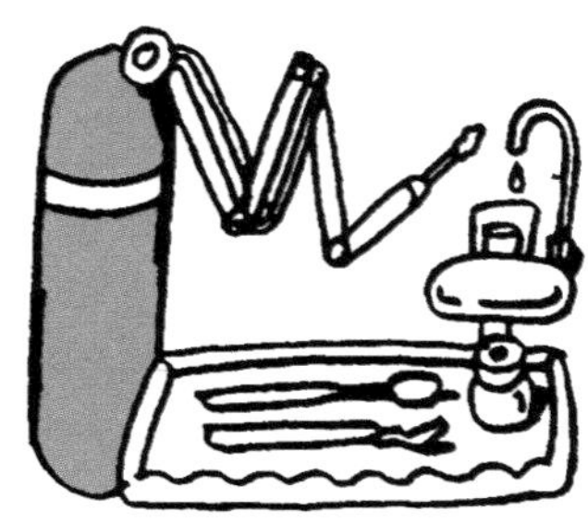

8. When you were at the hospital, what service was not provided?
   а. **Выписали рецепт на лекарство.**
   б. **Принесли водку и икру.**
   в. **Сделали операцию.**

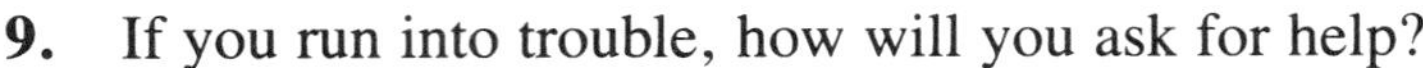

9. If you run into trouble, how will you ask for help?
   а. **Помогите!**
   б. **Читайте!**
   в. **Ложитесь!**

10. The nicest words in Russian for your hosts to hear is a polite "thank you" — **по-русски**.
   а. **Двадцать рублей.**
   б. **У меня маленькая проблема.**
   в. **Спасибо большое.**

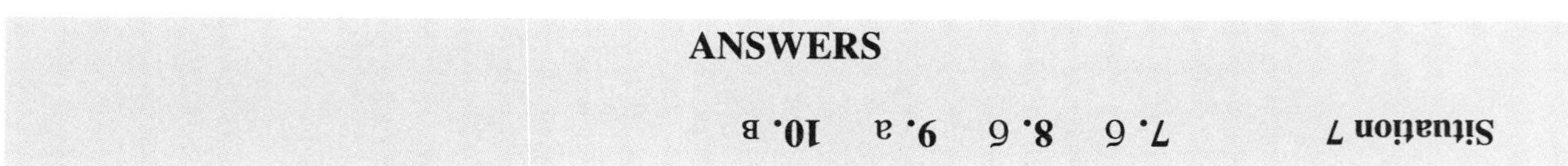

ANSWERS

Situation 7 **7.** б **8.** б **9.** а **10.** в

numbers
1–10

one	six
two	seven
three	eight
four	nine
five	ten

days of the week

Monday	Friday
Tuesday	Saturday
Wednesday	Sunday
Thursday	

months

January	July
February	August
March	September
April	October
May	November
June	December

numbers
11–20

eleven	sixteen
twelve	seventeen
thirteen	eighteen
fourteen	nineteen
fifteen	twenty

seasons of the year

spring	fall
summer	winter

in the morning	in the evening
during the day	at night

numbers
21–101

twenty one	seventy
thirty	eighty
forty	ninety
fifty	one hundred
sixty	one hundred one

to ride/drive
(to go by vehicle)

I am going	we are going
you are going	you are going
she/he is going	they are going

to go/walk

I am going	we are going
you are going	you are going
he/she is going	they are going

ме́сяцы

янва́рь
февра́ль
март
апре́ль
май
ию́нь
ию́ль
а́вгуст
сентя́брь
октя́брь
ноя́брь
дека́брь

дни неде́ли

понеде́льник
вто́рник
среда́
четве́рг
пя́тница
суббо́та
воскресе́нье

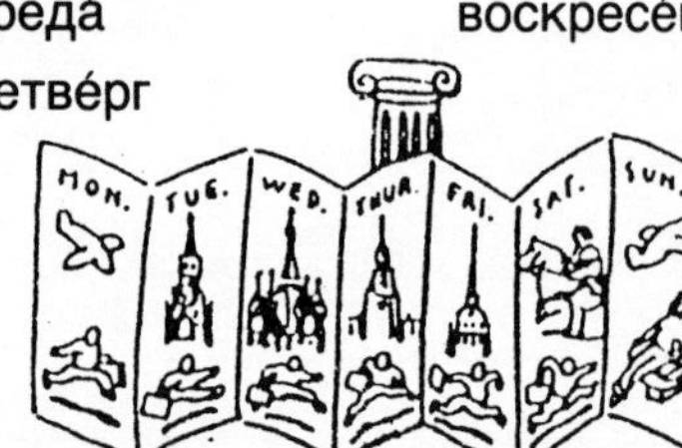

числа
1–10

оди́н
два
три
четы́ре
пять
шесть
семь
во́семь
де́вять
де́сять

у́тром
ве́чером
днём
но́чью

времена́ го́да

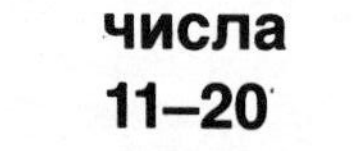

весна́
о́сень
ле́то
зима́

числа
11–20

оди́ннадцать
двена́дцать
трина́дцать
четы́рнадцать
пятна́дцать
шестна́дцать
семна́дцать
восемна́дцать
девятна́дцать
два́дцать

идти́

я иду́
ты идёшь
он/она идёт
мы идём
вы идёте
они иду́т

е́хать

я е́ду
ты е́дешь
она/он е́дет
мы е́дем
вы е́дете
они е́дут

числа
21–101

два́дцать один
три́дцать
со́рок
пятьдеся́т
шестьдеся́т
се́мьдесят
во́семьдесят
девяно́сто
сто
сто оди́н

Hello.

Goodbye.

Please.

Thank you.

You're welcome.

Excuse me.

What is your name?

My name is. . .

Russia

I am a Russian. (m)

I am a Russian. (f)

America
U.S.A.

I am an American. (f)

I am an American. (m)

Canada

I am Canadian. (m)

I am Canadian. (f)

England

I am an Englishwoman.

I am an Englishman.

to speak

I (don't) speak Russian.

Do you speak English?

to understand

Do you understand English?

I (don't) understand Russian.

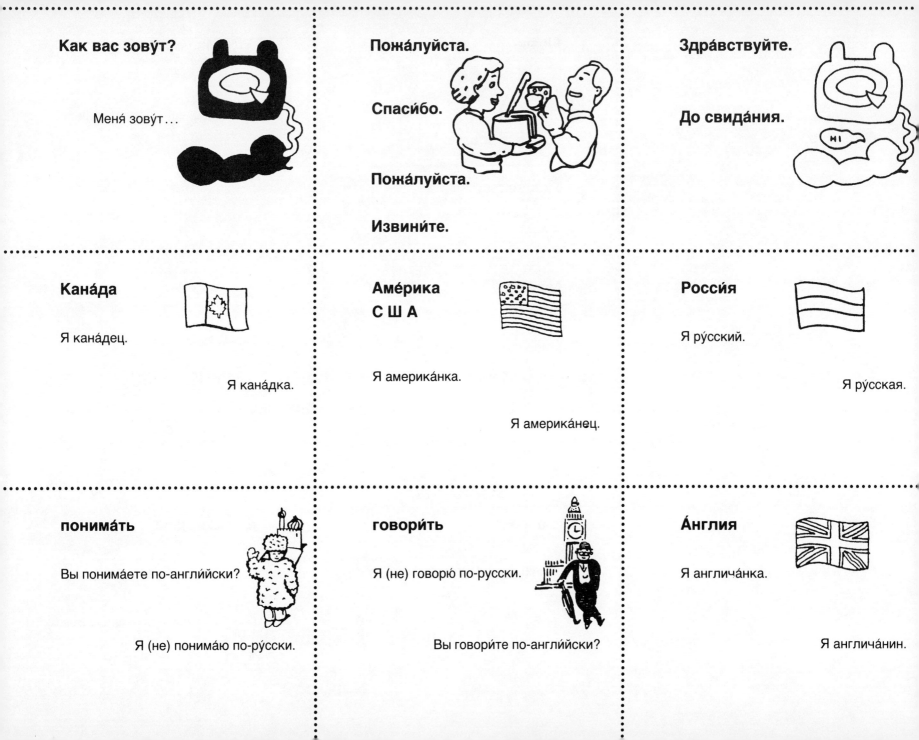

Как вас зову́т?

Меня́ зову́т . . .

Пожа́луйста.

Спаси́бо.

Пожа́луйста.

Извини́те.

Здра́вствуйте.

До свида́ния.

Кана́да

Я кана́дец.

Я кана́дка.

Аме́рика
С Ш А

Я америка́нка.

Я америка́нец.

Росси́я

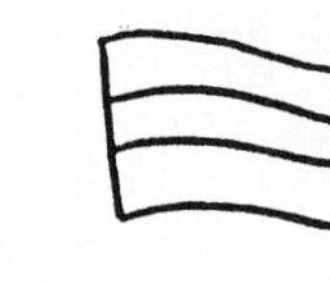

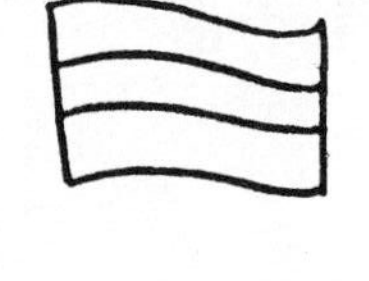

Я ру́сский.

Я ру́сская.

понима́ть

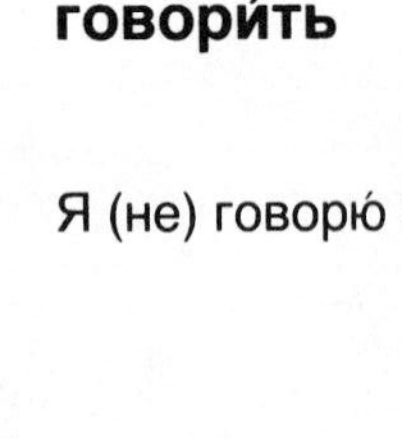

Вы понима́ете по-англи́йски?

Я (не) понима́ю по-ру́сски.

говори́ть

Я (не) говорю́ по-русски.

Вы говори́те по-англи́йски?

А́нглия

Я англича́нка.

Я англича́нин.

uncle aunt

sister brother

my family

grandmother grandfather
mother father
daughter son

questions

Who? How?
What? When?
Where? Where to?
How much/many?

What do you need?

I need . . .

What do you want?

I want

to see.

to buy.

Please tell me!

Please show me!

Please give me!

Whose is it?

mine(my) our(s)
your(s) your(s)
his, her(s) their(s)

Who is this?

I we
you you
he/she/it they

Can you?

Yes, I can.

No, I can't.

вопросы

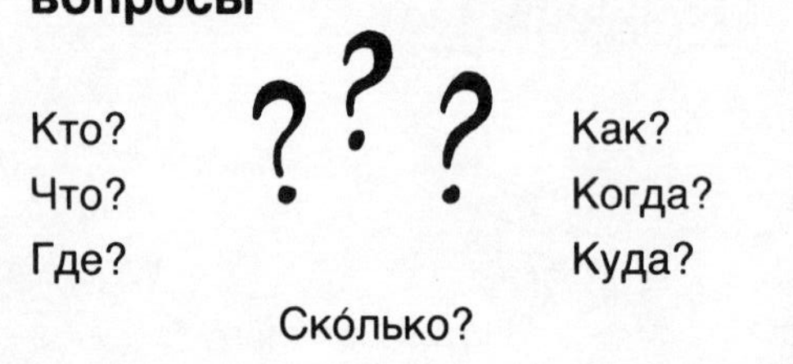

Кто?
Что?
Где?

Ско́лько?

Как?
Когда?
Куда?

моя́ семья́

ба́бушка
мать
дочь

де́душка
оте́ц
сын

дя́дя
сестра́

тётя
брат

Скажи́те, пожа́луйста.

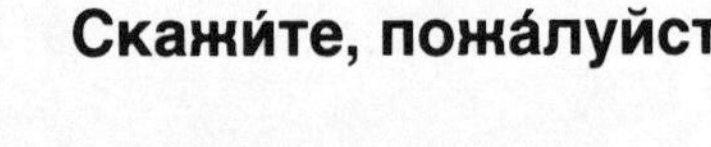

Покажи́те, пожа́луйста.

Да́йте, пожа́луйста.

Что вы хоти́те?

Я хочу́

посмотре́ть.

купи́ть.

Что вам ну́жно?

Мне ну́жно…

Вы мо́жете?

Да, я могу́.

Нет, я не могу́.

Кто э́то?

я
ты
он/она́/оно́

мы
вы
они́

Чей э́то?

мой, моя́
моё, мои́

твой, твоя́
твоё, твои́

его́, её

наш, на́ша
на́ше, на́ши

ваш, ва́ша
ва́ше, ва́ши

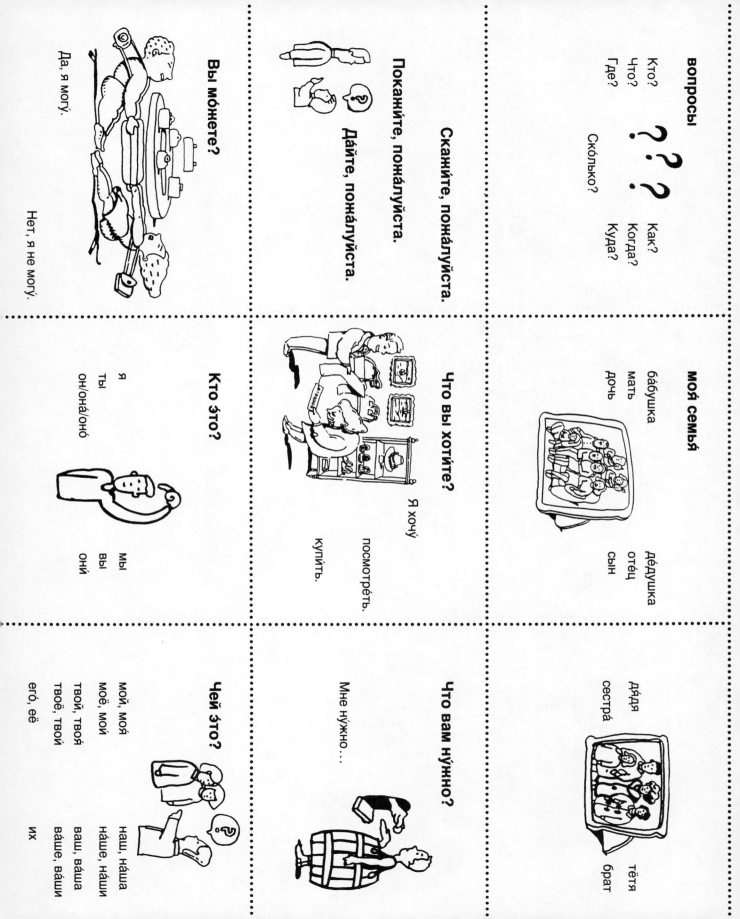

их

in the taxi

Are you available?
I (have to go) to the hotel Kosmos.
How much do I owe you?

on the metro

How do I get to the Kremlin?
How many stops to the theater?
How much does the trip cost?

at the hotel

Where is the key?
Where is the elevator?
I need another towel.
The shower doesn't work;
nor does the lamp.

directions

forward
to the left
to the right
backwards

on a train

Where are our seats?
Car 10, seats 7 and 8.
When does the train depart?

When?

At one.
At two.
At three.
At four.
At five.
At ten.
At twelve.
At thirteen (1:00 PM).

at the airport

Where is our luggage?
When do we take off?
When will we land?

What kind of weather?

Today it's . . . cold.
warm.
hot.

Is it raining or snowing?

the car

Please check the . . . oil.
tires.
brakes.

в гости́нице

Где ключ?
Где лифт?
Мне ну́жно ещё полоте́нце.
Душ не рабо́тает;
ла́мпа не рабо́тает.

на метро

Как прое́хать в Кремль?
Ско́лько остано́вок до теа́тра?
Ско́лько сто́ит прое́зд?

на такси́

Вы свобо́дны?
Мне в гости́ницу Ко́смос.
Ско́лько с меня́?

Когда?

В час.	В пять часо́в.
В два часа́.	В де́сять часо́в.
В три часа́.	В двена́дцать часо́в.
В четы́ре часа́.	В трина́дцать часо́в.

на поезде

Где на́ши места́?
Ваго́н 10, места́ 7 и 8.
Когда́ отправля́ется поезд?

направление движения

вперёд
нале́во
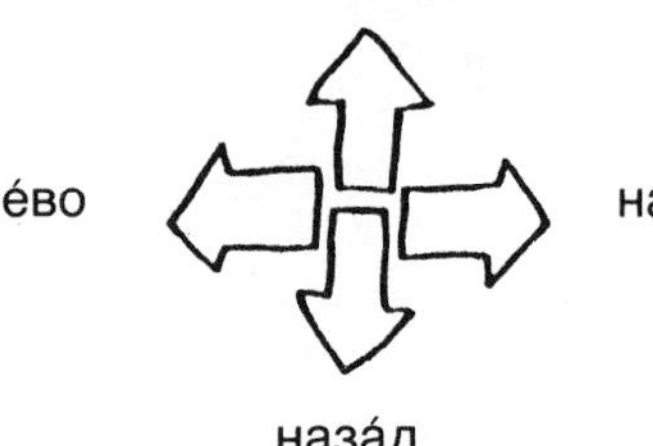
напра́во
наза́д

маши́на

Прове́рьте, пожалуйста… ма́сло.
шины.
тормоза́.

Кака́я пого́да?

Сего́дня… хо́лодно.
тепло́.
жа́рко.

Идёт дождь и́ли снег?

в аэропо́рту

Где наш багаж?
Когда́ вы́лет?
Когда́ мы приземли́мся?

How?

so pretty
very tasty
too expensive

What is that?

a good pharmacy
a poor snack bar
an interesting place
old books

What kind of people?

a big boy
a little girl

young people

The Bolshoi Theater

One ticket to the ballet?
Two tickets to the opera. Row 5, seats 7 and 8.
Opera glasses for me, please.

You

Do you have a city map?	genitive
I will telephone you.	dative
What's your name?	accusative
Who is with you?	instrumental
We know about you.	prepositional

I

I have some money.	genitive
Give it to me.	dative
My name is Oleg.	accusative
Will you go with me?	instrumental
What did you say about me?	prepositional

What's for breakfast?

juice
bread
cheese
butter
jelly
tea with sugar
coffee without milk

What do you like?

I like everything.

What do you love to do?

I love to play cards.

sport(s)

Who jogs?
I swim.
Papa watches soccer.
Mama rests and sunbathes.

Что за лю́ди?

большо́й ма́льчик
ма́ленькая де́вочка

молоды́е лю́ди

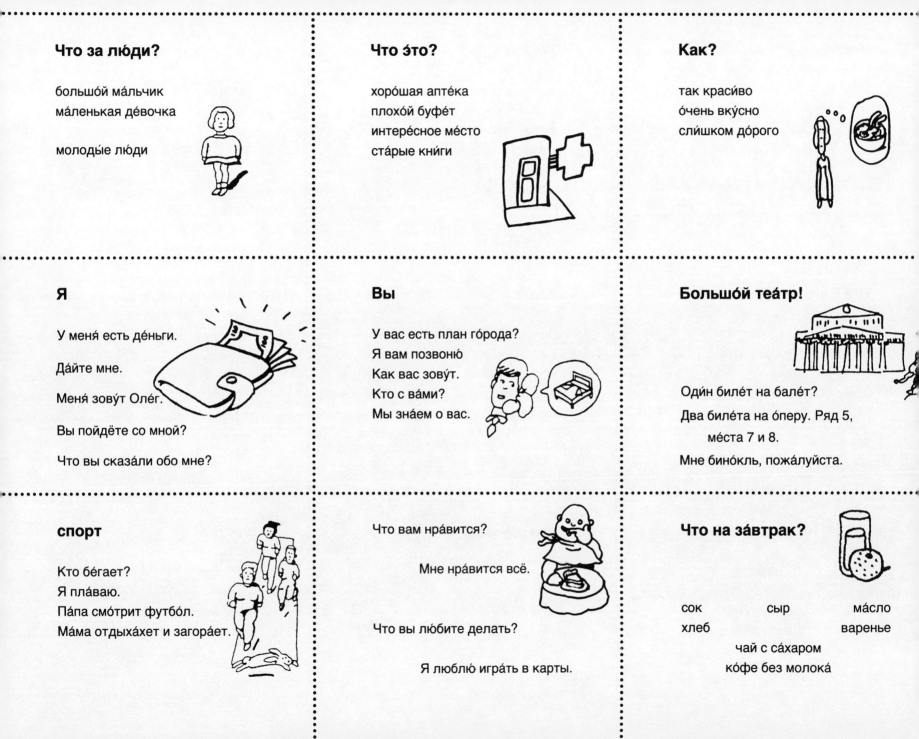

Что э́то?

хоро́шая апте́ка
плохо́й буфе́т
интере́сное ме́сто
ста́рые кни́ги

Как?

так краси́во
о́чень вку́сно
сли́шком до́рого

Я

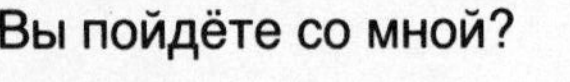

У меня́ есть де́ньги.

Да́йте мне.

Меня́ зову́т Оле́г.

Вы пойдёте со мной?

Что вы сказа́ли обо мне?

Вы

У вас есть план го́рода?
Я вам позвоню́
Как вас зову́т.
Кто с ва́ми?
Мы зна́ем о вас.

Большо́й теа́тр!

Оди́н биле́т на бале́т?

Два биле́та на о́перу. Ряд 5, ме́ста 7 и 8.

Мне бино́кль, пожа́луйста.

спорт

Кто бе́гает?
Я пла́ваю.
Па́па смо́трит футбо́л.
Ма́ма отдыха́хет и загора́ет.

Что вам нра́вится?

Мне нра́вится всё.

Что вы лю́бите делать?

Я люблю́ игра́ть в карты.

Что на за́втрак?

сок сыр ма́сло
хлеб варенье
чай с са́харом
ко́фе без молока́

the restaurant

menu waiter
first course second course third course
beverages

Bon appetit!

supper at the buffet

a sandwich with caviar
with cheese

I'll take
a glass of soda.
champagne.

What's for dinner?

soup salad
fish or meat
wine or beer

shops

Supermarket Bakery
Vegetables Fruits
Pastries Ice Cream

women's clothing

blouse skirt
dress shawl
bra slip
panties panty hose

men's clothing

shirt slacks
suit tie
underpants socks
undershirt

pharmacy

I need something for
a cough constipation diarrhea

Do you have
antacid aspirin bandages

toiletries

toothbrush toothpaste
comb tissues
soap shampoo

the market

How much does it weigh?
How much does it cost?

I'll take 100 grams.
Give me half a kilo (about a pound).

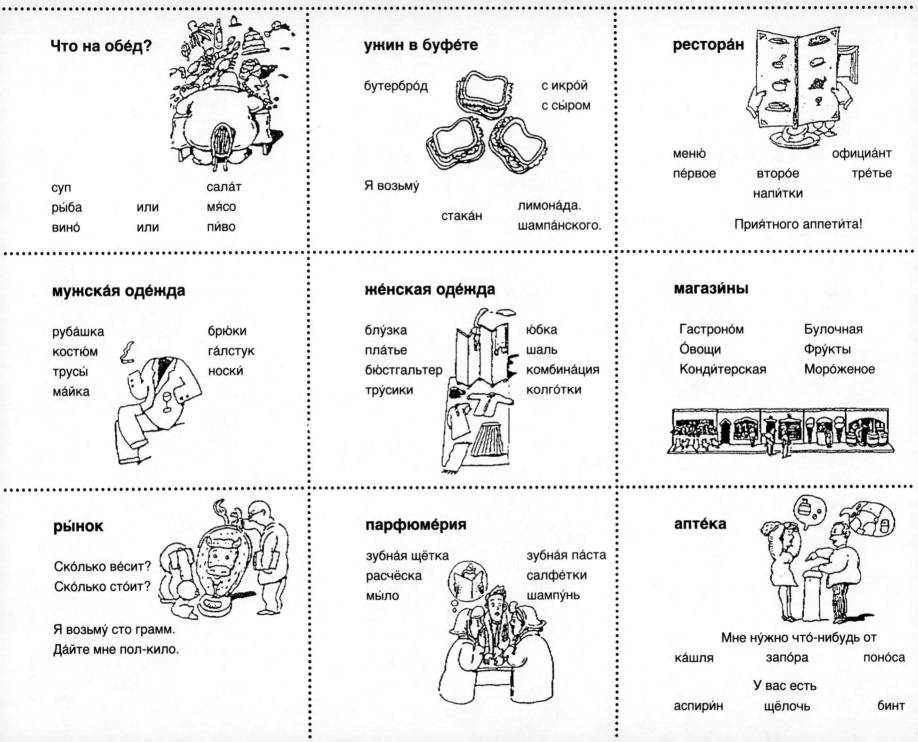

Что на обе́д?

суп — сала́т
ры́ба или мя́со
вино́ или пи́во

у́жин в буфе́те

бутербро́д с икро́й / с сы́ром

Я возьму́ стака́н лимона́да. / шампа́нского.

рестора́н

меню́ официа́нт
пе́рвое второ́е тре́тье
напи́тки

Прия́тного аппети́та!

мужска́я оде́жда

руба́шка — брю́ки
костю́м — га́лстук
трусы́ — носки́
ма́йка

же́нская оде́жда

блу́зка — ю́бка
пла́тье — шаль
бю́стгальтер — комбина́ция
тру́сики — колго́тки

магази́ны

Гастроно́м — Бу́лочная
О́вощи — Фру́кты
Конди́терская — Моро́женое

ры́нок

Ско́лько ве́сит?
Ско́лько сто́ит?

Я возьму́ сто грамм.
Да́йте мне пол-кило.

парфюме́рия

зубна́я щётка — зубна́я па́ста
расчёска — салфе́тки
мы́ло — шампу́нь

апте́ка

Мне ну́жно что́-нибудь от
ка́шля запо́ра поно́са

У вас есть
аспири́н щёлочь бинт

the barber shop

I want
a haircut and a shave.

Scissors-cut or razor cut?

the beauty salon

What can I do for you?

Give me a shampoo
and a cut and set.

laundry and dry cleaning

Can you wash my underwear?

Can you iron my shirts?

jewelry items

I would like to buy

a bracelet
a necklace
earrings
a ring

stationery section

I have to buy a

pencil
writing pad
paperclips

and a

pen
writing paper
notebook

the newsstand

Do you have
newspapers or magazines
in English?

records

Which music do you like?
Classical or folk music?

Do you need
records or cassettes?

souvenirs

nested doll
balalaika
lacquer box
fur hat

at the watchmaker

The watch is fast.
It is slow.
It doesn't run.
Can you replace the battery?

сти́рка и чи́стка

Вы мо́жете постира́ть моё бельё?

Вы мо́жете погла́дить э́ти руба́шки?

парикма́херская же́нский зал

Что вам сде́лать?

Вы́мойте мне го́лову,
сде́лайте стри́жку и укла́дку.

парикма́херская мужско́й зал

Я хочу́
постри́чься и побри́ться.

Но́жницами или бри́твой?

газе́тный кио́ск

У вас есть
газе́ты или жу́рналы
на англи́йском языке́?

канцеля́рский отде́л

Мне на́до купи́ть

каранда́ш		ру́чку
блокно́т		бума́гу для пи́сем
скре́пки	и	тетра́дь

ювели́рные изде́лия

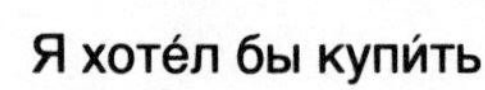

Я хоте́л бы купи́ть

брасле́т	се́рьги
ожере́лье	кольцо́

ремо́нт часо́в

Они спеша́т.
Они отстаю́т.
Они стоя́т.
Мо́жно поста́вить но́вую батере́йку?

сувени́ры

матрёшка	шкату́лка
балала́йка	ме́ховая ша́пка

пласти́нки

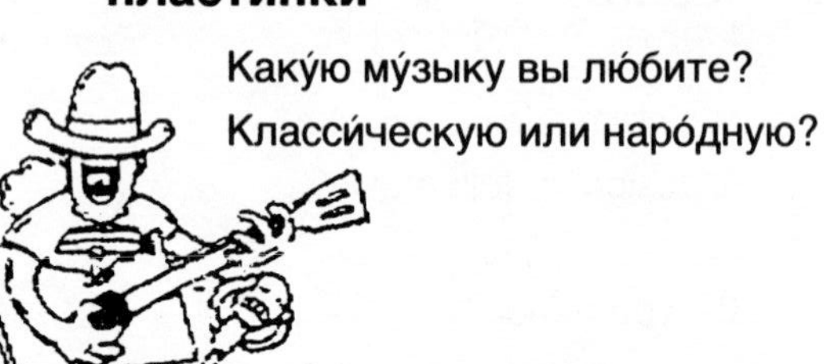

Каку́ю му́зыку вы лю́бите?
Класси́ческую или наро́дную?

Вам нужны́
пласти́нки или кассе́ты?

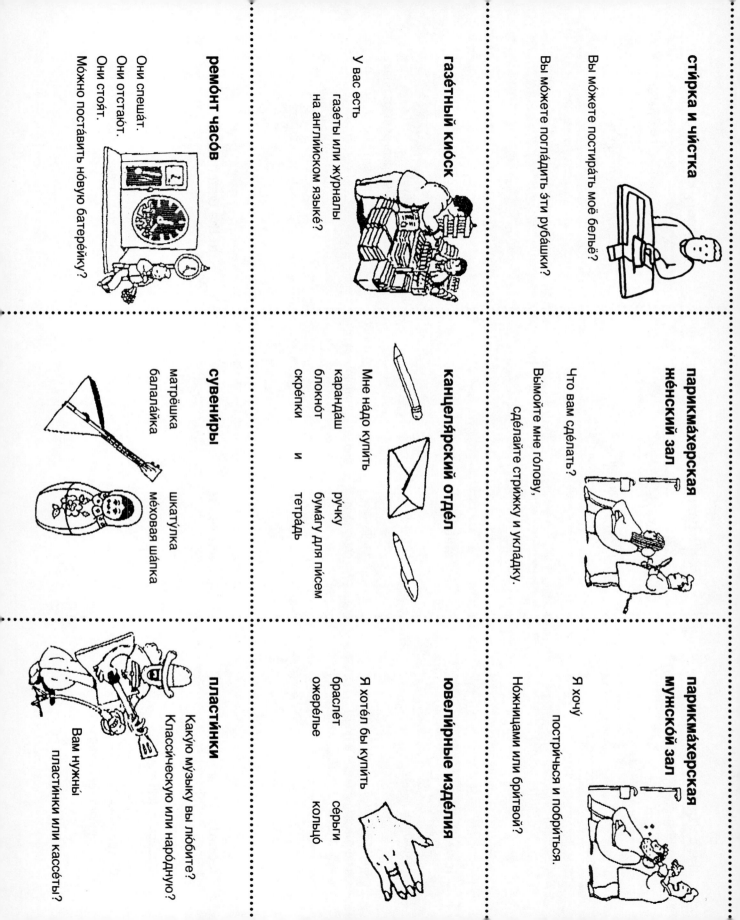

shoe repairs

heels — soles

shoelaces — insoles

repair of eyeglasses

Can you repair

the lens
the frame
the earpiece

photography supplies

Do you develop film?
Twenty or thirty-six exposures?
Black and white or color?
Prints or slides?

the post office

I want to send to the USA

an airmail letter
a telegram
a postcard
a fax

the bank

May I exchange money?
What is the exchange rate?

hard currency — travelers' checks
cash

money

one kopeck — one ruble
two kopecks — two rubles
three kopecks — three rubles
four kopecks — four rubles
five kopecks — five rubles

What else hurts?

eyes — ears
heart — shoulder

I have a high temperature.
I don't feel well.

at the doctor

Doctor, my ________ hurts.

head — throat
arm — stomach
back — leg

telephones

I want to make
an international call.

What is your telephone number?

Hello. This is Alexandra speaking.

I can't hear you. Speak louder.

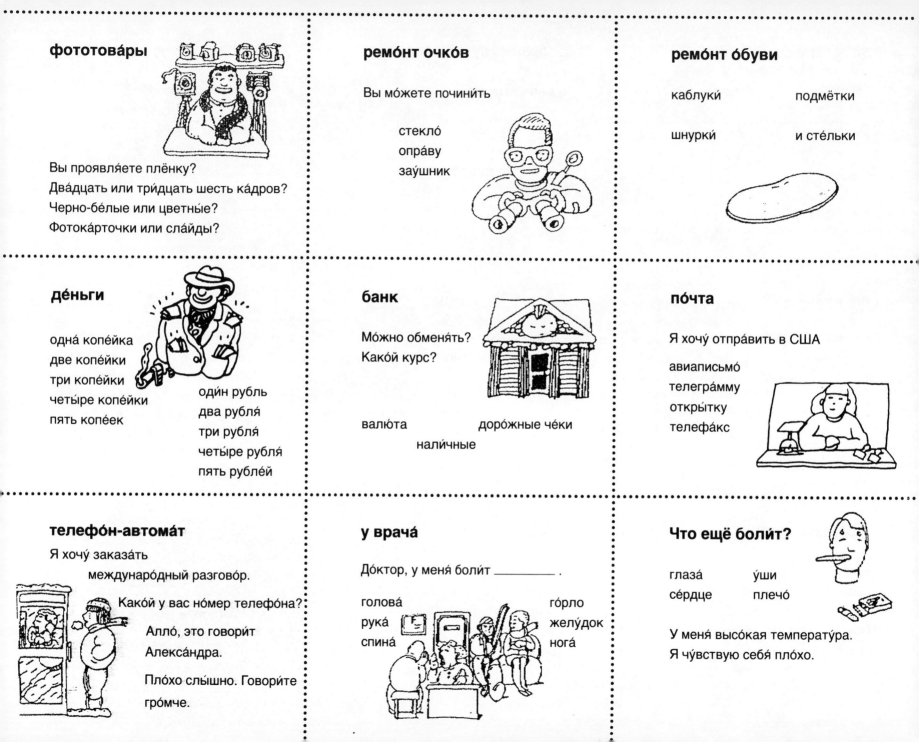

фототова́ры

Вы проявля́ете плёнку?
Два́дцать или три́дцать шесть ка́дров?
Черно-бе́лые или цветны́е?
Фотока́рточки или сла́йды?

ремо́нт очко́в

Вы мо́жете почини́ть

стекло́
опра́ву
зау́шник

ремо́нт о́буви

каблуки́ подмётки
шнурки́ и сте́льки

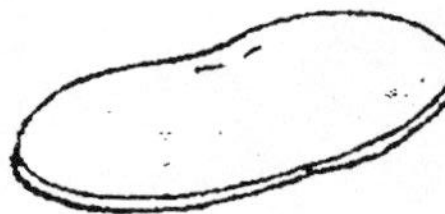

де́ньги

одна́ копе́йка
две копе́йки
три копе́йки
четы́ре копе́йки
пять копе́ек

оди́н рубль
два рубля́
три рубля́
четы́ре рубля́
пять рубле́й

банк

Мо́жно обменя́ть?
Како́й курс?

валю́та
нали́чные
доро́жные че́ки

по́чта

Я хочу́ отпра́вить в США

авиаписьмо́
телегра́мму
откры́тку
телефа́кс

телефо́н-автома́т

Я хочу́ заказа́ть
междунаро́дный разгово́р.

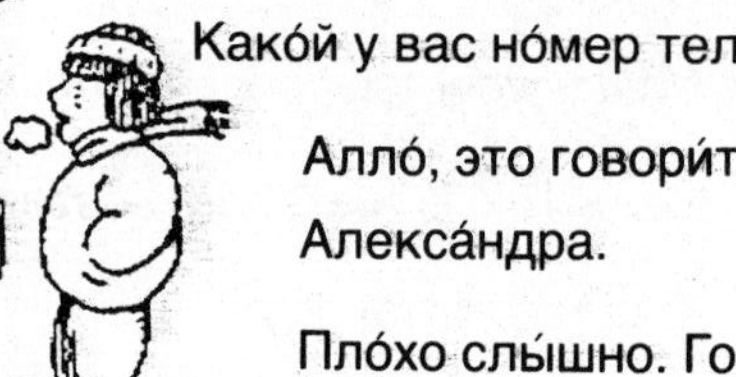

Како́й у вас но́мер телефо́на?

Алло́, это говори́т
Алекса́ндра.

Пло́хо слы́шно. Говори́те
гро́мче.

у врача́

До́ктор, у меня́ боли́т ________ .

голова́ го́рло
рука́ желу́док
спина́ нога́

Что ещё боли́т?

глаза́ у́ши
се́рдце плечо́

У меня́ высо́кая температу́ра.
Я чу́вствую себя́ пло́хо.

Help!

Call a doctor.
an ambulance.
the police.

the hospital

patient
operation
pulse
medicine
nurse
injection
blood pressure

at the dentist

I have a toothache.

I can put in a filling or pull the tooth!

colors

white
yellow
dark blue
red
black
green
light blue

Where is _______ ?

the restroom
the post office
the subway stop
the bus stop

Young man! (Waiter)

Miss! (Waitress)

important numbers

Fire 01
Police 02
Ambulance 03

My telephone number ______________

Yes.
No.
That's great!
That's bad!
Why?
Because

I'm hungry.

I'm thirsty.
(I want to drink something.)

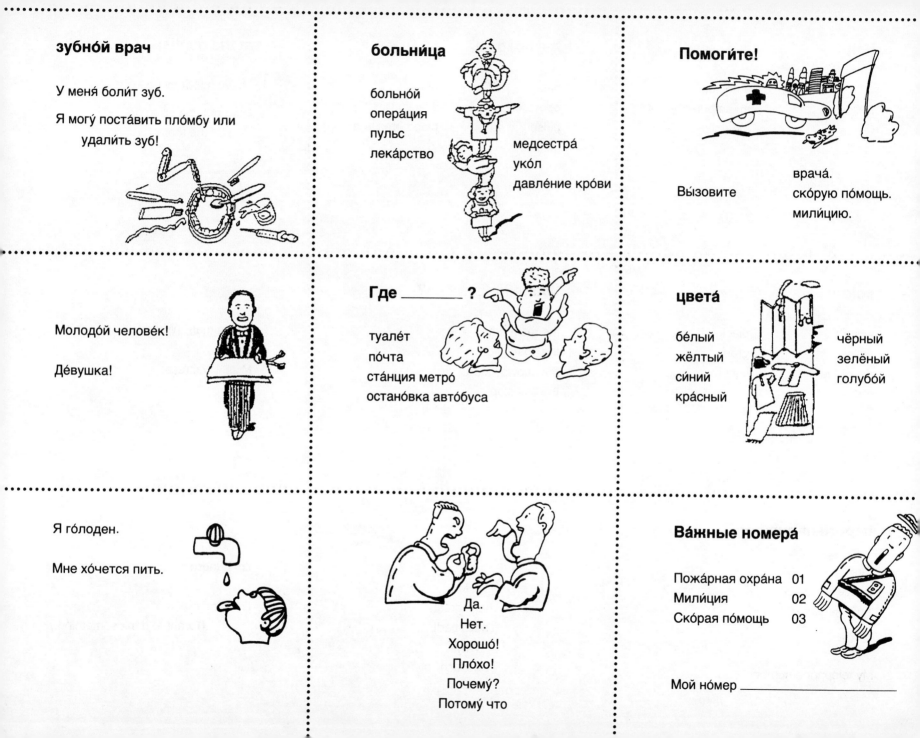

зубно́й врач

У меня́ боли́т зуб.

Я могу́ поста́вить пло́мбу или удали́ть зуб!

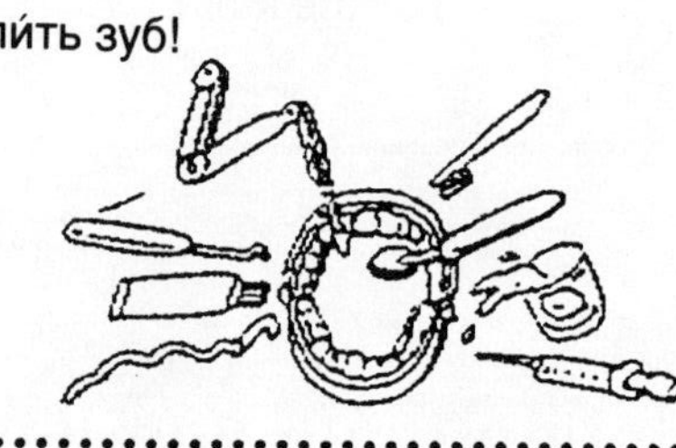

больни́ца

больно́й
опера́ция
пульс
лека́рство

медсестра́
уко́л
давле́ние кро́ви

Помоги́те!

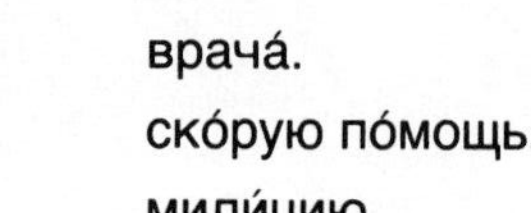

Вы́зовите врача́.
скóрую по́мощь.
мили́цию.

Молодо́й челове́к!

Де́вушка!

Где _______ ?

туале́т
по́чта
ста́нция метро́
остано́вка авто́буса

цвета́

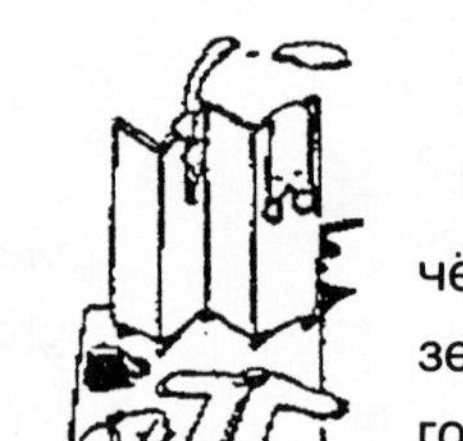

бе́лый
жёлтый
си́ний
кра́сный
чёрный
зелёный
голубо́й

Я го́лоден.

Мне хо́чется пить.

Да.
Нет.
Хорошо́!
Пло́хо!
Почему́?
Потому́ что

Ва́жные номера́

Пожа́рная охра́на	01
Мили́ция	02
Ско́рая по́мощь	03

Мой но́мер _______________

to live
(1st conjugation verb)

I live	we live
you live	you live
he/she lives	they live

to run, jog
(1st conjugation verb)

I run	we run
you run	you run
she/he runs	they run

to speak, say
(2nd conjugation verb)

I speak	we speak
you speak	you speak
she/he speaks	they speak

the past tense

I, you, he (masculines)
was, ran

I, you, she (feminines)
was, ran

we, you, they (plurals)
were, ran

(simple) future tense
with perfective verbs

I'll take	we'll take
you'll take	you'll take
he'll, she'll take	they'll take

future tense
with imperfective verbs

I will	we will
you will	you will
she will	they will

speak.

yesterday

today

tomorrow

From where?

I am coming from the park.
We are coming from Moscow.
They are coming from a concert.
Are you coming from Vadim's?

Where to?

I am going to the park.
We are going to Moscow.
They are going to a concert.
Are you going to Vadim's?

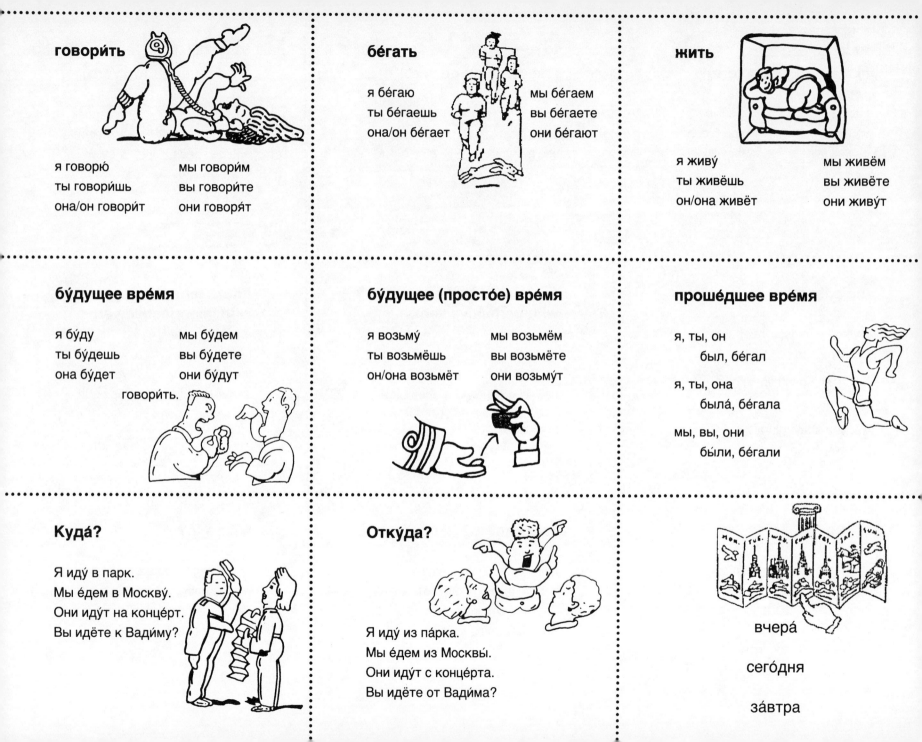

говори́ть

я говорю́ — мы говори́м
ты говори́шь — вы говори́те
она/он говори́т — они говоря́т

бе́гать

я бе́гаю — мы бе́гаем
ты бе́гаешь — вы бе́гаете
она/он бе́гает — они бе́гают

жить

я живу́ — мы живём
ты живёшь — вы живёте
он/она живёт — они живу́т

бу́дущее вре́мя

я бу́ду — мы бу́дем
ты бу́дешь — вы бу́дете
она бу́дет — они бу́дут
говори́ть.

бу́дущее (просто́е) вре́мя

я возьму́ — мы возьмём
ты возьмёшь — вы возьмёте
он/она возьмёт — они возьму́т

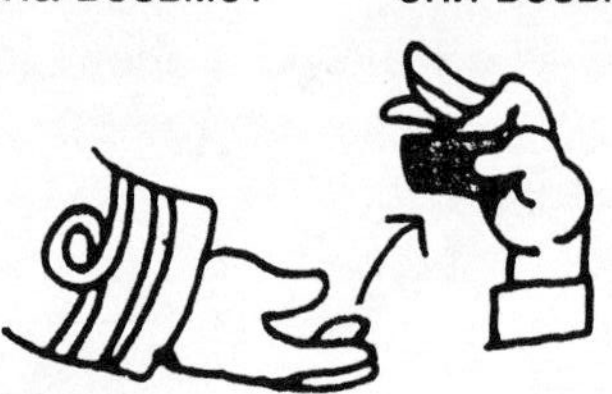

проше́дшее вре́мя

я, ты, он
был, бе́гал

я, ты, она
была́, бе́гала

мы, вы, они
бы́ли, бе́гали

Куда́?

Я иду́ в парк.
Мы е́дем в Москву́.
Они иду́т на конце́рт.
Вы идёте к Вади́му?

Отку́да?

Я иду́ из па́рка.
Мы е́дем из Москвы́.
Они иду́т с конце́рта.
Вы идёте от Вади́ма?

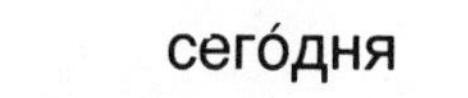

вчера́

сего́дня

за́втра

The Spelling Rules

1. After eight letters you may not write **я** or **ю**.
2. After seven letters you may not write **ы**.
3. After five letters you may not write **о** unless it is stressed.

Pronunciation Tips

1. When the letter **о** is not under stress it is pronounced as an **а**.
2. There are five "hard" vowels and five "soft" vowels.
3. At the end of a word, some consonants lose voicing; a **б** sounds like **п**.

A

B

C

Russian style!

neuter noun ending in о

window	Nominative case
Who is at the window?	Genitive
He approached the window.	Dative
They're looking out the window.	Accusative
This is next to the window.	Instrumental
The book is on the window.	Prepositional

feminine noun ending in а

Nina	Nominative case
Nina has time.	Genitive
They gave to Nina.	Dative
Who has seen Nina?	Accusative
What's with Nina?	Instrumental
What did you say about Nina?	Prepositional

masculine noun (hard)

Ivan	Nominative case
Ivan has money.	Genitive
They telephoned Ivan.	Dative
I know Ivan.	Accusative
We spoke with Ivan.	Instrumental
Mama is thinking about Ivan.	Prepositional

neuter noun ending in е

sea	Nominative case
Who was at the sea?	Genitive
He approached the sea.	Dative
They're looking into the sea.	Accusative
This is next to the sea.	Instrumental
The ship is on the sea.	Prepositional

feminine noun ending in я

Katya	Nominative case
Katya has time.	Genitive
They gave (it) to Katya.	Dative
Who has seen Katya?	Accusative
What's with Katya?	Instrumental
What did you say about Katya?	Prepositional

masculine noun (soft)

the driver	Nominative case
The driver has money.	Genitive
They telephoned the driver.	Dative
I know the driver.	Accusative
We spoke with the driver.	Instrumental
Mama's thinking about the driver.	Prepositional

азбука

а, б, в, г, д, е, ё, ж, з, и, й,

к, л, м, н, о, п, р, с, т, у, ф,

х, ц, ч, ш, щ, ъ, ы, ь, э, ю, я

1. ́о → а
2. а, э, ы, о, у
   я, е, и, ё, ю
3. б → п, г → к, д → т
   ж → ш, з → с

1. ж, ш, щ, ч, ц, к, г, х
   я → а ю → у
2. ж, ш, щ, ч, к, г, х
   ы → и
3. ж, ш, щ, ч, ц
   ́о → е

Ива́н

У Ива́на есть де́ньги.
Позвони́ли Ива́ну.
Я зна́ю Ива́на.
Мы говори́ли с Ива́ном.
Ма́ма ду́мает об Ива́не.

Ни́на

У Ни́ны есть вре́мя.
Да́ли Ни́не.
Кто ви́дел Ни́ну?
Что с Ни́ной?
Что вы сказа́ли о Ни́не?

окно́

Кто стои́т у окна́.
Он подошёл к окну́.
Они смо́трят в окно́.
Это ря́дом с окно́м.
Кни́га на окне́.

води́тель

У води́теля есть де́ньги.
Позвони́ли води́телю.
Я зна́ю води́теля.
Мы говори́ли с води́телем.
Мама ду́мает о води́теле.

Ка́тя

У Ка́ти есть вре́мя.
Да́ли Ка́те.
Кто ви́дел Ка́тю?
Что с Ка́тей?
Что вы сказа́ли о Ка́те?

мо́ре

Кто был у мо́ря?
Он подошёл к мо́рю.
Они смо́трят в мо́ре.
Это ря́дом с мо́рем.
Ло́дка на мо́ре.

NOTES

NOTES

NOTES

NOTES